141 Sitterson Hall
Dept. of Computer Science
U. of North Carolina

Sacrifices in the Sicilian

(Second edition)

Chapel Hill, NC
27599-3175

D. N. L. Levy

(919) 962-1756 work
490-2066 home

'He who attacks has the advantage' –
L. C. M. de la Bourdonnais

B. T. Batsford Ltd *London*

First published 1974
© D. N. L. Levy 1974
Second edition 1980
ISBN 2596 2 (cased)
ISBN 2597 0 (limp)

Typeset by Willmer Brothers Limited,
Birkenhead, Cheshire

and printed and bound in
Great Britain by
Billing & Son Ltd.,
Guildford & Worcester
for the publishers
B. T. Batsford Limited
4 Fitzhardinge Street, London W1H 0AH

To Jacq

A BATSFORD CHESS BOOK
Adviser: R. G. Wade
Technical Editor: P. Lamford

CONTENTS

PREFACE

The Sicilian Defence is the most popular opening at all levels of chess. In a recent survey of the twice-yearly Yugoslav publication *Informator*, I discovered that one quarter of their published games over a five year period were Sicilians. At club and county level, too, the Sicilian is at least as popular because of its exciting attacks and counter-attacks.

Many books have already been written on the Sicilian. In Batsfords 'Contemporary Chess Openings' series alone there has already been O'Kelly's book on the Najdorf Variation (*The Sicilian Flank Game*) and my own monograph *The Sicilian Dragon*. In addition, Hartston is preparing a book on the many systems in which Black plays an early . . . P–K3. Such specialisation is a necessary prerequisite for the modern match and tournament player who opens 1 P–K4 or who plays the Sicilian as Black. But it is also important to acquire a good understanding of the type of middle-game position that can arise from this double-edged opening.

There are a number of sacrificial ideas that can occur in Sicilian games, either in the game itself or in one or more of the variations that come to mind during the course of a player's at the board analysis. In order to be able to deal with these sacrificial possibilities when they arise, it is necessary for the player to have a certain feel for the kind of position that is produced by the sacrifice. He can then decide whether or not the sacrifice is likely to meet with success and he will be better equipped to find the correct continuation if and when the sacrifice is made.

Each chapter of this book deals with a different, typical Sicilian sacrifice, with the type of position that arises after the sacrifice has been made and with the way these positions should be handled. In the introduction to each chapter I have tried to describe the circumstances under which the sacrifice is most likely to succeed. I have also indicated the features that can give a good indication as to whether or not the sacrifice is sound. This introductory part of the chapter is illustrated with relatively simple examples.

The middle portion of each chapter contains further examples, examined in somewhat greater depth. Finally there are illustrative games which serve both to describe a sacrifice from its inception to the conclusion of the game and to act as a source of entertainment to the reader, providing him with lively, tactical games which he can study and enjoy.

This book then is both instructive and entertaining. The studious reader will benefit, time and again, as he acquires a better understanding of many important types of Sicilian position. The less serious reader will be able to enjoy the 127 sparkling, sacrificial examples and the 42 illustrative games, each for its own beauty.

In collecting the material for this book I have relied almost entirely on my own library and that of R. G. Wade who I would like to thank for his ever helpful assistance. I should also like to thank P. Poutiainen, C. W. Pritchett and H. Westerinen who readily contributed analyses, *The Chess Player* for permission to reproduce the Padevsky–Botvinnik example from *Botvinnik's Best Games 1947–70*, *Chess* for permission to use a translation that appeared in some of its 1963 issues, D. N. L. Levy for permission to quote from his excellent monograph *The Sicilian Dragon*, and lastly K. J. O'Connell for preparing the indexes and reading the proofs. Much of the analysis contained in this book stems from Soviet and Yugoslav sources. I would like to mention all those commentators whose notes I have used but there are too many of them. Perhaps one should also acknowledge the players who produced these sacrificial examples and games. While creativity of this kind exists in master chess the game will continue to appeal to an ever increasing number.

DNLL
London, February 1973

PREFACE TO THE SECOND EDITION

Following the success of the first edition the publishers have invited me to update *Sacrifices in the Sicilian*, to include examples and games from the period since February 1973. Although many more Sicilian sacrifices have been played in the intervening years, theory on these ideas has naturally remained unchanged, and so rather than alter any of the original material it has merely been necessary for me to add to the first edition.

In most chapters I have added one interesting game, and two 'test examples'. The purpose of the test examples is not for the reader to work out the next move—that is obvious from the theme of the chapter and the type of position—but to analyze the position in an attempt to find the salient factors that will determine the success or failure of the sacrifice. The reader may then compare his own analysis, which he should write down, with the game continuation and notes, to see if he has understood what was going through the sacrificer's mind.

I hope that this new edition will appeal to chess lovers everywhere and I should like to thank Len Perry who researched the recent examples.

DNLL
London, August 1979

SYMBOLS

+	Check
++	Double Check
±	Some advantage for White
∓	Some advantage for Black
±	Clear advantage for White
∓	Clear advantage for Black
±±	White has won position
∓∓	Black has won position
=	Balanced position
!	Good move
!!	Excellent move
!?	Interesting move
?!	Doubtful move
?	Inferior move
??	Losing move
1–0	Black resigned
½–½	Draw agreed
0–1	White resigned
Ch	Championship
Corres	Correspondence

W or *B* at the side of each diagram indicates which side is to move.

1 BLACK'S EXCHANGE SACRIFICE ... RxN(QB6)

Black's play along the semi-open QB-file is one of the main features of the Sicilian Defence. With a rook posted at QB1 Black can support a minor piece in its occupation of QB5, put pressure on White's QBP if his QN moves away or drastically alter the course of a game at his own convenience by sacrificing this rook for White's knight.

There are two principal ingredients in Black's compensation.

a) The doubling of White's QBP's and hence the demolishing of his neat Q-side pawnstructure (White is almost always compelled to recapture with the QNP); and

b) The increase in pressure on White's KP from a black knight situated at KB3 and/or Black's QB operating on the long diagonal—It is often the case that Black can capture this pawn immediately after the sacrifice is made.

A third compensatory factor, Black's use of the long dark-squared diagonal, will be dealt with in the section on the Dragon exchange sacrifice at the end of this introduction.

White has castled Q-side

With White's king installed on the Q-side, the exchange sacrifice must logically be of the greatest immediate danger to him since it shatters his protective shield. In Karaklajic–Joppen (*1*) Black's K2–QR6 diagonal is already open to use by his KB and the attack is swift—Black wins back the exchange by force and emerges with a clear positional advantage. If the K2–QR6 diagonal is blocked by Black's QP one of his first tasks after making the sacrifice will be to find an opportune moment for ... P–Q4, unmasking the KB.

B

16 ... **R×N!** 17 **P×R P–Q4** 18 **P×P 0–0!** 19 **Q×P** If 19 K–N2 N×QP threatening ... N×P∓∓ 19 ... **Q×P+** 20 **K–N1 B×N** 21 **P×B N×QP** 22 **Q–N2!** Drawing. Other moves lose at least the exchange. 22 ... **N–B6+** 23 **K–B1 N–R7+** 24 **K–N1 N–B6+** 25 **K–B1** ½–½ Spassky–Polugayevsky, USSR Ch 1960.

If Black's opening development has been restricted and his pieces are not placed particularly actively, the sacrifice should not meet with much success. In Ostojic–Sofrevsky, Skopje 1969, Black gets a pawn for the exchange but it is White who has the active position:

12 ... R×N? Better would have been 12 ... 0–0 13 P–N5 N–K1. **13 P×R N×KP 14 B–Q4 P–Q4 15 P–B3** If 15 B×NP B–KN4+ 16 K–N1 (or 16 K–N2 B–KB3 17 B×B—*17 B×R? N×QBP 18 B×B Q×B*—17 ... Q×B 18 Q–K3 Q×KBP with compensation for the exchange) 16 ... P–B3! and if 17 R–Q3 R–N1 18 P–KR4 B–Q7. **15 ... N–B3 16 P–QB4!** Undoubling his pawns and increasing the scope of his KB. **16 ... P×P 17 Q×BP 0–0 18 Q–K2 Q–B2 19 B–K5 Q–B1 20 B–N2 Q–B2   21 B–K5 Q–B1 22 B–N2 Q–B2   23 P–N5 B–N4 24 P–QB4! N–Q2 25 K–N1 B–QB3 26 KR–N1 R–K1   27 P–N6!** and White's attack was decisive.

In Bokuchava–Dzhindzhikhashvili (*3*) (yet another example of an early ... P–Q4 to unmask the KB) Black's sacrifice was probably the only way

to keep his game alive in view of the threatened pawn storm on the K-side. But although it succeeded in practice the sacrifice was probably not sound—Black's pieces achieved greater activity than they deserved.

When White can safely make the recapture Q×R, keeping his Q-side pawns intact, it is not so easy for Black to make immediate progress in his attack against the white king. Nevertheless, provided that Black's position is structurally sound and that White is unable to force the exchange of queens, Black's material deficit should not prevent him from continuing with his Q-side strategy as in Peretz–Benko, Netanya 1971:

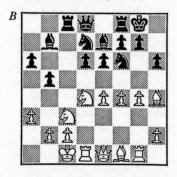

14 ... R×N The natural counter to White's K-side attack. **15 B×N?** Better is 15 Q×R N×KP 16 B×B N×Q   17 B×Q N×R   18 B–K7 R–K1   19 B×QP N–K6 with equal chances. **15 ... N×B** 15 ... R×RP 16 P×R N×B is unclear. It is probably better for Black to capture the important centre pawn rather than one on the wing. **16 Q×R N×KP 17 Q–K3 B–R5 18 R–N2** and now Black's best continuation would have been **18 ... P–Q4** followed by **... N–Q3** and **... N–B5**

with ample Q-side chances to compensate for the sacrificed material.

White has castled (or will castle) K-side
It is paradoxical that when White's king is safely hidden on the K-side, far away from the dangers of a Q-side attack, his Q-side pawns are somewhat more vulnerable—In many positions the white king can be a most valuable defensive piece on QN2.

A typical case is that of the over-ambitious K-side attack. In Barash-kov–Suetin (*4*) White has lashed out on the K-side without giving due care and attention to what is happening on the rest of the board. Padevsky–Botvinnik (*5*) is another, better known example.

Since an integral part of Black's plan frequently involves capturing the white KP, the exchange sacrifice is rarely possible when White can defend (or has defended) his KP by P–KB3 (The exception is the Dragon exchange sacrifice). The sacrifice is therefore seen most often when White's KBP has advanced at least as far as the fourth rank. Bednarski–Lehmann, Palma 1967 illustrates the frequently seen inflexible pawn pair at White's K4 and KB5:

15 . . . R × N! 16 Q × R After 16 P × R P–R5 17 N–K2 Q–N3 + 18 K–R1 N × P, White has the traditionally bad Q-side pawnstructure as well as the other problems which he has to face in the game. **16 . . . P–R5 17 N–K2 Q–N3 + 18 K–R1 N × P 19 Q–R3 N–N4!** This *zwischenidee* is even stronger than the immediate 19 . . . N–B7 +. **20 Q–N4 P–R6 21 R–KN1 N–K5 22 QR–KB1 N–B7 + 23 R × N Q × R 24 Q × NP P × P + 25 R × P Q × N! 26 B × P + K–Q1 27 Q × R + K–B2 28 Q–QB8 + K × Q 0–1**

This same pawn-structure appears in three further examples. In Karlson–Kozlov (*6*) White finds a counter-sacrifice which allows him to regain the initiative but which leaves him at a fatal material disadvantage. Hjuverinen–J. Szabo (*7*) shows that even though Black may not pick up the KP at once, a slow, methodical build up against this pawn can give enough counterplay to justify the sacrifice. Hohler–Klundt (*8*) is unusual in the way that Black intends to capture the KP with a rook which would then be instrumental in the final attack.

In Olafsson–Fischer, Bled 1959, Black could not capture the KP due to an unusual tactical stroke. Because of this the sacrifice was inadequate. Fischer should have continued in less optimistic vein:
See diagram next page
15 . . . R × N? Better is 15 . . . N–B5. **16 P × R N × N** Bad is 16 . . . B × P because of the surprising answer 17 N × P! K × N 18 B × N + K × B 19 Q–R5!! K–N2 20 Q–N4 + winning back the piece and remaining

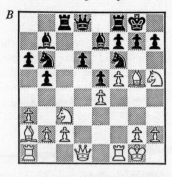

B

the exchange ahead for nothing.
**17 B×B Q×B 18 Q×N B×P
19 Q–N4!** A strong *zwischenzug* which
at once forces Black on the defensive.
**19 ... P–Q4 20 P–B6 Q–B4+
21 K–R1 P–N3 22 QR–K1! R–K1**
Not 22 ... Q×RP? 23 Q–R4 R–K1
24 R×B! P×R 25 B×P+! K×B
26 Q×P+ K–K3 27 Q×P±±
**23 Q–R4 P–KR4 24 Q–N5 N–B5
25 B×N NP×B 26 R–K3** Threat
27 R–N3. **26 ... Q–B1 27 R–QN1
and White won.**

In Mesing–Bukic, Yugoslav Ch
1968, Black's sacrifice was foolhardy
rather than optimistic. With his own
king still in the centre and White
having a lead in development and no
weaknesses in his position, the sacrifice could not possibly deserve to
succeed:

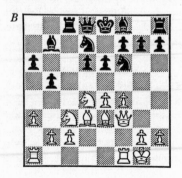

B

**11 ... R×N?! 12 P×R N–B4
13 P–B4! P×P 14 B×P N/3×P**
14 ... B×P 15 Q–K2 Q–R1
16 N–N3 is no better for Black
15 QR–N1! N–Q7? 15 ... Q–R1 or
or 15 ... Q–B1 would be better.
16 Q×B! N×Q 17 B×RP and
White wins—the threat is 18 B–N5+.

The Dragon Exchange Sacrifice

With a bishop on the long, dark-
squared diagonal, Black's sacrifice
possesses a new dimension—The
increase in pressure on White's QB3
square. In Gurfinkel–Archakova,
½-final USSR Ladies' Ch 1960, we see
the Dragon sacrifice at its very best:

B

White has played the Classical form
of the Dragon, throwing her K-side
pawns up the board in gay abandon
without first ensuring that her KP
was adequately protected. The result
... **12 ... R×N!** With White's king
on its original square this move is
particularly effective because of the
possibility of a later ... B×QBP+.
13 P×R If 13 P×N R×B 14 P×B
R–K1 15 Q–Q4 N×N 16 RP×N
Q–N3 and White loses at least two
pawns. **13 ... N×P 14 B–Q4 P–K4!
15 P×P P×P 16 B–B5 Q–B2!
17 B–QN4 N×N 18 BP×N P–QR4**

19 B–B3 P×B 20 B×N B–QB3
20 . . . Q×P+ is also rather strong.
21 B×B Q×B 22 0–0 P×P 23
R–B1 P–K5 24 R–QB2 Q–N3+
25 K–R1 R–Q1 26 Q–N4 Q–QB3
27 Q–B4 Q–Q4 28 R–KN2 B–K4
29 Q–B2 Q–K3 30 Q–K1 Q–R6+
31 K–N1 B–Q5+ **and Black soon
won.**

The Rauser (or Yugoslav) Attack
often witnesses the exchange sacrifice
. . . R×N. Although White's KP has
been protected by the move P–KB3
and is therefore not the object of
Black's counterplay, there are other,
equally valid reasons why the sacrifice
is such a frequently seen motif. Its
after-effects tend to distract White
from the pursuance of his traditional
K-side attack. The Dragon bishop
on KN2 puts additional pressure on
White's QB3 square. And as well as
the usual attacking chances on the
Q-side Black can be reasonably
optimistic about his endgame prospects—The typical Dragon pawn-
structure with the QP safely guarded
by its neighbour is more suited to an
endgame than pawn-structures which
contain a weakness at Q3 (pawns at
Q3 and K3, or at Q3 and K4 or even
no pawn at all on Q3—if Black has
played . . . P–K4 and White has
exchanged pawns, opening the Q-
file). With the Q-file only half-open
White's rooks have little scope in
most Dragon endings and to be the
exchange down is not, therefore, a
prospect which should fill Black with
dread.

If White does not develop his KB
at QB4 (the older form of the Rauser
Attack) his QR2 square is vulnerable
to an attack from Black's queen at
QR4. Smart–Levy, Herts Junior Ch
1962 is a simple example—Club and
county players are still falling into
this sort of quagmire even though the
idea has been well known for years:

13 . . . R×N! 14 Q×R Q×P+
15 K–B1 B×P! A second sacrifice, ①
but one which cannot be accepted
because of 16 P×B Q–R8+ 17 K–Q2
N×KP+ 18 K–K3 Q×R 19 K×N
Q×NP+ 20 K–K3 P–K4! 21
B×RP P–K5∓∓. The text threatens
16 . . . N×P! 16 B–N2 R–B1
17 Q–Q3 If 17 Q–R3 B–R3+
17 . . . B–K3 Threatening 18 . . .
B–N6 18 P–B3 B–N6 19 QR–K1
B–R3+ 20 B–K3 Q–R8+ 21 Q–N1
R×P+! and Black won.

The weakness on QR2 is also
apparent in Bellon–Adorjan (9) in
which White develops his KB on Q3.

Having stated that the capture of
White's KP does not form a part of
Black's plans, I must now give a
counter-example. It is not at all
unusual for White's attack to include
the move P–KN4, either to support
the advance P–KR5 or for one of a
couple of other reasons. By overload-
ing his KBP, White's P–KN4 sometimes introduces the possibility of a
typical Dragon combination:

① Sac #2 - undermine protection of W's KP by B×KNP.

B

Black first sacrifices a piece **17 ... B × P!!** so that after **18 P × B** White's KP is now vulnerable and he can sacrifice the exchange **18 ... R × N/6!** because 19 P × R loses at once to 19 ... N × KP and 20 ... N × P+ etc. So the game continued **19 N–K6 Q–K4 20 N × B N × KP 21 Q–Q4 R × B 22 Q × Q P × Q 23 N–K6 N–B7 24 QR–K1 R × R+ 25 R × R N × P** and Black was three pawns ahead, Litzberger–Whiteley, Harra-

chov 1967. It is precisely because of this type of combination that P–KN4 is no longer in fashion in the modern form of the Rauser Attack.

Cherepkov–Vasyukov (*10*) and Musil –Baretic (*11*) illustrate the successful handling of Black's Q-side attack. In the latter case Black conducts the attack without the use of his KB (this is often the case, since White normally aims at forcing the exchange of dark-squared bishops at the correct moment). Nevertheless, in this example Black's attack on the dark squares persists through the continued threat of the advance ... P–QR6.

The illustrative game Huguet–Wade is another excellent example of Black's attacking possibilities. The notes to that game show the sort of thing that happens in the type of endgame that so often arises after the Dragon exchange sacrifice.

Karaklajic–Joppen
Belgrade 1954

Botterill–Verber
Dresden 1969

| 15 ... | R ×N! |
| 16 B ×N | |

If 16 P ×R B–R6+ and mates.

| 16 ... | B ×B |
| 17 P ×R | B–K2! |

With the same idea as in the last note.

18 K–N1

18 Q–Q3? loses to 18 ... N ×B+ 19 Q ×N B–R6+ and 20 ... Q–N3+ and on 18 Q–R6 N ×B+ 19 K–N1 Q–N3+, Black exchanges queens into a won ending. **18 ... Q–N3+ 19 K–R1 N ×B 20 Q ×N B–R6 21 R–N1 B–N7+! 22 R ×B Q ×R/8+ 23 R–N1 Q–N6 24 R ×P?** Better 24 Q–B1 P–QN3! followed by ... R–Q1 and ... P–KR3 when Black has much the better game because of White's grotty pawns. **24 ... Q ×RP 25 P–QB4** 25 R ×RP? Q–R8+ 26 K–N2 R–N1+ 27 K–R3 Q–KN8 wins quickly for Black. **25 ... P–KR4 26 P–B5 Q–B1 27 Q–N5 P–R5 28 R–K7 P–R6 29 R ×KP Q–B2! 30 R–R5 R–N1 31 Q–Q3** White's queen must be able to meet 31 ... Q–N2 with 32 Q–N3. **31 ... Q–B5! 32 Q–Q1 Q–K6 0–1.** There is no defence to the threat of 33 ... Q–B6+.

15 ...	R ×N!
16 P ×R	P–Q4!
17 P ×P	B ×RP+
18 K–N1	B ×P
19 Q–R3	

If 19 Q ×B N ×Q 20 B ×Q N ×P+ 21 K–R1 N ×R 22 R ×N R ×B 23 P–B6 P–N3! and Black has a good pawn more.

Now the whole of Black's army rushes to the Q-side.

19 ...	Q–B2
20 B–K2	R–B1
21 P–N4	N–K5
22 B–K1	N–N3

Threatening 23 ... N–R5 24 K–R1 B–N7+ 25 K–R2 N/K5 ×P+ 26 B ×N N ×B+ 27 K ×B N ×B∓ ∓

| **23 K–R1** | **B–K2!** |

Threatening 24 ... Q–Q3! and 25 ... Q–R6+

24 P–N5	**B ×P**
25 P–B6	**B ×P**
26 Q–B5	**Q–K2!**
27 R ×B	

Or 27 K–R2 N ×P+ 28 B ×N R ×B 29 B–Q3 P–K5!∓ ∓
27 ... Q–R6+ 28 K–N1 N–R5! 29 Q ×R+ K–R2 30 R ×KNP+ K ×R 31 Q–N4+ B–N4 0–1

Bokuchava–Dzhindzhikhashvili
USSR 1970

Barashkov–Suetin
USSR Ch ¼-final 1948

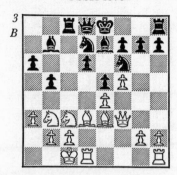

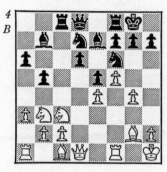

13 ... R × N 14 P × R 0–0 14 ...
P–Q4!? 15 K–N2 P–Q4? 16 P × P
P–K5 17 Q–N3 Not 17 B × KP?
N–K4 18 Q–B4 N–B5+ 19 K–R2
B–Q3! 20 Q–B3 N3 × B 21 Q × N
R–K1∓∓. 17 ... P × B 18 P–Q6
P × P 19 R–Q3 If 19 K × P N–Q4
20 P × B Q × P 21 B–B1 R–B1
22 KR–K1 Q–B3 23 B–N2 P–N5
with the better game for Black.
19 ... B–K5 20 R–Q2 B × BP
21 P × B Q × P 22 B–Q4? Correct
was 22 R–K1 N–K5 23 B–Q4, when
Black is forced to exchange queens
and White's material advantage
should then be decisive. Now the
pendulum swings the other way.
22 ... R–K1 23 R–KB1 B–N3
24 Q–B7 Q–K5 25 R–B1 P–KR4
26 R/1 × P Q–K3 27 R–K2 N–K5
28 N–Q2 Q–B4 29 Q–B6 N/5–B3
30 R × R+ N × R 31 R–B1 Q–Q6
32 N–N3 Q–K7+ 33 K–R1 N/2–B3
34 B × N N × B 35 Q–B3 Q–B5
36 N–Q4? After 36 K–N2 White's
Q-side has more chances of holding
together. 36 ... N–K5 37 K–N2
N–B4 38 Q–R8+ K–R2 39 Q–B6
N–Q6+   40 K–R1 and White
Resigned.

14 ... R × N! The logical counter to
White's last, extravagant K-side
gesture (13 P–N4). 15 P × R N × KP
16 Q–K1 B–R5 17 Q–K3 Q–R1
Black's queen is most effectively
placed on the long diagonal. The
threat now is 18 ... N–N6+ 18
K–N1 R–B1 19 B–Q2 If 19 B–N2
B–Q1! and 20 ... B–N3+ 19 ...
B–N4 20 Q–K2 N × B 21 B × B
Q × B Not 21 ... Q–R2+ 22 R–B2
R × P 23 N × N R × BP 24 R–Q1
Q × B 25 Q–Q3, when White has
some counterplay. 22 N × N R × P
Restoring the material equilibrium.
Now White's exposed king, his split
Q-side pawns and his over-extended
K-side all combine to bring his down-
fall. The immediate threat is 23 ...
B–K6+ 23 N–B3 B–K6+ 24 K–R1
N–B3 25 Q–N2 Q–B3 26 QR–Q1
Threatening 27 N × P! 26 ... P–R3
Not 26 ... R × BP 27 R × P!
27 N–K1 N × P 28 Q × Q R × Q
29 R–QN1 B–Q5 30 R–B3 N–K6
31 P–B6 P–N4 32 R–R3 N–N5
33 K–N2 K–R2 34 P–B3 N–K6+
35 K–R1 R × P 36 N–N2 R × P 0–1

Padevsky–Botvinnik
Moscow 1956

| 13 ... | R × N! |
| 14 P × R | |

Now White loses an important centre pawn, the long white diagonal is opened and his position becomes critical. Undoubtedly 14 P × N R × B 15 Q × R (but not 15 P × B R × Q 16 P × Q=Q R × R+ 17 R × R R × Q) was better, but after 15 ... B × BP the open position of the white king makes Black's position preferable —his two bishops are very strong.

Padevsky kept his KNP, hoping for an attack.

| 14 ... | N × P |
| 15 Q–N4 | Q–B1! |

After 15 ... P–N3 White could complicate matters by the rook sacrifice 16 P–B5 KP × P 17 R × P P × R 18 N × P. Now 16 P–B5 can be met by 16 ... P–K4 17 N–B3 N × B 18 RP × N Q × P 19 QR–K1 P–Q4 followed by ... B–B4.

| 16 R–B3 | N × B |

| 17 RP × N | P–B4 |
| 18 Q–R4 | |

Black would have a more complex task after 18 P × Pep. For example 18 ... N × KBP 19 Q × KP+ Q × Q 20 N × Q B × R 21 N × R K × N 22 R × P P–QN4 23 B–Q4, and Black has considerable technical difficulties to overcome.

However, after 18 ... R × P 19 P–B5 P × P 20 N × P B–B1 21 N–R6+ (21 R/1–KB1 R–N3 22 N–R6+ P × N) 21 ... R × N 22 Q × Q R–N3+ 23 K–B1 B × Q 24 R × P B–N5 25 R/3–B7 B–R6+ 26 K–K1 R–K3 Black will undoubtedly win.

18 ...	P–K4
19 R–R3	P–KR3
20 Q–R5	

His last chance. The threat is NP × P followed by RP × P, but his own king proves to be in more danger.

| 20 ... | Q × P |
| 21 R–Q1 | P × N |

Meeting White's main threat of 22 NP × P which is now countered by 22 ... P × B defending KN2.

| 22 B–Q2 | |

Also hopeless is 22 B × P Q × BP 23 P × P N–B3.

| 22 ... | Q–B3 |
| 23 P × P | N–N4 |

More accurate than 23 ... N–B3 24 Q–N6.

24 R–N3	Q–R8+
25 K–B2	N–K5+
0–1	

Karlson–Kozlov
Candidate Masters' Tournament
Moscow 1971

Hjuverinen–J. Szabo
Leningrad 1960

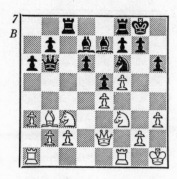

14 ...	**R × N!**
15 P × R	**N × P**
16 N × P+	

A counter-sacrifice which drives Black's king into the open without any useful effect. But if 16 Q–Q3 Q–R4 or 16 ... B–R5+! with a tremendous game for the exchange.

16 ...	**K–B1**
17 Q–R5	**K × N**
18 Q × BP+	**K–R3**

Now Black threatens 19 ... N–N4 trapping the queen.

19 P–B6

If 19 P–KR4 R–B1 20 Q–K6+ R–B3 21 Q–N8 Q × Q 22 B × Q R × P and Black should win without much difficulty.

19 ... N × KBP 20 0–0 B–K5! Now Black quickly consolidates his material advantage. **21 QR–K1 B–N3 22 Q–K6 K–N2 23 R–K3 R–B1 24 R/3–B3 P–K5! 25 R–B4 P–Q4 26 Q × RP B–Q3 27 R–R4 B–QB4+ 28 K–R1 N–N5!! 29 Q–N7+ K–R1 30 R × R+ Q × R/1 31 Q × NP** Defending against the mate threat, but ... **31 ... N–B7+ 0–1** If 32 K–N1 N–Q6+.

20 ...	**R × N!**
21 P × R	**R–B1**
22 P–B4	

Avoiding material loss but leaving his bishop without scope.

22 ...	**B–B3**
23 N–Q2	**Q–Q5**
24 KR–K1	**N–Q2**
25 Q–Q3	**Q–N3**
26 R–K2	**N–B4**
27 Q–QB3	**B–KN4**
28 R/1–K1	**Q–B2**

Bad is 28 ... B × N 29 Q × B N × B 30 P × N Q × P 31 Q × QP etc. Black's plan is to intensify his pressure against White's KP.

29 N–B3	**B–K2**
30 Q–Q2	**P–QN3**
31 Q–B3	**Q–N2**
32 N–Q2	**B–KR5**
33 R–KB1	

If 33 P–N3 B–KN4 34 K–R2 R–Q1 followed by ... B × N and White's KP falls.

33 ... B × P 34 N × B 34 K–R2 is a little better but White's position would still be in shreds. **34 ... N × N 35 Q–B3 N–N6+ 36 K–R2 Q × Q 37 R × Q N × R 0–1**

Hohler–Klundt
Berlin 1968

Bellon–Adorjan
Groningen 1969

21 . . .	**R/1×N!**
22 N–R5	

If 22 P×R R×P 23 Q–B2 (23 Q–B3 R–KB5∓) 23 . . . N–N5 24 Q–N3 B×B 25 Q×B N–K6 26 Q–Q8+ K–R2 and Black has many threats (27 . . . N×QBP, 27 . . . N×KBP, 27 . . . N×NP etc.)

22 . . .	**R×NP**

Not 22 . . . Q–R1 23 P×R R×P 24 Q–B3!

23 N×Q	**R×R**

Although material is evenly balanced Black's pieces are so active that White's position collapses almost at once.

24 R–QN1

Or 24 R–QB1 R–B2 25 R–QN1 R/2×P.

24 . . .	**R/6×P**
25 Q–B1	**N×P!**
26 B×B	**N–Q7**
27 Q–Q1	**N×R**
28 Q×N	**R/R–N7**
29 Q–Q1	**R–Q7**
30 Q–QB1	**R/Q–QB7**
31 Q–Q1	**R×P!**
32 Q×P	**R×P+**
33 K–N1	**R/R–Q7**
34 Resigns	

15 . . .	**R×N!**
16 P×R	**Q×BP**
17 K–B1	

If 17 Q–Q2 (or B–Q2) 17 . . . N×P! or 17 B–Q4 Q–N5+ 18 K–B1 N–N5!

17 . . .	**R–B1**
18 B–Q4	**Q–N5**
19 Q–N1	**B–K3**
20 R–Q2	**B×P**
21 K–Q1	**P–K4!**
22 B–R1	

If 22 B–K3 P–Q4! 23 P×P B×P 24 K–K2 P–K5 and White's king will soon be devoid of shelter.

22 . . .	**B–R3**
23 Q–K1	

23 R–B2 loses to 23 . . . Q–N8+ 24 K–K2 R×P+

23 . . .	**B–QB5**
24 B×B	

Or 24 R–B2 Q–N8+ 25 K–K2 Q×P+

24 . . .	**R×B**
25 K–K2	**N×P!**
26 Resigns	

Dragon Endgame

Cherepkov–Vasyukov
Spartakiad 1967

16 ...   R × N!
17 P × R

Exchanging queens leaves White with a bad endgame: 17 Q × R Q × Q 18 P × Q B–N2 (18 ... B–B5 also gives Black the better ending) 19 KR–K1 P–R4   20 P–R4 R–QB1 21 K–N2 N–B5   22 P–N3 N–K3 23 R–K3 N–B4   24 K–R3 B–R3 25 P–KB4 P–K4   26 N–K2 B–B3 27 B–Q5 B × RP 28 R–B3 B × QBP 29 R–KR1 B–B1   30 P × P B × P 31 B × B N × B   32 P × P B × P+ 33 K–R4 R–B5+   34 K–N5 R–B4+ 35 K–N6 B–B2+   36 K × NP N–Q3+ 37 K–R8 P–R5 0–1 Hartston–Westerinen, Havana Olympiad 1966.

17 ...   R–QB1
18 N–B5!   B–KN4
19 P–KB4!   R × P

Not 19 ... N × P 20 Q–N3 N–K3 21 B × N B × B   22 Q × B Q × RP+ 23 K–B1, and Black's attack soon peters out: 23 ... R × P 24 N–K3 B–N6 25 K–Q2!; or 23 ... Q–R8+ 24 K–Q2 Q × P+   25 K–K2 Q × P+ 26 R–Q2 Q × P+   27 N–K3.

20 Q–Q4   B–KB3
21 N–R6+   K–B1

22 P–K5   B–N2
23 P–N4

Even worse is 23 N × P? R × B+ 24 RP × R K × N 25 KR–K1 B–N5 26 R–Q2 N–N6   27 P–B3 Q–R6 28 R–N2 B–B4+ 0–1 Jansa–Vasyukov, 'Fraternal Armies' Ch, Havana 1967.

23 ...   N–N6
24 N × P

Now there is nothing better, e.g. 24 R–R3 R × B+ followed by 25 ... N–K7 and 26 ... N–B6+

24 ...   N–K7

Not 24 ... N × R? 25 N × P ± ±

25 Q–Q2

Or 25 Q–Q5 Q × Q   26 B × Q R–B4! ∓ ∓

25 ...   R × B+
26 BP × R

Or 26 RP × R N–B6+   27 K–N2 N × R+ ∓ ∓

26 ...   Q × Q
27 R × Q   N–N6
28 R–N1?

There are two plausible alternatives though neither prevents Black from getting the better endgame:
a) 28 P–K6 B × P 29 N–N5 B × KNP 30 R–N1 B–B4+; or
b) 28 R–K1 K × N 29 R–N2 B × NP 30 R × N B–B4+   31 K–B1 P × P 32 P × P K–K3. In each case Black's active bishop and mobile pawns give him the advantage.

28 ... N–K5   29 R–Q4 N–B6+
30 K–N2 N–K7   31 N × P N × R/5
32 N × P N–K7   33 R–KB1 B × NP
34 N–B5 K–K1   35 P–N4 N × P
36 R–K1 N–N7   37 R–K4 B–B6
38 R–QB4 and 0–1

Musil–Baretic
Cateske Toplice 1968

Malevinsky–Annikayev
Novosibirsk 1976

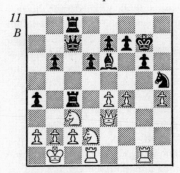

23 ...	R×N!
24 P×R	

If 24 Q×R Q×Q 25 P×Q N×P and White has too many weak pawns.

24 ...	N×P!

The knight cannot be captured because of 25 Q×N Q×P 26 R–QB1 P–R6 followed by mate.

25 QR–KB1?

After 25 QR–K1 Q×P, Black is clearly better. But the text makes matters much easier.

25 ...	N–K7!!
26 Q×N	Q×P
27 Q–Q3	Q–N5+
28 K–B1	

28 K–R1 loses to 28 ... R–B6! 29 R–N1 Q–B4! and 28 N–N3 to 28 ... P×N 29 BP×P R–B6! and 30 ... B×P.

28 ...	R–B6
29 Q–K2	Q–R6+
30 K–Q1	Q×P
31 K–K1	R×P
32 R–B3	

If 32 P–R5 B–B5 33 Q–K3 Q–N7!∓∓

32 ... Q–N7 Or 32 ... Q–R8+ at once. **33 P–R5 Q–R8+ 34 K–B2 Q–Q5+ 35 K–N3 R×N 36 P–R6+ K–R2 37 Q–K3 Q×Q 38 R×Q K×P 39 R–N1 B–N6 40 P–K5 P×P 0–1**

12 ...	R×N!?
13 P×R	P–Q4

White cannot now protect the QRP because after 14 K–N2 Black can quickly build up a devastating attack with 14 ... Q–B4 15 R–R1 N–N3 and ... N–R5+.

14 P–B5	B×P+
15 K–N1	P×KP
16 P×P	P×P
17 B×N	N×B
18 P–N5	N–Q4
19 Q–R5+	P–N3
20 Q–R3	N–B5
21 Q–N3	0–0
22 KR–K1	N×B
23 Q×N	

The complications are over. Black has rook and two bishops for two rooks and a knight—in itself a perfectly satisfactory arrangement—but in addition Black has two pawns and a promising Q-side attack. In other words, White is helpless.

23 ... B–Q4 24 R–KB1 Q–B2 25 R×R+ B×R 26 Q–B2 Q×BP 27 R–KB1 Q–N5+ 28 N–N3 P–K4 29 K–R1 P–QR4 30 Q–N6 B×N 31 R×B+ K×R 32 Q–N8+ K–B2 33 Q–R7+ Q–K2 34 Q–B2+ K–N1 35 P×B Q–R6+ 36 K–N1 Q×P+ 37 K–R1 Q–KB6+ 38 K–R2 Q–B5+ 0–1

Ljubojevic–Ribli
Portoroz / Ljubljana 1975

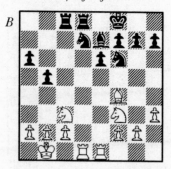

20 ...   **R×N!**

In return for the exchange Black develops strong pressure against White's shattered Q-side pawns. This motif can be very effective even when queens have already been exchanged.

21 P×R	N–Q4
22 B–Q2	N/2–N3
23 N–Q4	N–QB5

23 ... N–R5 was also a possibility.

24 R–KB1   **P–K4**

Now Black has a strong initiative and White must fight for a draw. The extra material is worthless at the moment because White's rooks and bishop are so inactive while Black's minor pieces have great dynamic potential.

25 N–N3	P–QR4
26 B–K1	P–B4
27 P–N4	P–B5
28 R–Q3	P–R5?

Driving the knight towards a better square (K4). Black should have continued 28 ... P–K5 29 R–Q4 P–R5 30 N–B1 (now N–Q2 leaves the QB3

pawn hanging) 30 ... B–B3 31 R×P B×P 32 R×P+ N×R 33 B×B N–Q7+ 34 B×N R×B, when despite being a pawn down Black has the better ending because of his actively placed pieces.

29 N–Q2	K–B2
30 N–K4	K–K3
31 B–Q2	N×B+
32 N×N	

Not 32 R×N?? N×P+!

32 ...   **N×P+**
33 K–N2

Black would again have the better ending after 33 R×N R×N.

33 ...	N–Q4
34 N–K4	R–QN1
35 R/1–Q1	N–N3
36 P–QB3	N–B5+
37 K–B2	N–R6+
38 K–B1	P–N5
39 P×P	B×P
40 N–N5+	

Other continuations permit Black to establish his rook on the seventh rank (... QB7) via ... QB1.

40 ...   **K–B3**
41 N–K4+   **K–K3**
                        ½–½

If 42 R–Q8 R–N3 43 R–QB8 B–K2, threatening ... R–N8+

Although Black mishandled his position with 28 ... P–R5 this example does serve to demonstrate that the exchange sacrifice on ... QB6 does not always need to find compensation in a mating attack a là the Dragon, but that pure positional considerations, such as the inactivity of White's forces, is often sufficient compensation in itself.

Gipslis–Simagin
USSR Ch ½-final
Sverdlovsk 1957

1 P–K4 P–QB4 2 N–KB3 P–Q3
3 P–Q4 P × P 4 N × P N–KB3
5 N–QB3 P–QR3 6 B–QB4 P–K3
7 0–0 B–K2 8 B–N3 N–B3 9 P–B4
9 B–K3 0–0 10 P–B4 N × N 11 B × N
transposes to the fourth game of the
1972 World Championship match in
which Spassky laid bare the inade-
quacies of White's opening strategy.

9 ...	N × N
10 Q × N	0–0
11 K–R1	P–QN4
12 P–QR3	

More active is 12 P–B5 at once.

12 ...	B–N2
13 P–B5	P–K4
14 Q–Q3	P–R3
15 B–K3?	

White should overprotect his KP by
15 B–Q2 R–B1 16 QR–K1.

15 ...	R–B1
16 QR–Q1	

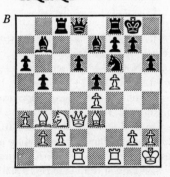

16 ...	R × N!
17 P × R	

If 17 Q × R B × P (threatening
18 ... Q–Q2 winning the KBP)
18 Q–Q2 Q–B1 19 Q–B2 N–N5 etc.

17 ...	B × P

18 Q–K2	Q–B1
19 P–B4	

Indirectly saving the KBP.

19 ...	P × P
20 B × BP	B–N2
21 B–N3	P–Q4

Threatening the QRP.

22 B–B1	

If 22 P–QB4 P–Q5 23 B × QP
(23 B–B1 B–Q3 is even better for
Black than the text because he would
be the proud owner of two passed
pawns) 23 ... P × B 24 Q × B R–K1
25 Q–Q6 R–K7 26 R–KN1 N–K5
and Black wins.

22 ...	B–Q3
23 B–N2	B–N1!

With the idea of 24 ... Q–B2 and
25 ... P–K5.

24 R–Q3	

Naturally not 24 B × KP? R–K1.

24 ...	P–Q5
25 R–N3	R–Q1

Black must defend the QP before
advancing the KP. If 25 ... P–K5?
26 B × QP B × R 27 B × N! P × B
(otherwise 28 Q–N4) 28 P × B, and
White will win through the manoeuvre R–B4, Q–R5 and R–R4.

26 B–B1	P–K5
27 B–KB4	B × B
28 R × B	

Threatening 29 R/4–N4! N × R
30 Q × N P–N3 31 Q × NP+ etc.

28 ...	B–Q4!

See diagram next page

As well as defending against the
threat, the text improves Black's endgame prospects by exchanging bishops
and thereby highlighting the weakness of White's split pawns.

29 B × B	R × B
30 R × KP!	

The best chance. 30 R/4–N4 can

now be met by 30 ... N×R   31 Q×N P–N3 or even 30 ... P–Q6.

If Black is allowed to keep both central pawns the win would be only a matter of simple technique. Now, however, Black must play the rook and pawn endgame with great accuracy. (All rook endings are drawn— Russian Proverb)

30 ... N×R   31 Q×N Q×KBP 32 Q×Q R×Q   33 K–N1 R–B4 34 R–Q3 R–B5   35 K–B1 P–B4 36 R–Q2 K–B2   37 K–K2 K–K3 38 K–Q1 White cannot activate his king: 38 K–Q3 R–R5 and 39 ... K–Q4. **38 ... K–Q4 39 R–K2 R–R5** At last the vulnerability of White's Q-side pawns makes itself felt. **40 R–K7!** The last chance. **40 ... P–N4 41 R–KR7 R×P 42 R×P** White has defended well, but now comes a neat winning manoeuvre. **42 ... P–Q6!   43 P×P R–R7 44 P–N3 K–Q5   45 R–KB6 K×P 46 K–K1 K–K5   47 P–R4 P–N5 48 K–B1 K–B6!   49 R×BP+ K×P 50 P–R5 R–R8+   51 K–K2 P–R4 52 P–R6 R–R8   53 R–B6** After 53 R×P R×P   54 K–B1 K–R7 the ending is a simple 'book' win. **53 ... P–R5   54 R–R6 R–R4!** Not 54 ... K–N7?? 55 R×P

drawing. **55 K–K3 K–R7 56 R–KN6 P–N6   57 K–B3 R–R6! 0–1**

Drag on Endgame

Huguet–Wade
Monte Carlo 1967

1 P–K4 P–QB4   2 N–KB3 P–Q3 3 P–Q4 P×P   4 N×P N–KB3 5 N–QB3 P–KN3   6 B–K3 B–N2 7 P–B3 N–B3 8 Q–Q2 0–0 9 B–QB4 B–Q2   10 P–KR4 Q–R4   11 0–0–0 KR–B1   12 B–N3 N–K4   13 P–R5 N×RP

14 P–N4

After 14 B–R6 Black can choose between the incredibly complex 14 ... N–Q6+!? (which may lead, by 15 Q×N B×B+   16 K–N1, to the position of Hartston–Westerinen [cf example 10]), or 14 ... B×B 15 Q×B R×N   16 P×R R–QB1! which can be shown to be good for at least a draw, e.g. 17 N–K2! (not 17 K–N1? N–QB5   18 R–Q3 Q–R6 19 B×N R×B 20 N–N3 B–K3 when Black has a decisive attack. Wood-cock–Whiteley, Oxford 1966; nor 17 P–N4 N–KB3   18 P–N5 N–R4 19 R×N P×R   20 Q×P/R5 Q×BP 21 K–N1 N–B5! 22 B×N R×B∓ ∓)

17 ... N–KB3   18 K–N1 B–N4
19 N–B4 B–B5!   20 N–R3 R–B3
21 N–N5 B×B   22 BP×B Q×BP
23 N×RP Q–B7+ ½–½ Timperly–
Hollis, British Corres Ch 1966/67.

14 K–N1 R×N 15 Q×R Q×Q
16 P×Q R–QB1 leaves Black with an
impregnable position and modest
winning chances in the endgame.
Some examples:
a) 17 B–N5 B–KB3! 18 B×B
(18 R×N P×R 19 B×B P×B
20 K–N2 N–N3 is certainly not bad
for Black) 18 ... N×B 19 K–N2,
and now Black can secure good
chances by remaining passive on the
Q-side and starting a K-side advance
with ... N–KR4–N6, ... P–KR4,
... P–KN4 and ... P–R5; Black's
knights would then be more active
than White's rooks;
b) 17 N–K2 P–R4 18 P–R3 P–R5
19 B–R2 B–N4 20 KR–K1 N–QB5
21 B×N B×B 22 B–Q4 N–B3
23 N–B1 P–K4 24 B–K3 P–Q4
25 B–N5 P×P 26 P×P B–K3 and
Black was gaining the upper hand.
Scholl–Tatai, Beverwijk 1967;
c) 17 K–N2 (best) 17 ... P–R4
18 P–R3 N–KB3 19 B–KB4 N–K1
20 B–N5 P–R5 21 B–R2 N–QB3!
22 R–Q2 N–B3 23 N×N B×N
24 R–Q4 P–R4 (leaving his RP safely
defended so as to free his king for its
travels to the Q-side) 25 K–B1 K–B1
26 K–Q2 R–R1 27 R–N4 R–R4
28 B–K3 P–K3 29 P–QB4 N–Q2
30 P–B3 B–B3 (Black's position has
absolutely no weaknesses) 31 B–QN1
B–KN4+ 32 B–K3 B×B+ 33 K×B
K–K2 34 K–B2 N–B4 35 R/N4–N1
N–Q2 36 R–N4 N–B4 37 R/N4–N1
N–Q2 ½–½ Spassky–Stein, RSFSR–
Ukraine match 1967. A fine example

of the resilience of Black's position in
the endgame despite his material
deficit.

14 ... **N–KB3**
15 B–R6
   15 K–N1 R×N 16 Q×R Q×Q
17 P×Q R–QB1 18 K–N2 P–QB4
produces a typical Dragon exchange
sacrifice endgame which bears a
marked affinity to that of the
Spassky–Stein game given in the
previous note. Here, however, there
is the important difference that White
has already committed himself to the
advance P–N4 which leaves White
with an inflexible pawn-structure and,
in particular, a weak pawn at KB3.
Ezmakov–Keene, USSR–GB Corres
match 1967/70 continued: 19 P–R3
(not 19 P–R4? when this pawn will
soon be lost) 19 ... P–R5 20 B–R2
B–K1 21 R–R3 N/3–Q2 22 N–K2!
R–B3 23 B–Q5 R–R3 24 B×P
N–B5+ 25 K–B1 R–R4 26 B–Q4
N×P 27 B–Q5 N–K4 28 R/1–R1
P–R3 29 B–R2 R–N4 30 N–B4 K–B1
31 N–Q3 R–N1 32 N×N P×N
33 B–K3 N–N4 34 B–Q2 P–N4
35 P–QB4 N–Q5 36 P–B3 N–K7+
37 K–B2 N–B5 38 R/3–R2 P–R6
39 B–N3? (Correct was 39 B×N!
KP×B with an unclear position—
Black's chances should be no worse.)
39 ... B–R5! 40 B×B (40 R–QN1
P–R7∓∓) 40...R–N7+ 41 K–B1
(41 K–Q1 P–R7∓∓) 41...N–Q6+
42 K–Q1 P–R7 43 K–K2 N–B4!!
44 R–R1 N×B 0–1. There is little to
be done. If 45 R/2–R1 N–B4 46
K–K3 P–R4! 47 P×P (47 R×P
N–N6∓∓) 47 ... B–R3∓∓. If
White ignores Black's KRP there
follows ... P–R5 when Black's two
passed RP's are decisive.

Don't allow opening of d-file

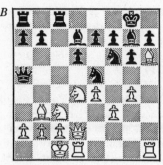

15 ...   **R×N!**

16 P×R

On 16 Q×R Q×Q 17 P×Q B×B 18 R×B, Black can either play it safe with 18 ... P–QN4 which probably leads to no more than a draw, or try for more with 18 ... N–R4 19 P×N K–N2 20 P×P K×R 21 P×BP R–KB1 when his outside passed pawn should give him the better ending but 22 R–N1 may pose some nasty problems on the way.

16 ...   **B×B**

16 ... N×BP 17 B×P+ K×B 18 N×N Q–R6+ 19 K–N1 N×KP 20 Q–B4+ B–B4 should lead to a draw after running through a maze of intricacies, e.g. 21 B×B P–K4! 22 N×P+ (if 22 B×P P×B 23 R×P+ K–N1 24 R–R8+ K×R 25 Q×P+ K–N1) 22 ... K×B 23 Q–R6+ K–B3 24 N–Q7+ K–K3! 25 P×B+ K×N 26 R–Q3 N×P+ 27 R×N Q×R 28 Q×P+ K–B3 29 P×P Q–N5+ etc.

17 R×B

17 Q×B R–QB1 leads to a position reached in the note to White's fourteenth move.

17 ...   **R–QB1**

18 K–N2   **Q–N3**

Not 18 ... P–QN4? 19 R/1–KR1 N–B5+ 20 B×N P×B 21 R×RP!

N×R 22 Q–R6±± Tal–Wade Palma 1966.

Another possibility is 18 ... N–B5+ 19 B×N R×B 20 N–N3 (20 R/1–KR1 R–R5!) 20 ... Q–K4 21 Q–K3 B×P! 22 P×B N×NP 23 Q–Q3 R×KP 24 R–R4 N–B7 25 R×R N×Q+ 26 P×N with a difficult game for both sides. Analysis by Tal.

19 K–B1

19 Q–R2 Q–B4 20 R×RP Q×P+ 21 K–N1 N×R 22 R–R1 P–K3 23 Q×N+ K–B1 24 Q–R6+ K–K2 25 Q–N5+ P–B3 26 R–R7+ N–B2 27 Q×NP Q–K8+ draws by perpetual check.

19 ...   **Q–R4**

20 K–N2   **Q–N3**

21 K–B1   **Q–B4**

22 K–N2   **P–R4!**

23 R/1–KR1   **P–R5?**

23 ... P–K3!, a suggestion of Larsen's, gives Black the advantage. The text should lead to no more than a draw.

24 R×RP   **N×R**

25 Q–R6   **P–K3**

26 P–N5

With the threat of 27 Q×N+ K–B1 28 Q–R8+ K–K2 29 Q–B6+ and 30 R–R8 mate.

26 ...   **N–N5!**

If White captures this knight, 27 ... Q×P+ and 28 ... Q×N leave Black's queen defending the K-side.

27 Q×N+   **K–B1**

See diagram next page

28 N–K2??

This move leads to a lost position. 28 B×P also loses after 28 ... Q×BP+ 29 K–N1 B×B 30 N×B+ K–K2.

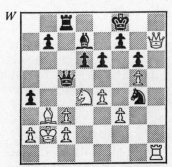

White can draw however by 28 N × P+!! B × N 29 B × B, when Black is obliged to take a perpetual check.

28 ...	P × B
29 P × N	Q × NP

Taking away the threat of mate.

30 R–KB1	B–K1
31 N–B4	K–K2
32 RP × P	R–R1!

White's threats have mostly disappeared and Black starts to bounce back. White can never afford to play an endgame, an unfortunate state of affairs because with queens on his king is faced with unsurmountable problems.

33 P–N4	Q × P
34 Q–N7	Q–N4
35 Q–Q4	Q–N4
36 N × NP+	

Desperation! But otherwise Black's queen comes to QR3 with a vengeance.

36 ...	P × N
37 Q–N7+	K–Q1
38 Q–B6+	K–Q2
39 R–KR1	Q–R3
40 R–R7+	K–B3
41 K–B1	Q–K7

Threatening mate in three by 42 ... Q–K8+ etc.

42 K–N2	Q–Q8
43 P–N5+	K–N3??

A cure for which there is no disease. It is criminal that Black, having played impeccably for so long, should lose half a point by playing one bad move. Clearly there is no justice in chess.

Simply 43 ... K × P 44 R × P+ K–B3 forces White's resignation. Now it is Black who must be careful.

44 Q–B2+	K–R4!
45 R × P	K–R5
46 Q–N6	

46 P–K5 P–Q4 47 Q–B4+ P–Q5 48 P × P K–R4 also draws.

46 ...	R–R4
½–½	

47 R–QR7 R × R 48 Q × R+ K × P 49 Q–QN7+ K–B4 50 Q–QB7+ B–B3 51 Q–R5+ draws by perpetual check. 47 Q–B7 also draws after 47 ... R × P+ (not 47 ... B × P 48 Q–B4+ with mate to follow) 48 R × R K × R!

Just as one of the principal aims of White's N–Q5 sacrifice is to take control of KB5 with the Q4 knight, so the point of the N–KB5 sacrifice is usually to capture the Q5 square with the QB3 knight as in Erikson–Maricic, Corres 1961:

10 N–B5! 0–0 If 10 ... P×N 11 B×N P×B 12 N–Q5 B×B 13 R×B+ K–B1 14 Q–R5±± **11 N×B+ Q×N 12 N–Q5 Q–Q1 13 N×N+ P×N 14 B–KR6 K–R1 15 B×R and White won.**
This particular example is rather drastic—White's winning sequence is all forced from the moment that he plays N–B5. That Black was unable to capture the knight is not an uncommon occurrence. The exchange of this knight for Black's KB (the normal continuation when Black has

not captured on KB4) is usually advantageous to the first player. Geller–Filip (*12*) is an example in which Black cannot afford to capture the knight and so retreats his KB to avoid having it exchanged.

In Tolush–Lehmann, W. Germany–USSR match 1960, White's attacking prospects were enhanced by the fact that the KB-file was half-open:

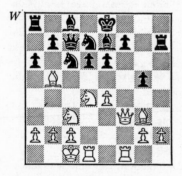

15 N–B5! P×B If 15 ... P×N 16 N–Q5 Q–Q1 17 B×N P×B 18 N×B Q×N 19 B×P Q–Q1 20 P×P and 21 KR–K1+ **16 N×NP Q–R4 17 N/N5×P+ B×N 18 N×B+ K–K2** and now White could have forced an immediate win by **19 Q×P+!! R×Q 20 R×R+ K–Q1 21 N×P+! B×N 22 R–B8+! K–K2 23 B–Q6 mate.**

A more typical example of the attack on the K-file is Shamkovich–Lebedev, USSR Ch ½-final 1956:

17 N–B5! P×N   17 ... N/1–N3 18 R/4–B1 0-0-0 would be inadequate because of simply 19 N×B+ N×N   20 B×N P×B   21 R×P. **18 N–Q5 Q–N1** If 18 ... Q–R4 19 P×P R–B1   20 B–K1! Q–N4 21 P–B4 Q–B3   22 N×B K×N 23 B–N4! and Black is crushed. **19 P×P B–QB3   20 N×B K×N 21 P–B6+   K–K1   22 R/4–Q4 N/1–N3   23 R×P K–B1   24 B×N and White won.**

Palmiotto–Primavera (*13*) and Matulovic–Bertok (*14*) are two more examples of successful attacks along the K-file.

White's Q4 knight can sometimes be offered on KB5 when Black has played ... P–KN3 instead of ... P–K3. This theme occurs occasionally in the Dragon Variation when White plans to attack along the open KN-file as in Bokor–Sapi, Hungarian Ch ½-final 1967:

19 N–B5! P×N   20 NP×P B–R5 21 QR–N1 N–K1 22 R×B+! N×R 23 Q–R6 K–B1   24 Q–B6! K–K1 25 Q×QP 1–0

Another example of this idea is the Levy–Whiteley game at the end of this chapter. White's sacrifice does not lead to a forced win as in the above example but Black is sufficiently immobile to make his defensive task very difficult.

Geller–Filip
Curaçao 1962

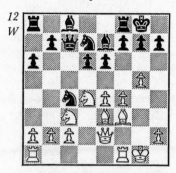

12
W

14 N–B5!   B–Q1

After 14 ... P×N 15 N–Q5 White
wins back the piece and retains the
more active position. Best was 14 ...
R–K1, a move which Filip rejected
because he felt that after 15 N×B+
R×N White's initiative was too
dangerous.

15 B–Q4!

Very powerful. If now 15 ... P×N
(15 ... P–K4 16 N–Q5 is almost as
bad as 15 ... P–KN3 16 N–R6
mate) 16 N–Q5 Q–B3 17 P×P!
with a very strong attack.

15 ...   P–B3

16 K–R1

Hoping to continue the attack
along the KN-file.

16 ...   N/2–N3

Not 16 ... P–N4 17 P×P P×P
(17 ... B×P 18 P–K5!) 18 Q–N2+
K–B2 19 B–R5 mate.

17 P×P?!

17 N–N3 is good for White.

17 ...   B×P?

After 17 ... P×N 18 BP×P R–K1
19 B–R5 B–Q2 it is not at all clear
that White has enough for the piece,
e.g. 20 B–B7+ K×B 21 P–N8=Q+
R×Q 22 Q–R5+ K–B1. Possibly

Geller had been counting on Filip's
cautious nature.

18 B×B   R×B

19 N×QP!   R×P

Bad is 19 ... N×N 20 P–K5 R×P
21 P×N Q×P 22 QR–Q1 Q–B2
23 B–K4! with dangerous threats.

20 N×N   N×N?

Correct is 20 ... Q×N 21 Q–Q2
R–B1 22 B–K2! R×R+ 23 R×R
Q–B2 with roughly equal chances.

W

21 P–K5!!

A very strong move, introducing a
new attacking possibility in N–K4.
There is also the threat of 22 N–Q5
P×N 23 B×P+ and 24 R×R.

21 ...   B–Q2

There was no satisfactory defence:
a) 21 ... Q×P 22 B–K4;
b) 21 ... N×KP 22 N–Q5 P×N
23 B×P+ R–B2 24 R×R N×R
25 Q–K8 mate;
c) 21 ... R–B2 22 N–Q5 Q–B4
23 P–N4!; or
d) 21 ... Q–B2 22 B–R5 R×R+
23 R×R Q–B2 24 B–B7+ K–R1
25 B–K8! P–KN3 26 R–B7 Q–B4
27 N–K4 and White wins.

22 N–Q5   1–0

After 22 ... P×N 23 B×P+
K–R1 24 R×R N×KP 25 R–K1,
White has a winning attack.

Palmiotto–Primavera
Italian Ch 1965

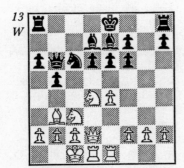

Matulovic–Bertok
Yugoslavia 1966

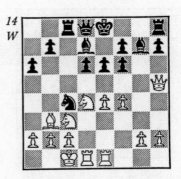

13 N–B5!   **P×N**
14 N–Q5   **Q–Q1**

On 14 ... Q–R4 comes 15 Q–R6 (threatening 16 P×P, 17 N×B and 18 Q×BP) 15 ... 0–0–0 16 P×P KR–K1 17 N×B+ R×N 18 R×R N×R 19 Q×BP and if 19 ... N×P 20 P–N4 traps the knight in broad daylight.

     15 P×P   **0–0**
     16 R×B!   **N×R**
     17 N×P+   **K–N2**

If 17 ... K–R1 18 Q–R6 B×P 19 N–R5 R–KN1 20 Q–B6+ and mate next move.

     18 Q–B3

Not 18 Q–N5+ N–N3! 19 N–R5+ K–R1 20 Q–R6 R–KN1∓∓. But now White threatens mate by 19 N–K8++ K–R3 20 Q–N7+ etc.

18 ... N×P   **19 N×B+**   Since Black's KN2 square is now defended.
19 ... K–N1   **20 N×R Q×N**
21 Q–B3 N–N2 If 21 ... N–R3 simply 22 Q–N3+ and 23 R×P.
22 B×P+ K–R1   **23 R×P R–R2**
24 R–KB6 Q–K2 25 B–Q5 Q–K8+
26 Q–Q1 Q–N5 27 P–QB3 Q–K2
28 Q–B3 1–0

14 N–B5!   **P×N**
15 P×P+   **K–B1**
16 N–K4

Threatening 17 B×N R×B 18 N×QP±±.

     16 ...   **Q–B2**
     17 K–N1!

Still with the same threat.

     17 ...   **B–K1**

If 17 ... P–Q4 18 B×N Q×B (or 18 ... P×B 19 N–Q6 B–B3— *19 ... B–K1 20 Q–K2 B–B3 21 N×R Q×N 22 Q–K7+ etc.*— 20 N×R Q×N 21 R–Q2 followed by R/2–K2 or R/1–Q1 as appropriate) 19 N–Q6 Q×QBP+ 20 K–R1 B–K1 21 R×B+±±
18 B×N Q×B 19 N×Q P Q×QBP+
20 K–R1 Q–B2   **21 N×R Q×N**
22 Q–K2 B–R3 23 Q–K7+ K–N2
24 R–K6! R–B1 25 Q×P/6+ K–N1
26 R–K3 B×P 27 R–QB3 B–B3 If
27 ... Q–N1 28 R–Q8 Q–R2 29 P–QR3 followed by R/3–B8. **28 P–KN3 B–B2**   **29 R–Q4 R–K1**
30 R–KN4+ K–B1   **31 Q–N7+ K–K2**   **32 R–K3+ K–Q3**   **33 Q–B6+ 1–0**

Balashov–Gheorghiu
Leningrad 1977

16 N/4×P!

An unusual form of the knight sacrifice. White does not secure the opening of the KN-file but instead establishes his other knight on the dominating square KB5.

16 ...   **P×N**
17 N×P   **B–KB1**

If 17 . . . R–KN1 18 N×B+ R×N 19 B–Q4 R–N3 20 KR–B1, etc.

18 KR–B1   **Q–Q2**
19 B–Q4

Increasing the pressure, almost to breaking point.

19 ...   **Q–K3**

Threatening, quite simply, to take the QRP.

20 K–N1!

Safeguarding everything. Now there is no threat on QR2, no check by Black's rook on . . . QB1 , and Black cannot resist the pressure for very much longer.

20 ...   **N×KP**

What else? If 20 . . . R–KN1 21 B×N Q×B 22 N×P+ Q×N 23 Q×P+ K–Q1 24 Q×R, with a fairly easy win.

21 Q–B4   **R–KN1**
22 KR–K1   **0–0–0**
23 P×N   **P–B3**

Preventing 24 P–K5.

24 P–KR3   **R–K1**
25 K–R1   **P–KR4**
26 B–B2!   **P×P**
27 P×P   **B×P**
28 N×P+   **B×N**
29 R×KB   **Q×NP**
30 R–QB1+   **K–N1**
31 R–QN6+   **1–0**

Nicolaide–Ghiricuta
Rumania 1975

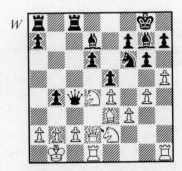

18 N–B5!   **P×N**
19 NP×P

Here, as in the Levy–Whiteley example, Black has to face a fierce attack along the KN-file.

19 ...   **P–KR3?**

19 ... K–R1 would offer more resistance, though after the obvious build-up 20 QR–N1 R–KN1 21 Q×QP Q–B3 22 Q×NP, White still has pressure along the KN-file and he now has three pawns for the piece.

20 B×KRP!   **Q×BP+**

Exchanging into a lost ending, but what else can Black do. If 20 ... B–R1 21 QR–N1+ K–R2 22 B–N7! B×B 23 P–R6 B–R1 24 Q–N5 with a mating attack.

21 Q×Q   **R×Q**
22 B×B!   **R×N**
23 B×N

Even without queens on the board White's mate threats persist.

23 ...   **R–QB1**
24 P–R6   **K–R2**
25 QR–N1!   **R/1–B7**
26 R–N7+   **1–0**

If 27 ... K–R1 28 R–N8+! K×R 29 P–R7+ and mate next move.

Ulyanov–Lepeshkin
Sochi 1965

1 P–K4 P–QB4   2 N–KB3 P–Q3
3 P–Q4 P×P   4 N×P N–KB3
5 N–QB3 P–QR3   6 B–KN5 P–K3
7 P–B4 B–K2   8 Q–B3 Q–B2
9 0–0–0 QN–Q2   10 P–KN4 P–N4
11 B×N N×B   12 P–N5 N–Q2
     13 P–QR3   R–QN1!

The logical way for Black to seek counterplay in view of White's last move.

14 B–R3

Not best. It is currently thought that 14 P–KR4 is the correct move, defending the KNP in preparation for P–B5. After 14 P–KR4 P–N5 15 P×P R×P 16 B–R3, Black has three serious possibilities:

a) 16 ... Q–N3 17 N–B5! P×N 18 N–Q5 Q–B4 19 P×P B–N2 20 KR–K1 B×N 21 R×B/5 Q–B3 22 B–N2! Q–R5 23 R×P 0–0 24 R×B R–QB1 when Boleslavsky evaluates the position as good for Black but Gipslis points out that after 25 R–QB6! it is White who has the advantage:

b) 16 ... 0–0 17 N×KP!? (in Minic–Fischer, Rovinj/Zagreb 1970, White sacrificed thematically with

17 N–B5 but after 17 ... N–B4! 18 N×B+ Q×N 19 P–R5 B–N2 20 P–R6 B×KP! 21 N×B N×N 22 P×P R–B1 23 R–R2 R–R5 24 K–N1 P–Q4! Black had parried White's attack and went over to a powerful counter-attack.) 17 ... P×N 18 B×P+ K–R1 19 N–Q5 Q–B5! (weak is 19 ... Q–N2 20 N×B! N–K4 21 B×B R×B 22 P×N R×BP+?! 23 K×R R×NP+ 24 K–B1!±±) 20 B×N B×B 21 N×B R/1–QN1, and according to Gligoric has sufficient active possibilities to compensate for his material deficit; or

c) 16 ... N–B4 17 P–B5! Q–N3 (other moves are no better) 18 BP×P P×P 19 N×KP N×N 20 N–Q5 Q–N2 21 N×R Q×N 22 K–N1! (with the threat of 23 P–K5) and White may have some advantage.

     14 ...   N–B4

15 N–B5?!

Extant master games lead us to conclude that this sacrifice is unsound. The most popular continuation is 15 KR–N1 P–N5 16 P×P R×P 17 P–B5 Q–N3 which is thought to offer equal chances.

     15 ...   P×N

15 ... 0–0 also seems to be good

for Black (compare the Minic–Fischer game cited above). Parma–Buljovcic, Yugoslav Ch 1965 continued 16 N × B+ Q × N 17 P–B5?! (better 17 KR–N1) 17 ... Q × P+ 18 K–N1 P–N5 19 P × P R × P 20 KR–B1 P × P 21 B × P B–N2 22 N–Q5 B × N 23 R × B P–N3 24 Q–B3 Q–N7 25 R/1–Q1 R–N3 26 Q–B6 R/1–N1 27 R × N R × P+ 28 K–R1 R7–N5 29 B–K6 R–R5+ 30 B–R2 R × B+ 31 K × R P × R and Black was two pawns ahead.

| 16 N–Q5 | Q–Q1 |
| 17 P × P | B–N2! |

This is why White's sacrifice is doomed. He has too much wood on the long diagonal, most of which belongs on the K-file.

| 18 P–B6 | P × P |
| 19 Q–R5 | |

What else? After 19 KR–K1 B × N and 20 ... 0–0, White has no real attack.

19 ...	B × N
20 R × B	P–N5
21 P–R4	P–N6
22 R–K1	Q–B2

Threatening 23 ... N–Q6+ 24 K–N1 Q × P+ and mate.

| 23 P–B3 | R–N5! |

Intending to exchange one pair of rooks, thereby reducing White's pressure on the K-file and taking advantage of the fact that White's king is more exposed than his own.

24 P × P	R–K5
25 R × R	N × R
26 P × B	N × P

Decisive.

27 P × N Q × BP+ 28 K–Q1 Q–B7+ 29 K–K1 P–N7 30 R–Q1 P–N8=Q 31 R × Q Q × R+ 32 K–B2 Q–B7+ 33 K–K3 Q–B6+

34 K–K4 Q–QB3+ 35 K–Q3 Q × P 36 B–K6 Q–N4+ 0–1

Jovcic–Zlatan
Yugoslav Corres Ch 1959

1 P–K4 P–QB4 2 N–KB3 P–Q3 3 P–Q4 P × P 4 N × P N–KB3 5 N–QB3 P–QR3 6 B–QB4 P–K3 7 0–0 P–QN4 8 B–N3 P–N5 9 N–R4 N × P
10 R–K1!

10 P–B4 would transpose to the famous game Fischer–Tal, Belgrade 1959: 10 ... P–N3? 11 P–B5! NP × P 12 N × BP R–N1 (not 12 ... P × N? 13 Q–Q5 R–R2 14 Q–Q4 forking two rooks, nor 12 ... B–QN2 13 N–R6 B × N 14 Q–R5! Q–K2 15 B × B R–N1 – threatening 16 ... R × P+ 17 K × R N–KB3+ – 16 P–N3 N–Q2 17 QR–K1 with a strong attack. Szeles–Sax, Hungary 1972. But a better defence is 12 ... P–Q4 13 N–R6 B × N—Fischer) 13 B–Q5! R–R2, and now Fischer gives 14 B–K3! N–B4 15 Q–R5! R–N3 16 QR–K1! with a strong attack.

| 10 ... | N–KB3 |

Not 10 ... B–N2? 11 N × P P × N 12 B × P with a winning attack, e.g. 12 ... Q–R4 13 Q–B3 B–K2 14 R × N Q × N 15 B–N5!

10 ... N–B4? is also bad: 11 N × N P × N 12 B–R4+ B–Q2 13 N × P.

Probably the best defence is 10 ... P–Q4 11 B–KB4 (threatening 12 B × N followed by 13 N–B6) 11 ... B–N2 (in Nei–Chukaev, Voroshilovgrad 1955, Black played 11 ... B–Q2 with a view to a later ... Q–R4, winning a piece. The game continued 12 P–B4 NP×Pep 13 N×BP N×N 14 P×N B–K2 15 N–B5! 0–0—*not 15 ... P×N 16 Q–Q5*—16 B×P N–B3 17 N×B+ Q×N 18 B–K4±. 11 ... B–Q3 fails to 12 B×B Q×B 13 P–KB3! N–KB3 14 N–KB5 Q–B2 15 Q–Q2 0–0 16 N×P!) 12 Q–R5! with excellent attacking chances for the pawn.

11 B–N5   **B–K2**

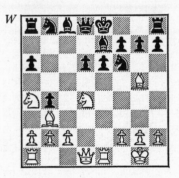

12 N–KB5!   **0–0**

After 12 ... P×N White wins by 13 B×N P×B 14 Q–Q5 R–R2 15 Q×BP+ K–Q2 16 N–N6+ etc.

13 N×B+   **Q×N**
14 N–N6   **B–N2**

On 14 ... R–R2 15 N–Q5 Q–Q1 16 B×N P×B 17 Q–Q4, White wins the exchange under circumstances that are much better than in the game.

**15 N×R B×N   16 B×N Q×B
17 Q×P N–B3 18 QR–Q1 P–KR4
19 Q–B5 Q–N3   20 P–KB3 P–R5
21 P–KR3 R–K1 22 R–Q6 Q–N6
23 R/1×P! R–KB1** If 23 ... P×R 24 R×P R×R 25 B×R+ K–R2 26 Q–KR5 mate **24 Q–B5 N–K2
25 R×N Q×R   26 B×P+ K–R1
27 R–K6 1–0**

Velimirovic–Bukal
Yugoslav Team Ch, Pula 1971

**1 P–K4 P–QB4   2 N–KB3 P–Q3
3 P–Q4 P×P   4 N×P N–KB3
5 N–QB3 N–B3   6 B–QB4 P–K3
7 B–K3 B–K2   8 Q–K2 P–QR3
9 0–0–0 Q–B2 10 B–N3 0–0**

The older variation was 10 ... P–QN4 11 P–N4! N–QR4 12 P–N5 N×B+ 13 RP×N N–Q2

14 N–B5!? (Thematic but unsound. Correct is 14 P–R4 P–N5 15 N–R4, e.g. 15 ... B–N2 16 P–KB3 N–B4 17 P–R5 Q–R4 18 K–N1 N×N 19 P×N Q×RP 20 P–N6 R–QB1 21 Q–N2 B–KB3 22 B–N5! with a winning attack. Platonov–Polugay-evsky, 35 USSR Ch 1967) 14 ... P×N (Medina–Pomar, Malaga 1969 went instead: 14 ... P–N5 15 N×NP+ K–B1 16 Q–R5! K×N 17 B–Q4+ N–K4 18 P–B4 P×N 19 B×P with a dangerous attack) 15 N–Q5 Q–Q1 16 P×P B–N2 (Velimirovic–Sofrevsky, Yugoslav Ch 1965 went 16 ... 0–0 17 P–B6! P×P 18 B–Q4 N–K4 19 P×P B×P 20 KR–N1+ B–KN2 21 B×N with a winning attack. The text exchanges White's powerful knight.) 17 P–B6

P×P 18 KR–K1 B×N! 19 R×B R–KN1! Gheorghiu–Hamann, Vrnjacka Banja 1967. In the game White's attack was rebuffed after 20 P–R4 R–QB1 21 B–B4 K–B1 22 P×P N×P 23 R–KB5 R–B4! 24 B–R6+ K–K1 25 R×N R–K4! Afterwards Gheorghiu pointed out the drawing possibility 20 B–B4 K–B1 21 Q–R5 Q–R4 22 Q–K2 Q–Q1 etc. So far no improvement has been found for White and the 14 N–B5 sacrifice has almost disappeared from master chess.

Because of the Platonov–Polugayevsky game and the various possibilities open to White because of Black's king being in the centre, Larsen prepared a different plan for his game against Fischer at the 1970 Interzonal Tournament in Palma.

11 P–N4

11 KR–N1 has become popular again thanks to the game Ostapenko–Zhartsev (see page 121).

11 ...   **N–Q2**

Larsen's move.

12 N–B5!?

Typical Velimirovic—When in doubt, sacrifice something! The Fischer–Larsen game went 12 P–KR4? (described at the time as 'Criminal' by Velimirovic who had once recommended 12 P–N5 to Fischer in this position) 12 ... N–B4 13 P–N5 P–N4 (so far Larsen had consumed only three minutes) 14 P–B3 B–Q2 15 Q–N2 P–N5 16 N/3–K2 N×B+ 17 RP×N P–QR4 and Black's attack was the stronger.

When I visited Belgrade only a week or so after Velimirovic had played this game, the entire chess fraternity of the city was endeavouring to persuade me that N–B5 was unsound but no-one could show me a refutation.

The notes which follow are based on Velimirovic's own analysis in *Informator 11*.

12 ...   **P×N**
13 N–Q5   **Q–Q1**
14 NP×P   **N–R4**

After 14 ... N–B3 15 B–N6 Q–Q2 16 KR–N1 K–R1 17 R–Q3, White has sufficient compensation for the sacrificed material.

15 N×B+   **Q×N**
16 B–Q5   **K–R1**
17 KR–N1   **N–KB3**
18 Q–B3

Not 18 B–Q4? B×P

18 ...   **N×B**
19 R×N

If 19 R×P K×R (not 19 ... N×B 20 R×RP+ K×R 21 Q–R5+ K–N2 22 R–N1+ K–B3 23 Q–R4+) 20 R–N1+ K–R1 21 Q–N4 Q–B3 22 P×N N–B5! and Black wins because he can meet 23 B–Q4 with 23 ... N–K4.

19 ...   **N–B5**
20 P–B6 !

20 R×NP K×R 21 B–R6+ K×B 22 P–B6 looks tempting, but after 22 ... Q–K4! 23 R×Q P×R

24 Q–N3 B–K3! 25 Q–N7+ K–R4 26 Q×RP+ K–N5 27 Q–N7+ K–B6 28 Q–N3+ K×KP White soon runs out of checks.

20 ...   Q×BP
21 Q×Q   P×Q
22 B–Q4

Even with so little material on the board Velimirovic is still trying to weave a mating net.

22 ...   N–K4
23 P–KB4   N–Q2
24 R×P

Threatening 25 R×N B×R 26 B×P mate.

24 ...   R–KN1
25 R–Q1

Still with the threat of 26 R×N.

25 ...   R–K1

If 25 ... K–N2 26 B–B3 and Black is still under pressure, e.g. 26 ... R–K1? 27 R–N1+ K–R3 (27 ... K–B1 28 B–N4± ± or 27 ... K–R1 28 R×N± ±) 28 B×P and Black is being mated.

26 P–B5   R×P
27 R–N1   P–KR4
28 R–N5!   R–N5?

After 28 ... K–R2 29 B×P N×B 30 R×N R–K2 31 R–Q6 R–K1 32 R×KRP+ K–N2 33 R–N5+ K–R2 (not 33 ... K–B1 34 P–B6

B–K3 35 R–KR5) 34 P–KR4, according to Velimirovic, White has a clear advantage. Clearly White should not lose this position but there seems no good winning plan either. After 34 ... P–N4 for example, if 35 P–R5 R–KN1!

29 R×BP!   R–N8+

29 ... K–R2 loses to 30 R×KRP+ K–N1 31 R–R8+ K×R 32 R–R6++ K–N1 33 R–R8 mate, 29 ... R×R to 30 R–R6++ K–N1 31 R–R8 mate, 29 ... R×B to 30 R–R6 mate and 29 ... N×R to 30 B×N+ K–R2 31 R×P+ K–N1 32 R–R8 mate.

'With Velimirovic all variations lead to mate'—Bent Larsen.

30 K–Q2

30 R×R N×R 31 B×N+ K–R2 32 R–N7+ and 33 R×P leaves White only two pawns ahead. The text retains all the mating possibilities mentioned in the previous note.

30 ...   R–N7+
31 K–K3   1–0

Levy–Whiteley
Southern Counties Junior Ch 1963

1 P–K4 P–QB4 2 N–KB3 P–Q3
3 P–Q4 P×P 4 N×P N–KB3
5 N–QB3 P–KN3 6 B–K3 B–N2
7 P–B3 0–0 8 Q–Q2 N–B3 9 B–QB4 N–Q2 10 P–KR4 N–N3
11 B–N3 N–R4 12 Q–K2

Not good because it deprives White's Q4 knight of its natural retreat square. But in 1963 I knew little about the finer points of the Dragon and had not encountered Black's next move before. Correct is 12 Q–Q3.

12 ...   **P–QR3!**

This move threatens 13 ... P–K4, winning the knight, but instead of saving the piece by 13 Q–Q3, which would be an admission that my last move was bad, I decided to sacrifice the knight in a way that is not uncommon in this opening.

13 P–KN4   **P–K4**

14 N–B5   **P × N**

15 NP × P

In return for the piece White has one pawn, good attacking chances on the K-side, and the advantage that Black's pieces are somewhat tied up.

15 ...   **K–R1**

This move must be played sooner or later.

16 O–O–O   **Q–B2**

17 P–R5!   **B–B3**

If 17 ... N/4–B5 18 B/N3 × N N × B 19 N–Q5 Q–B3 20 P–B6 ± ±. If 17 ... N/N3–B5 18 N–Q5 ± ±. If 17 ... P–KR3 18 QR–N1 and

Black is helpless against the threat of R–N3, R/1–N1 and Q–N2 etc.

18 K–N1

This quiet move carries the threat of 19 Q–B2 N–Q2 20 B–R6 B–N2 (if the rook moves, 21 B × BP) 21 B × B+ K × B 22 QR–N1+ K–R1 23 Q–N2 ± ±.

The text must be played first so that Black cannot play 20 ... N × B with check.

18 ...   **N × B**

19 BP × N

19 RP × N would give Black attacking chances by 19 ... P–R4 followed by ... P–R5.

19 ...   **B–Q2**

20 Q–KB2   **N–B1**

21 N–Q5   **Q–Q1**

22 QR–N1   **R–KN1**

23 R × R+   **K × R**

24 R–N1+   **K–R1**

25 N × B   **N–K2**

If 25 ... Q × N 26 B–N5 Q–N2 27 P–R6 Q–B1 28 B–B6+

26 B–N6   **Q–QB1**

27 Q–N2   **N × P**

28 P × N   **B × P+**

29 K–R1   **Q–B1**

30 Q–N5   **B–K3**

31 P–R6   **1–0**

Black cannot prevent 32 Q–N7+ Q × Q 33 P × Q mate. Even if not entirely sound, White's sacrificial idea posed too many practical problems for Black to solve over the board.

Sibarevic–Antunac
Yugoslavia 1977

1 P–K4 P–QB4 2 N–KB3 P–K3 3
P–Q4 P×P 4 N×P N–KB3 5 N–QB3
P–Q3 6 P–B4 P–QR3 7 B–K2 Q–B2 8
0–0 B–K2 9 K–R1 0–0 10 Q–K1
P–QN4 11 B–B3 B–N2 12 P–K5 P×P
13 P×P KN–Q2 14 Q–N3 K–R1 15
B–B4 N–QB3

White clearly has the game under
control. So long as he can maintain his
KP he will be able to increase his
pressure against the black king, and the
indicated continuation is 16 N×N B×N
17 N–K4, with some advantage.
Instead Sibarevic gets carried away by
an attractive sacrificial idea.

16 N–B5?!

Expecting 16 ... P×N 17 P–K6
Q–Q1 18 P×N Q×P 19 QR–Q1, with a
fine game for the sacrificed pawn. But
White has overlooked a neat resource.

| 16 ... | P–N4! |

Undermining White's control of K5.

17 N×B

The only move.

17 ...	P×B
18 Q–R4	N×N
19 Q×N	QR–K1
20 Q–R4	B×B

| 21 R×B | Q×P |
| 22 R×P?! | |

White should first activate his other
rook, since the KB4 pawn will not run
away. After 22 R–K1 Q–B3 (not 22 ...
Q–KB4? 23 R×BP Q×P 24 R–Q1, and
White wins because of the threat to the
knight, or if the knight moves, the move
Q–B6+ is killing.) 23 Q×Q+ N×Q 24
R×BP, the position would be a dead
draw. Perhaps White had deluded
himself that with the black king
exposed there was still the prospect of a
strong attack, but with his K-side well
consolidated Black has little to fear.

22 ...	P–B4!
23 R–K1	Q–N2
24 Q–B2	R–KN1
25 P–QR4	N–K4
26 P×P	P×P
27 P–R3	

White cannot afford to permit ...
N–N5.

| 27 ... | N–N3 |
| 28 R–QN4 | P–K4! |

Now it is Black who is sacrificing
material for an attack. The advance of
the KP and KBP, combined with the
pressure against White's KN2 square,
give Black the better game.

29 N×P

Even more unpleasant would have
been 29 Q×P N–B5 30 Q–K4 N×NP 31
R–KN1 Q–R3.

29 ...	N–B5
30 N–Q6	R/K–KB1
31 R–KN1	

31 R×N P×R 32 N–B4 would have
left Black with many technical
problems to solve, and the lack of a
passed black pawn might have led to an
eventual draw.

| 31 ... | R–B3 |
| 32 R–N6 | Q–QB2 |

Stronger is 32 . . . N–R4!, followed by . . . N–N6+, . . . P–B5, . . . P–K5 and . . . P–K6.

33 N–B4 **R–B2**
34 P–QN3 **R/2–N2**

Threatening 35 . . . N×RP.

35 Q–K3??

An elementary oversight in time trouble. Best was 35 R–KR6 R×P (if 35 . . . N×NP 36 Q×P Q–N2 37 K–R2!, and then if 37 . . . N–K8 38 R×P+! R×R 39 Q–B6+, drawing.) 36 R×R R×R 37 Q–N6 Q×Q 38 R×Q when White has good drawing chances.

35 . . . **N–Q4**

A move that no self respecting computer program would have overlooked.

36 Q–B2 **N×R**
37 Q×N **Q×Q**
38 N×Q **P–B5**
39 N–B4 **P–K5**

Because of this pawn the win is now easy.

40 R–K1

Otherwise simply . . . P–K6–K7 and . . . R×P is curtains.

40 . . . **R×P**
41 N–Q6 **R×P**
42 N×P **R–K1**
0–1

One of the morals of this story is that if you see an enticing sacrifice, first ensure that your opponent cannot find a refutation by not accepting it.

3 THE SACRIFICE ON KB6

The black knight on KB3 is a most useful piece in the Sicilian Defence. It guards the K-side where Black usually castles, it controls the important Q4 square and it attacks White's most vulnerable unit—his KP. Because this piece is so useful, White often tries to exchange it off so long as Black cannot immediately reoccupy KB3 with his remaining knight.

If White has castled K-side (or played R–KB1) and if, after White's often thematic P–KB4, the KB-file becomes semi-opened, it is possible for White to destroy Black's KB3 knight with the exchange sacrifice R × N.

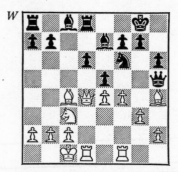

This combination, stemming from an analysis by Schmid, illustrates the sort of disaster that can befall Black once the bastion of his defence is removed in this way: **15 P × P P × P**

16 Q × R + B × Q 17 R × B + K–R2 18 R × N! P × R 19 N–Q5 and White wins.

White's compensation for the exchange sacrifice comes in two distinctive wrappers:

a) Provided that Black cannot recapture with his QN, White will derive great benefit from occupying his Q5 square with his QN (which is on QB3). The Nezhmetdinov–Tal combination (*16*) is a fine example of the use that White's knight can make of the Q5 square;

b) If Black is forced to recapture with his KNP as is often the case, his K-side becomes exposed to a dangerous attack from White's queen and minor pieces—The black pawn-structure (pawns at KB2, KB3 and usually K4) gets in the way of his pieces, preventing them from coming to the aid of his besieged monarch. In addition, Black's dark square weaknesses often give rise to mating threats on his KN2 square.

It may be that White's sacrifice on KB6 involves capturing a bishop rather than a knight (e.g. if White has previously exchanged bishop for knight on KB6). In this case it will be the K-side attack that is foremost in White's mind rather than the use of his Q5 square (which he already has).

A typical case is Borodiansky–Korzin (*15*) in which Black quickly finds himself the victim of a mating attack—The move N–Q5 is used by White to distract Black's QB from its control of a square needed by White's remaining rook. In Parma–Capelan (*17*) White's knight takes a more personal role in the mating attack. This example is unusual in the way that White's rook comes to be attacking the KB6 square—Instead of sitting on the semi-open KB-file it is on the Q6 square where it recently captured a pawn.

In Karasev–Yoffe (*18*) both of White's knights play a part in the attack. The Q4 knight jumps into KB5 where it must immediately be exchanged for Black's QB. Since this bishop was also guarding White's Q5 square the way is left open for White's QN to occupy this key outpost at once. An additional, useful feature of White's position is the fact that his QRP has advanced beyond the third rank. This allows White to bring his QR to the K-side one move quicker than usual (R–QR3–KR3 rather than R–KB1–KB3–KR3 or R–Q1–Q3–KR3), particularly important here since Black's knight guards White's KB3 and Q3 squares.

An example of the value of a white knight situated permanently on KB5 is Voynov–Tatayev, Central Chess Club Ch semi-final 1961.

See diagram next column

Here Black's defensive task is even more difficult than usual (in this case impossible) because his move . . . QR–K1 has left him without hope of removing his king to the centre by first vacating KB1. **17 R×B N×B**

W

**18 P×N P×R   19 N–B5 K–R1
20 Q–R4 Q–Q1 21 R–KB1 R–N1
22 R–B3 R–N4 23 N–K2 R/1–N1
24 Q×P+! K×Q 25 R–R3+ R–R4
26 R×R+ K–N3 27 R–R6+ K–N4
28 P–KR4+ K–N5 29 N–K3 mate**

In Stein–Parma (*19*) Black's K-side appears relatively secure but his dark square weaknesses still prove fatal. Litvinov–Koblencs (*20*) shows how the attack on the dark squares can triumph even when White is unable to get a knight posted on Q5 or KB5.

Other examples are rife of the exchange sacrifice being followed by a quick mate on the dark squares, for example Zhurakhov–Sakharov, Kiev 1959:

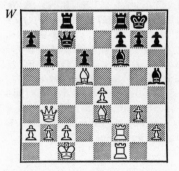

W

**22 R×B! P×R   23 B–Q4 KR–K1
24 R×P B–N3** If 24 . . . R–K4

25 B×R P×B   26 P–N4 B–N3
27 P–KR4 Q–K2 28 Q–KB3 K–N2
29 P–N5 P–KR4 30 P×Pep+±±
25 Q–Q3 Heading for KR6 while keeping the QB2 square protected.
**25 ... Q–K2   26 Q–Q2 R–B4
27 R×B+ RP×R   28 Q–R6 1–0**

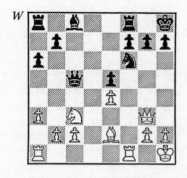

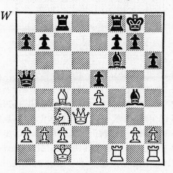

This position stems from analysis by Pisek **17 R×B! P×R 18 N–Q5 K–N2** If 18 ... KR–Q1 ·19 N×P+ K–N2 (or 19 ... K–B1 20 B–Q5) 20 N–Q5 B–K3 21 Q–KN3+ K–R2 22 N–B6+ K–R1 23 Q–K3 K–N2 24 N–R5+ K–R2 (24 ... K–N3 25 Q–KN3+ K×N 26 B–K2+ and mates) 25 Q–KN3 R–KN1 26 N–B6+±± **19 Q–KN3 P–B4** If 19 ... R×B? 20 Q×B+ K–R1 21 Q–R4±± **20 B–N3 K–R2 21 P–KR3 B–K7 22 Q×P Q–Q1 23 N–B6+ K–R1 24 R–K1!** Not 24 Q×P? K–N2 25 P–K5 B–Q6! **24 ... B–B5 25 Q×P K–N2 26 R–K3 Q×N 27 R–N3+ 1–0**

Small differences in White's position can seriously affect the success of his sacrifice, an example is Portisch–Matulovic, Palma 1967:

Were White's bishop on Q3 (protecting the QBP) instead of K2 he would almost certainly have a winning position, but ... **17 R×N** Black was intending to consolidate his position by 17 ... B–K3, 18 ... N–Q2 and 19 ... P–B3. Possibly White should play 17 B–Q3 B–K3 18 R×N but then his N–Q5 would not be a threat. **17 ... P×R 18 Q–R4 R–KN1 19 N–Q5** In Liberzon–Moiseyev, Moscow 1968, White tried 19 Q×BP+ R–N2 20 R–Q1 B–K3 21 R–Q8+ R×R 22 Q×R/8+ R–N1 and the game was drawn. **19 ... R–N2 20 Q×BP B–K3?!** Better 20 ... Q×BP! 21 B–B3 Q×QNP! **21 Q×KP Q×BP** After 21 ... B×N 22 P×B Q×PB 23 B–B3, White's passed pawn is very dangerous. **22 N–B4 R–QB1!** Not 22 ... K–N1 23 P–R3!± **23 N–R5 Q–B8+ 24 B–Q1 Q–N4 25 Q×R+ Q×Q 26 N×Q K×N 27 K–N1 R–Q1** and although White is a pawn ahead Black's active rook provided sufficient compensation. The game was drawn on move 39.

Borodiansky–Korzin
Moscow 1960

Nezhmetdinov–Tal
29th USSR Ch 1961

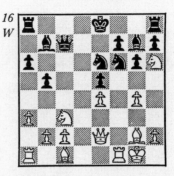

18 R×B!   **Q–K2**

If 18 ... P×R at once, 19 Q×BP and 19 R–KB1 should both lead to a winning attack.

19 R/1–KB1   P×R
20 R–B3   K–R1

There are two other defensive tries:

a) 20 ... P–B4 21 R–N3+ K–R1 22 Q–R6 R–KN1 23 P×P P–K5! 24 P–B6 (not 24 B×KP B×P) 24 ... Q–B1 25 R×R+ Q×R 26 B×KP when White has two pawns for the exchange and Black's game is full of holes; or

b) 20 ... KR–Q1 21 Q–R6 K–R1 22 N–Q5 B×N 23 P×B (23 R–R3? B×P) 23 ... P–B4 (or 23 ... P–K5 24 B×KP P–B4 25 R×P R–Q3— *25 ... R–K1 26 R–K5*—26 Q–B4 R–K1 27 R×P Q×B 28 R–B8+ K–N2 29 Q–B7+ ± ±) 24 B×BP P–B3 25 B×P Q×B (or 25 ... Q–KN2 26 Q–R4) 26 Q×P+ Q–KN2 27 R–R3+ K–N1 28 Q–K6+ winning.

21 N–Q5   Q–B1

Or 21 ... B×N 22 R–R3.

22 R–N3   1–0

17 R×N!

Because Black has fianchettoed his KB and advanced his KP his KB3 square is particularly vulnerable.

17 ... B×R 18 N–Q5 Q–Q1 19 Q–B2 N–B5 20 B×N P×B 21 P–K5! Opening another file and the long diagonal. **21 ... B×P**

Not 21 ... B×N 22 P×B B×B 23 R–K1+ K–B1 24 Q–B5+ and mate next move, nor 21 ... B–K2 (or 21 ... B–N4) 22 N–B6+ B×N 23 P×B threatening both 24 R–K1+ and 24 B×B. And on 21 ... B–R5 22 Q–Q4 R–KB1 23 R–Q1, White has a tremendous game for the exchange.

22 R–K1 P–B3 If 22 ... B×N 23 R×B+ B–K3 24 R×B+ P×R 25 B–B6+ K–B1 (25...K–K2 26 Q–B5+ Q–Q3 27 Q–N5+ K–B1 28 Q–B6 mate) 26 B×R Q×B 27 Q×P+ K–N2 28 P–N5 Q–R2+ 29 K–N2 Q–N2+ 30 K–R3± ± **23 N× P/B6+ Q×N 24 Q–Q4 K–B1 25 R×B Q–Q1** Or 25 ... R–Q1 26 R–K8+ K–N2 27 R–K7+ **26 R–KB5+ P×R 27 Q×R+ K–K2 28 Q–N7+ K–K3 29 P×P+ 1–0**

Parma–Capelan
Solingen 1968

Karasev–Yoffe
Leningrad 1969

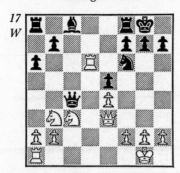

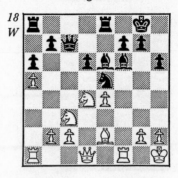

17 R×N!	**P×R**
18 N–Q5	**R–Q1**

Making way for the king to escape.
If 18 ... K–N2 19 Q–N3+ K–R1
20 N×P and 21 Q–R4, or 18 ...
B–K3 19 N×P+ K–R1 and 20
Q–R6.

19 N×P+	**K–B1**
20 R–QB1	**B–K3**
21 P–KR4!	

Not only avoiding the possibility
of any nasties on the back rank but
also preparing for a deep winning
idea.

21 ...	**Q–Q6**
22 Q–R6+	**K–K2**
23 Q–N5	**K–Q3**

If 23 ... K–B1 24 R–B7 forces
mate, or 23 ... B×N 24 N–Q5++
K–B1 25 Q–R6+ K–K1 26 N–B6+
K–K2 27 R–B7+++

24 N–B5	**Q–N4**
25 N×B	**P×N**

Or 25 ... K×N 26 N–N4 R–KB1
27 Q–B6+ K–Q2 28 N×P+ K–K1
29 R–B7 etc.

26 Q–Q2+	**1–0**

After 26 ... K–K2 White mates by
27 R–B7+ K×N 28 Q–N5—The
point of his 21st move.

17 R×B!	**P×R**
18 Q–Q2	**N–B3**

There is no way for Black to defend
against the threats on the K-side:
a) 18 ... K–B1 19 N–B5 B×N
20 Q×RP+ K–N1 21 N–Q5++;
b) 18 ... K–R2 19 N–Q5 Q–Q1
(19 ... B×N 20 N–B5) 20 Q–B4
(20 R–KB1 is also possible) 20 ...
N–Q2 21 N–B5 B×N/B4 22 Q×B+
K–R1 (or 22 ... K–N1 23 R–R3)
23 B–N4++; or
c) 18 ... K–N2 19 N–Q5 Q–Q1
20 R–R3 P–B4 (if 20 ... N–N3
21 N–B5+ B×N/B4 22 P×B N–K4
23 R–KN3+ K–R2 24 R–KR3, or
20 ... R–KN1 21 Q–B4 N–N3
22 R–KN3 with 23 N–B5+ to follow)
21 R–KN3+ K–R2 22 N×P
B×N/B4 23 P×B (threat 24 R–
KR3) 23 ... R–KN1 24 R×R++

19 N–B5	**B×N**
20 N–Q5	**Q–Q1**
21 Q×P	**B–N3**
22 R–R3	**1–0**

Since there is no defence to the
threat of 23 R–R3 and mate at KR8.

Stein–Parma
USSR–Yugoslavia Match 1962

Litvinov–Koblencs
Parnu 1964

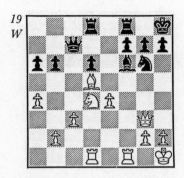

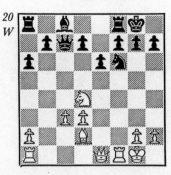

28 R×B!

Although Black's king appears to be quite secure, this sacrifice is still decisive because Black's pieces are passively placed and White controls the two important squares Q5 and KB5.

28 ...   **P×R**
29 Q–B2   **K–N1**

If 29 ... K–N2 30 R–KB1 puts White a tempo ahead of the game continuation.
30 R–KB1 Shamkovich prefers 30 Q–K3 when 30 ... N–K2 loses to 31 Q–R6 and 32 R–Q3 etc. and 30 ... K–R1 31 Q–R6 leaves White with a strong initiative. **30 ... R/Q1–K1 31 N–B5 Q–Q1 32 Q–N3 K–R1** Otherwise comes 33 P–R4 P–KR4 34 Q–B3. **33 N×P R–K2 34 R×P** As well as a strong attack White has two pawns for the exchange. **34 ... R×P 35 N×P+** Not 35 B×R? Q×R nor 35 N×R Q×B. **35 ... R×N 36 R×R R–K4 36 ... Q×B?? 37 Q–N8+ 37 P–B4 Q–K1 38 R–B1 Q×P 39 Q–QB3 Q–K1 40 B–B7 Q–KB1 41 R–B5 Q–Q3 42 P–R3 1–0** B×N will be decisive.

19 R×N!   **P×R**
20 Q–R4

Also good is 20 B–R6 P–B4 21 Q–R4 P–B3 22 B×R K×B 23 Q×BP+ K–N1 24 N–B3, but the text is even stronger.

20 ...   **Q–Q1**
21 B–R6   **K–R1**
Forced
22 B×R   **Q×B**
23 Q×BP+   **Q–N2**
If 23 ... K–N1 24 R–KB1.
24 Q–Q8+   **Q–N1**
25 Q–B7   **Q–B1**
26 R–KB1   **P–B3**

White was threatening 27 R–B6 Q–N2 (otherwise 28 Q–KB4 wins) 28 Q–Q8+ Q–N1 29 Q–K7 K–N2 30 R–B3±± and if 26 ... Q–N2 27 Q–Q8+ Q–N1 28 Q–K7 P–B4 29 R×P! P×R 30 N×P±± **27 N–B3 Q–K2 28 N–Q2 P–N4 29 N–K4 P–B4 30 N–Q6 Q–B1 31 P–Q4 K–N1 32 R–B3 P–R3 33 P–Q5 P×P** Otherwise 34 P×P P×P 35 R–N3+ K–R1 36 N–B7+ K–R2 37 N–K5+ and 38 N–N6+ **34 N×BP Q–B3 35 N×P+ 1–0** After 35 ... Q×N 36 Q–Q8+ Black soon loses his queen for nothing.

Schweber–Quinteros
Argentine Ch 1969

Kaykhmov–Vaulin
USSR 1978

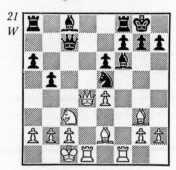

17 R×B!	**P×R**
18 Q–B2	

Aiming for mate on the dark squares as usual.

18 ...   **Q–R2**

Black cannot defend both weak points (KB3 and K4). If 18 ... Q–K2 19 B–R4 K–N2 (19 ... N–Q2 20 R×N B×R 21 B×BP) 20 R–B1 N–Q2 21 P–K5 ± ±

19 Q×P   **N–N3**

Controlling the weak K4 square and so preventing White from bringing his dark squared bishop to the long diagonal.

20 B–Q6	**Q–K6+**
21 K–N1	**P–N5**

If 21 ... R–K1 22 P–KR4.

22 B–R5!   **B–Q2**

22 ... P×N loses to 23 B×R forcing mate.

23 B×P

Bringing the bishop nearer to the crucial diagonal.

23 ... B–B3   24 B×N RP×B 25 R–Q3 Q–R3 If 25 ... Q–K8+ 26 N–Q1 Q–K7 27 B–B3. **26 N–Q5!** Clearing the way for the bishop at last. **26 ... P×N 27 R–KR3 Q–N2 28 B–B3 P–Q5 29 B×P 1–0**

15 R×N!

A classic example. White's domination of Q5 will prove decisive.

15 ...   **B×R**

If 15 ... P×R, White can win with ease after 16 N–Q5, e.g. 16 ... Q–N2 17 N×B+ Q×N 18 Q–N1!, threatening the knight.

16 N–Q5	**Q–B3**
17 N×Bch	**P×N**
18 Q–K1	

18 Q–N1 is also rather effective.

18 ...	**B–N2**
19 N–B5	**K–R1**
20 B×N	**Q×B**
21 Q–R4	**Q–N3**
22 R–KB1	**B–B1**
23 N–K7!	

A novel echo theme. The second knight now comes in on Q5.

23 ...	**P–B4**
24 N–Q5	**Q–Q1**
	and 1–0

Sax–Hulak
Vinkovci 1976

17 R×B! Opening up Black's king position and taking advantage of the fact that most of Black's pieces are on the opposite side of the board, unable to come to the rescue of the king. **17 . . . P×R 18 Q–R5 P–B4 19 Q–N5+ K–R1 20 Q–B6+ K–N1** It is always useful when planning a deep sacrifice to have an intermediate stage in the proceedings where, if necessary, one can take a draw. This allows the player making the sacrifice to take stock of the

position a few moves further on and to confirm in his own mind that he wishes to play for a win. **21 R–K1 R–K1 22 N–B5 P–K5 23 R–K3 N–K4 24 B–B4!** Overworking the knight which must now guard . . . KB2 while being able to interpose on the KN-file. **24 . . . P–B5** Forced. By giving up this pawn Black gets his bishop into the game. **25 Q×P/4 B–B4 26 B–Q5 N–N3 27 Q–Q6 R–K4 28 P–B4?** Simply 28 B×NP is crushing, e.g. 28 . . . Q–N1 29 Q–QB6 N–K2 30 Q–R6, winning back material and retaining the attack. **28 . . . Q–B1 29 N×NP B–K3! 30 B×P B×P 31 Q–Q4 B–K3 32 B–B7 R–KN4 33 N–Q6 R–Q1 34 Q–B6 R×N 35 B×R? Q×B 36 Q×R Q–Q5??** Trying for too much. 36 . . . Q–Q8+ 37 K–B2 Q–Q7+ 38 K–B1 B–B5+ 39 K–N1 Q–Q8+ 40 K–B2 P–B3! 41 Q–R6 P–B4 leaves White with all the problems. **37 B×N RP×B 38 Q–K5** Simple and effective. White forces mate or a won ending. 38 . . . Q×RP 39 R–Q3 K–B1 40 Q–R8+ K–K2 41 Q–Q8 mate.

Umansky–Cherepkov
Spartak TU Ch 1967

1 P–K4 P–QB4   2 N–KB3 P–K3
3 P–Q4 P×P   4 N×P N–QB3
5 N–QB3 Q–B2   6 B–K3 P–QR3
7 B–Q3 N–B3   8 0–0 N–K4   9 P–KR3
B–B4   10 Q–K2 N–N3   11 K–R1
11 P–B4 is also not bad, e.g.:
11 ... N×BP   12 R×N B×N
13 B×B Q×R   14 R–KB1 Q–Q3
15 Q–K3 P–K4   16 B–B5 Q–B3
17 B–R3 R–KN1   18 Q–N3 with a
winning position. Tseitlin–Cherepkov,
Leningrad Ch 1970. If 18 ... Q–K3
19 R×N! and 20 N–Q5. The game
continued 18 ... P–Q3   19 R×N!
1–0. In both games White sacrifices
his KBP and the exchange in order
to open up the KB-file. **11 ... 0–0
12 P–B4 B×N   13 B×B N×BP
14 R×N Q×R   15 R–KB1 Q–R5**

16 R×N!   **P×R**
17 Q–B3   **P–K4**
Making White's knight a present
of the Q5 square. A better defence
might have been offered by 17 ...
P–B4 followed by ... P–B3.
18 B–K3   **P–Q3**
19 N–Q5   **B–K3**
If 19 ... R–K1   20 N×P+ K–B1
21 B–KN5!

20 N×P+   **K–N2**
21 N–R5+   **K–R1**
Or 21 ... K–N3   22 P–KN4
threatening a piquant mate by
23 Q–B5+ B×Q   24 KP×B.
22 B–B2   **Q–N4**
23 P–KR4   **Q–N3**
24 N–B6   **R–KN1?!**
The audacity of the man, playing
for a win! He should be content to
play 24 ... K–N2 when White has
nothing better than to take the draw
by 25 N–R5+ K–R1   26 N–B6 etc.
25 B–K2
Depriving Black's queen of her
KN5 square ...
25 ...   **QR–B1**
26 P–B3   **B×P**
27 K–R2!
... and her KN6 square ...
27 ...   **B–K3**
28 B–K3
... and her KN4 square. So one
would now expect Black to notice
White's threat and play 28 ... K–N2,
when 29 P–R5? Q×N   30 P–R6+
Q×P   31 B×Q+ K×B leaves him
with more than enough material for
the queen. So again White would be
forced to repeat the position: (28 ...
K–N2)   29 N–R5+ K–R1   30 N–B6
etc.
28 ...   **P–QR4?**
Call this a counter-attack?
29 P–R5   **Q–N2**
30 P–R6   **Q–N3**
After 30 ... Q–B1   31 N×R K×N
32 Q–B6! White would be assured of
at least a draw and he would still
have some winning chances. **31 Q–B2!
P–R5   32 B–R5 Q×NP+   33 Q×Q
R×Q+   34 K×R P–R6   35 P×P
R×P   36 B–QN6** The start of an
amusing mating idea. **36 ... R×P**

37 B–Q8 P–N4   38 B–K7 R–Q6
39 B–B8 1–0

Rossolimo–Nestler
Venice 1950

1 P–K4 P–QB4   2 N–KB3 P–K3
3 P–Q4 P×P   4 N×P N–KB3
5 N–QB3 P–Q3   6 B–K2 P–QR3
7 0–0 Q–B2 8 P–B4 N–B3 9 B–K3
B–Q2 10 Q–K1 P–QN4 11 P–QR3
N×N   12 B×N B–B3   13 B–Q3
Q–N2

By applying additional pressure to
White's KP, Black prevents the
thematic manoeuvre Q–N3.

   14 Q–K2   N–Q2
If 14 ... P–N5 15 P×P Q×P
16 B×N P×B 17 N–Q5!

   15 P–QN4?!
Better was 15 Q–R5 so as to
prevent Black's next move.

   15 ...   P–K4!
   16 P×P   P×P
   17 B–K3   N–B3!
Otherwise 18 N–Q5!

   18 R–B5
On 18 Q–B3 Black should not
reply 18 ... B–K2 because of 19
Q–N3 and 20 B–R6. Instead he
should play 18 ... Q–Q2 followed by
... Q–K3 or ... Q–N5.

   18 ...   Q–B2
   19 R/1–KB1   B–K2
Not 19 ... B–Q2? 20 R×N P×R
21 N–Q5.

   20 R/5–B2
Black was threatening 20 ... B–Q2
winning the exchange.

   20 ...   0–0
Black could have avoided his
coming difficulties by 20 ... Q–Q2!

followed by 21 ... Q–K3 and only
then 22 ... 0–0.

   21 R×N!   B×R
21 ... P×R allows White to win
back the exchange at once by 22
B–R6.

   22 R×B   P×R
   23 N–Q5!   B×N
Even though this exchange opens
up the QN1–KR7 diagonal for
White's bishop, Black cannot avoid
it as otherwise his queen would be
overworked defending the attacked
KBP. Thus, 23 ... Q–Q3 24 Q–R5!
(threatening 25 Q–R6) and now:
a) 24 ... K–R1   25 B–B5! Q–K3
26 B–K7!! R–KN1   27 B×BP+
R–N2 28 Q–N5 R/1–KN1 29 N–K7!
Q×N 30 B×R+ and 31 Q×Q±±;
b) 24 ... P–B4   25 B–B5! Q–K3
26 Q–N5+ K–R1 (26 ... Q–N3??
27 N–K7+) 27 B×R Q–N3! (not
27 ... R×B 28 N–B6 and there is
no defence to 29 Q–R6 threatening
mate at both KR7 and KB8) 28 Q×Q
RP×Q (or 28 ... BP×Q 29 B–Q6
R–K1   30 N–K7 and if 30 ... B
moves 31 B×KP+ P–B3 32 B×BP
is mate) 29 B–Q6, and White's
material advantage will prove decisive;
c) 24 ... B×N   25 P×B KR–B1

(otherwise 26 Q×RP+ K–B1 27
B–QB5. And Black cannot save
himself by giving up pawns on the
K-side, e.g.: 25 ... P–B4 26 B×BP
KR–B1—*or 26 ... P–R3 27 B×P
Q–KB3 28 Q–N4+ K–R1 29 B–N5
Q–N2 30 B–B6!! Q×B 31 Q–R5+
and mates in two*—27 B×R R×B
28 Q–N4+; or 25 ... P–K5 26
B×KP P–B4 27 B×P P–R3 28
Q–N4+ K–R1 29 B–Q4+ P–B3
30 Q–N6 R–R2 31 Q×RP+ K–N1
32 B–K6+ R/2–KB2 33 B×P and
34 Q–R8 mate) 26 Q–R6;

d) 24 ... QR–K1 25 B–B5 Q–Q1
26 B×R B×N (or 26 ... K×B
27 Q–R6+ K–N1   28 N×P+)
27 Q–R6! R×B 28 P×B and mate
on R7; or

e) 24 ... KR–K1 25 B–B5! Q–Q1
(if 25 ... Q–K3 26 Q–R6 B×N
27 P×B winning the queen) 26
B–N6! Q–Q3 27 B–B7! Q–B1 28
N×P+ K–N2 29 B–Q6!! Q×B (or
29 ... R–K2   30 B×R Q×B
31 Q×RP+ K×N 32 Q–R6 mate)
30 Q–N5+ K–R1 31 Q–R6 Q×N
32 Q×Q+ and 33 Q×B±±.

From this maze of variations the
studious reader will be able to glean
a profound understanding of the
problems facing Black when trying
to defend his ruptured K-side pawn
complex (pawns at KR2, KB2, KB3
and K4) against a mating attack on
the diagonals.

**24 Q–N4+   K–R1
25 Q–B5!**

Blocking the KBP and threatening both 26 P×B (followed by mate
at KR7) and 26 Q×BP+ (followed
by 27 B–R6 and mate at KN7).

25 ...   R–KN1!
The best defence. After 25 ...

Q–B1   26 Q×BP+ K–N1   27 P×B
Q–N5 28 B–KB5 Q–N2 29 Q–R4,
White's fine bishops give him good
chances despite his material deficit.

**26 Q×BP+   R–N2
27 B–R6   R/1–KN1
28 P×B   Q–B6!**

After 28 ... Q–Q2   29 Q×KP
Q–N5   30 P–N3 Q–B6 (threatening
31 ... P–B3) White may be able to
win at once by 31 B–K2 followed by
the advance of the QP.

29 K–B1

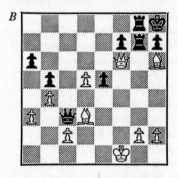

29 ...   Q–Q5?

Missing a draw by 29 ... Q–R8+
30 K–K2 Q–KN8! when White must
take the perpetual check 31 B×R+
R×B   32 Q–Q8+ etc.

Now White has a vital extra
tempo.

**30 P–Q6   Q–Q4
31 B–B5!**

Preventing 31 ... Q–K3 and
threatening simply to advance the
QP to the eighth rank.

**31 ...   Q×NP+
32 K–K1   Q–N8+
33 K–Q2   Q–B7+
34 K–B1   Q–N8+
35 K–N2   Q–Q5+
36 K–N1   Q–Q8+**

37 K–N2   Q–Q5+
38 K–R2?

In acute time trouble Rossolimo misses an easy win by 38 P–B3! Q–B7+ 39 K–N3 and 40 P–Q7.

38 ...   Q–Q4+
39 K–R1   Q–Q8+
40 K–R2   Q–Q4+
41 K–N1   Q–Q8+
42 K–N2

and **Black claimed a draw by repetition of position.**

Pritchett–Adams
British Universities' Ch 1970
Notes by Pritchett specially contributed for this volume

1 P–K4 P–QB4   2 N–KB3 P–Q3
3 P–Q4 P×P   4 N×P N–KB3
5 N–QB3 P–QR3   6 B–K2 P–K4
7 N–N3 B–K2   8 0–0 0–0   9 B–K3
Q–B2

Prepares ... P–QN4 which, on this move, fails to 10 N–Q5 B–N2 11 N–N6 R–R2 12 N–Q7 winning the exchange, a tactical point overlooked by O'Kelly in his recent book on the Sicilian Defence.

10 P–B4!?

Both 10 P–QR4 and 10 Q–Q2 deter the aggressive reply 10 ... P–QN4. The first of these restrains Black directly. 10 Q–Q2 issues a more subtle, positional restraint. After 10 Q–Q2 P–QN4, for example, an analysis by Geller runs 11 KR–Q1 B–N2 12 N–Q5 N×N 13 P×N N–Q2 14 N–R5 when White has good squares and prospects of play against Black's extended Q-side pawns.

Over the board in a game from a

match between Glasgow and Edinburgh Universities, it occurred to me that 10 P–B4 also probably deterred 10 ... P–QN4, this time for tactical reasons.

10 ...   P–QN4?!

Nevertheless! Of other possible replies here, 10 ... B–K3 might be the best. 11 P–B5 B–B5 12 P–QR4 QN–Q2 would then transpose into another main line of the 6 ... P–K4 defence. 10 ... QN–Q2 would also be better than the text.

11 P×P   P×P

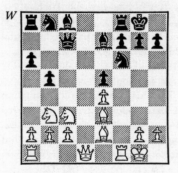

12 R×N!

The only consistent positional continuation. White's immediate brutality is only a means to an end. Ahead in development, he hopes to regain the sacrificed exchange and remain in a position to exploit his structural advantages. His potential lies in his latent Q-side pawn majority and control of Black's weakened Q-side dark squares and, especially, Black's Q4 square.

12 ...   B×R
13 N–Q5   Q–B3

Deflecting the knight to R5. Some alternatives:

a) 13 ... Q–Q1 14 N–N6 B–N2! 15 N×R B×N is less critical. After

16 B–B3, White's chances on the Q-side and more active pieces give him the edge;

b) 13 ... Q–Q2 14 N–N6 Q–R2 (14 ... Q×Q+ 15 R×Q ±) 15 B–B2! etc.

14 N–R5   **Q–Q3?**
15 N–N6?

Overlooking a chance to gain an immediate material advantage. Although Black could still struggle, after 15 N×B+ Q×N 16 Q–Q5 N–B3 17 Q×N Q×Q (if 17 ... B–K3 18 P–B3) 18 N×Q B–N2 19 N×P (alternatively 19 N–K7+ K–R1 20 B–Q3 P–N3! 21 N–Q5 B×N, with an unbalanced position which White should win) 19 ... KR–K1 20 B–KB4 P–B3 21 N–Q3 B×P he should ultimately lose.

The most accurate continuation for Black would therefore have been 14 ... Q–Q2 15 N–N6 Q–B2, reaching the game position but without allowing White this resource.

15 ...   **Q–B2**

Or 15 ... Q–N5. If 15 ... Q×Q+ 16 R×Q R–R2 17 N×B R–B2 18 N–N6 R×P 19 R–Q2 ±.

16 N×R   **Q×N**
17 N–N6   **B–N4**

If 17 ... B–N2 18 P–QR3! B–N4 19 B–B2! Q–Q7 20 Q×Q B×Q 21 R–Q1 B–N4 22 N–Q5 ±.

Or 17 ... Q–N5 after which the original game (as far as I know) in this variation, Pritchett–George, Glasgow Univ.–Edinburgh Univ. 1967, continued: 18 P–B4! B–N2 (not 18 ... Q×NP 19 N–Q5 R–K1 —*What else? If 19 ... P×P 20 R–N1 or 19 ... B–Q1 20 B–B5 R–K1 21 P–QR3! and the queen is trapped*— 20 R–N1 followed by 21 N×B+

gives White a winning attack) 19 Q–B2 P×P 20 B×P R–Q1 21 N–Q5 B×N 22 B×B N–Q2 23 P–QR3 Q–N1 24 P–QN4! (White has a strategically won game) 24 ... N–N3 25 B–N3 Q–N2 26 Q–B2! N–B1 27 B–Q5 Q–N4 28 Q–R2! Q–Q6 29 B–B5 N–Q3 30 Q–N1! Q×Q+ 31 R×Q N–N4 32 R–N3 N–Q5 33 R–Q3 N–K7+ 34 K–B2 N–B5 35 R–Q1 R–Q2 36 P–QR4 N×B (Loses quickly but, if 36 ... N–K3 37 B–N6 B–Q1 38 P–R5! soon wins) 37 R×N R×R 38 P×R B–Q1 39 P–Q6 P–B4 40 P–N5? (A pity, 40 P–R5! was much more aesthetic) 40 ... P×P 41 P×P 1–0.

18 B–B5   **R–Q1**

18 ... B–K2 19 B×B also favours White.

19 N–Q5   **N–B3**
20 P–QR3!

Thematic and powerful. Black must now opt for the exchange of queens and a difficult ending.

20 ...   **Q–Q7**
21 Q×Q   **B×Q**
22 R–Q1   **B–N4**
23 P–B4   **P×P**
24 B×P   **P–N3**
25 P–QN4   **K–N2**
26 B–N6!

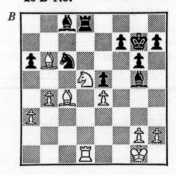

Initiating a period of light manoeuvring to disrupt Black's piece position before breaking on the Q-side.

26 ...	R–Q2

If 26 ... R–B1 27 N–B7 B–Q1 28 R–Q6 B–N2 29 B–Q5 etc.

27 P–N5	P × P
28 B × P	B–N2
29 R–KB1	

Threatening 30 N–N4 and bearing down on KB7.

29 ...	R–Q3
30 B–B7	R–K3
31 B–B4	

White has achieved a strong bind (which is not alleviated by 31 ... B–Q1 32 R–N1 B–R1 33 R–N6!) and is threatening the powerful advance of his QRP.

31 ...	R–K1
32 P–QR4	P–R4
33 P–R5	P–B3

If 33 ... R–QR1 34 N–N6 R × P 35 R × P+ K–R3 36 N–Q5 R–R8+ 37 K–B2 and there is no defence to B–Q6–B8+ winning quickly.

34 P–R6	B–R1
35 P–N3!	

A vital move. The threat 36 P–R4 may be parried only by deflecting the KB from its present important diagonal.

35 ...	P–R5
36 P × P	B × P
37 N–N6!	

The point: Black's key defensive piece is his blockading QB. With his KB on KN4, Black could prevent its exchange by ... B–K6+ and ... B × N.

37 ...	B–N4
38 N × B	R × N
39 R–N1	B–K6+
40 K–N2	R–R2
41 B–N6	B × B
42 R × B	N–K2

Other knight moves meet with the same deadly reply.

43 B–Q5	K–R3

What else? If 43 ... P–B4 44 P × P P × P 45 P–R4 soon wins—Black's rook being locked in at a timely stage by B–N7. Or 43 ... P–N4 44 K–N3 K–N3 45 B–N7 and White's king ultimately penetrates. Finally, 43 ... N × B 44 R–N7+ etc.

44 R × P	K–N4

The rook and pawn ending after 44 ... N × B 45 P × N K–N4 46 R–N6 is equally hopeless.

45 R–B7	R × P

Fighting to the last. If 45 ... N–B1 46 R × R N × R 47 K–N3! N–B1 (47 ... K–B3 48 K–N4) 48 B–K6 N–R2 49 B—Q7 etc.

46 R × N K–B5 47 R–KB7+ K–N4 48 K–N3 R–R6+ 49 R–B3 R–R8 50 P–R4+ K–R4 51 B–B7 R–KN8+ 52 K–B2 R–N5 53 R–B6! K × P 54 B × P K–N4 55 R–Q6 K–B5 56 B–B5 R–N6 57 R–KN6 R–KB6+ 58 K–N2 R–KN6+ 59 K–R2 R × R 60 B × R **and Black resigned after a few more moves.**

Ilijin–Vaisman
Rumanian Championship 1975

1 P–K4 P–QB4 2 N–KB3 P–Q3 3 P–Q4 P×P 4 N×P N–KB3 5 N–QB3 P–QR3 6 B–K2 QN–Q2 7 B–K3 P–K3 8 P–QR4 P–QN3 9 P–B4 B–N2 10 B–B3 R–B1 11 0–0

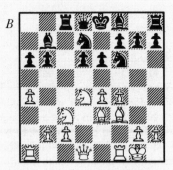

11 ...   R×N!?

An idea of Walter Browne's. In return for the exchange Black gets a pawn and some counterplay, but he must be careful to consolidate his position otherwise his king will suffer in the centre.

12 P×R	**N×P**
13 Q–K1	**P–Q4**
14 B×N	**P×B**
15 P–R5	**P–QN4**

If 15 ... P×P 16 P–B4, when the QR5 pawn will fall, sooner or later.

16 P–B5	**P–K4**
17 N–K6!	

Being ahead in material it is easier than usual for White to make this piece sacrifice. If Black declines he loses his right to castle, so Vaisman makes the correct decision.

17 ...	**P×N**
18 P×P	**N–B3**
19 R–Q1	**Q–B1?**

Black is under so much pressure that he should take the opportunity to simplify the position. Correct is 19 ... B–Q4!, when if Black is given time for ... B–K2 and /or ... Q–R1 White will be hard pressed to conclude his attack successfully. Possibly White's best course would be to trade off into a level ending by (19 ... B–Q4) 20 Q–Q2 B–K2 21 R×N B×R 22 Q×B Q×Q 23 R×Q.

20 R×N!

Now Black's king will never escape from the centre.

20 ...	**P×R**
21 Q–R4	**K–K2**

If 21 ... Q×KP 22 Q–R5+ K–K2 (or 22 ... Q–B2 23 R–Q8+!) B–B5+

22 Q–R3!   B–R3

And here 22 ... Q×KP fails to 23 B–B5+ K–B2 24 R–Q7+, winning the queen.

23 R–Q7+	**Q×R**
24 B–B5+!	

An important zwischenzug. If 24 P×Q B×B+ 25 Q×B R–Q1, and it is not at all clear how White continues.

24 ...	**Q–Q3**
25 B×Q+	**K×B**
26 Q×B	

The difference now is that White's queen is more active than in the previous variation and Black's pieces are not co-ordinated.

26 ...   R–K1

If 26 ... K×P 27 Q–N7 R–QN1 28 Q–QB7, winning more material.

27 Q×BP	**R×P**
28 Q–Q8+	**K–B4**
29 Q–B7+	**B–B3**
30 K–B2	**K–B5**
31 Q×RP	**R–B3+**
32 K–K3	**K×P**
33 Q–K7	**R–R3**
34 Q–B5+	**K–N7**
35 K–Q2	

Threatening 36 Q–B3+ and a quick mate.

35 ...	P–K6+
36 K×P	K–B8
37 K–Q3	P–K5+

38 K–B3	P–N5+
39 K×P	R–K3
40 Q–K3+	K–N7?

Speeding the end.

| 41 Q–QN3+ | 1–0 |

4 BxQNP (AND B–QN5)

The sacrifice of White's KB on QN5 is normally associated with positions in which Black has played . . . P–QN4. In return for the piece White usually gets three pawns because after . . . P × B the recapture N/Q4 × NP forks Black's queen at QB2 and his QP at Q3. When White does win this third pawn is it correct to call the move B × NP a sacrifice? The answer is 'yes' because in the middle-game a piece is usually of more value than three pawns.

White's compensation can take one of two forms. If he has picked up all three pawns for the piece and if he can force the exchange of queens under favourable circumstances, he may play the ending in which his three united Q-side pawns will eventually win, once sufficient material has been exchanged.

See diagram next column

This is better for White than the typical situation because, even with the queens exchanged, White has a strong attack:
13 B × P P × B 14 N/4 × NP Q–Q1 15 N × P + B × N 16 Q × B Because of the exposed position of his QB4 knight, Black is forced to exchange queens. **16 ... Q × Q 17 R × Q** And now White has the initiative because that knight is still under fire. **17 ... N–Q2 18 R/1–Q1 0–0–0**

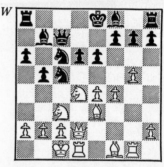

19 N–N5 KR–B1 20 R/1–Q3 B–R1 21 R–R3 B–N2 22 R–B3 N/2–N1 23 N–R7+ K–B2 24 N–N5+ K–B1 25 B–N6 B–R3 26 R × R+ R × R 27 B × R B × N 28 B–N6 K–N2 29 B–B2 B–B8 30 R–KN3 N–Q2 31 K–Q2 N–Q1 32 B–Q4 P–N3 33 K–K3 P–K4 (otherwise 34 K–B2 followed by 35 R–KR3 N–B1 36 B–N7) **34 B × P N × B 35 P × N B–B5 36 R–R3 N–K3 37 P–N3 B–N4 38 R × P N × P 39 R–N7 B–K1 40 R–N8 B–Q2 41 R–KB8 B–K3 42 P–KR4 N–R6 43 R–KR8 1–0** with the time scramble over. There will be no stopping White's passed pawns.

The Bronstein–Najdorf game (page 56) is possibly the best known example. That Bronstein won may be attributed to the fact that this type of ending was not very well understood in 1954 and that Najdorf failed to realise how powerful White's Q-side pawns would be even with two pairs of rooks on the board. The Vasyukov–Averbakh game (page 61) puts these endings into correct perspective. If Black keeps his king within easy reach of the Q-side he should be able to stem the flow of passed pawns.

With these endings now known to offer White few real prospects, he has, since the late 1950s, sought compensation in an attack against Black's king. This attack is particularly effective if Black's KB does not guard the QP, for then, when White's knight lunges in to Q6 it cannot be exchanged. Instead, Black must move his king which is then exposed to attack:

13 B×P! P×B 14 N×P Q–N1 15 N×P+ K–K2 16 B–B5 B–Q2 17 P–K5 N–Q4 After 17 ... N–K1 follows 18 N–N7+ and after 17 ... N–KN1 18 N×P+ **18 R×N! P×R 19 Q×P R–R4 20 R–Q1** Threatening 21 N–B5+ against which Black has no good defence. **20 ... R×B 21 Q×R** Threatening, among other things, 22 N–B5+ **21 ... R–KN1 22 N×P+ 1–0** If 22 ... K×N

23 R×B+ and 24 Q×N etc. or if 22 ... K–K1 23 P–K6, van den Berg–van Soom, Sinaia 1965.

An even more drastic example is Bozic–Molerovic, Yugoslavia 1966, in which White wins back the piece immediately because Black's knight on K2 introduces a new hazard—the possibility of being mated on the back rank:

11 B×P! P×B 12 N/4×NP Q–N3 13 N×P+ K–B1 14 N×B QN–B3 15 N–Q6 R–Q1 If 15 ... Q×NP 16 Q–B3 **16 N–B4 Q–N5 17 Q–K2** and White soon won.

White's attack is likely to go wrong if his initiative is not strong enough. For this reason it is very important that Black's queen be on QB2 so that White's N/4×NP comes with tempo. If Black has an extra move with which to defend himself he can either play to consolidate or he can launch an immediate counter-attack as in the following position:

See diagram next page

10 B×P? P×B 11 N/4×NP N–QN5! **12 P–QR3** If 12 B×N P×B 13 N×P+ B×N 14 Q×B N×RP+ 15 N×N R×N 16 K–N1 R–R2 and White has nothing to show

for the sacrificed material. **12 ...
B×N 13 N×B P–Q4! 14 P–K5**
Or 14 N–B3 Q–N3 15 B×N P×B
16 P×P R×P!∓∓ Vorobeyev–
Mazurenko, Moldavia – Ukraine
match 1962. **14 ... Q–N3! 15 P×N**
15 N–B3 allows 15 ... R×P! as in
the last note. **15 ... Q×N 16 P×P
N–R7+ 17 K–N1 B×NP 18 P–B4
Q–N6** and White can resign. Analysis
by Kogan and Mazurenko.

White's attack can also fail if he
does not have enough active pieces.
In Kapengut–Faibisovich, USSR
Student Ch 1967, White has
exchanged off his active QB and his
KN is passively placed on QN3:

**13 B×P? P×B 14 N×P Q–N1
15 N×P+ K–B1 16 P–K5 B–K2
17 Q–QB3 N–N3** Not 17 ... B–N2?
18 N×P **18 P–B5** The only way to
keep the initiative. **18 ... P×P
19 N–Q4 R×P 20 P–QN3 N–Q4!
21 Q–B6 B–K3 22 N×B+ P×N
23 R×N P×R 24 Q×P B×N
25 P×B Q–B1!** If Black grabs the
rook at once he allows a perpetual
check. **26 P–B4 R–R8+ 27 K–B2
R×R 28 P–Q7 Q–Q1 29 P–B5
K–K2** and White had only a few
checks to compensate for being two
rooks down.

The bishop sacrifice on QN5 is
sometimes seen even when there is no
black pawn to be captured. In
Tal–Tolush *(23)* White develops his
bishop by sacrificing it. As compensation he gets a beautifully posted
knight on QN5 and the way is opened
for his KR to support the attack from
K1.

Zhaudrin–Pikhanov
Corres 1970/71

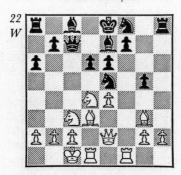

22
W

Tal–Tolush
USSR Ch 1956

23
W

16 B–N5+!! In Ree–Kavalek, Amsterdam 1968, White missed this crushing sacrifice and continued instead 16 Q–B2 N/1–N3 17 N–B3 R–KR2 18 N–QR4 B–Q1 19 Q–Q4 B–Q2 20 N–B3 Q–N3! **16 . . . B–Q2** If 16 . . . P×B 17 N/4×NP Black's position is virtually hopeless:
a) 17 . . . Q–N3 18 B×N P×B 19 Q–B2! N–Q2 (19 . . . Q×Q 20 N–B7 mate) 20 Q×P+ K–Q1 21 Q–N7 R–K1 22 Q×KP with a big plus for White;
b) 17 . . . Q–B3 18 B×N P×B 19 N–Q5! P×N 20 P×P Q–QN3 21 P–Q6 P–B3 22 N–B7+ K–B2 23 N×R±±;
c) 17 . . . Q–B4 18 P–N4! Q×P (18 . . . Q–N3 and 18 . . . Q–B3 come to the same thing as variations **a** and **b** respectively) 19 B×N±±; or
d) 17 . . . Q–R4 18 B×N P×B 19 Q–B4 N–Q2 20 N–B7+ K–B1 (or 20 . . . K–Q1 21 N×R Q×N 22 R×P) 21 Q×P R–KR2 22 N×R Q×N 23 R×N±± **17 B×N QP×B 18 N×P! P×N 19 R×N+! B×R 20 R×B Q×R 21 B×Q+ K×B 22 N–R4! R–K1 23 Q–Q2+ 1–0** 23 . . . K–B2 24 Q–B3+±±

15 B–N5! The best way to complete his development. **15 . . . P×B 16 N×NP P–B3** Not 16 . . . N–R3 17 N/5–Q6+ B×N 18 Q×B±± **17 P×P!** After 17 N/4–Q6+ B×N 18 N×B+ K–K2 Black has no threats to face. **17 . . . P×P** If 17 . . . Q×N/K5 18 P×P and now:
a) 18 . . . B–B4+ 19 K–N3 Q–K4+ (if 19 . . . R–N1 20 R–K1) 20 K–R3 Q×NP 21 N–B7+ K–B2 22 R–KB1+ K–N1 23 B–R6 winning the queen; or
b) 18 . . . Q–B4+ 19 R–KB3 B–B4+ 20 K–N3 Q–K4+ 21 K–R3 R–N1 22 R–K1. **18 R–K1 R–R3** Bad is 18 . . . P×B because of 19 N–B7+ K–Q1 20 N×KP+ K–K1 21 N/6–B5±± **19 B×P N×B 20 N×N+ K–B2 21 R–KB3!** **Q–R5+** If 21 . . . Q×N 22 N–Q5+ K–K1 23 N–B7+ **22 K–B1 P–K4** 22 . . . Q–QB5+ 23 K–N1 B–B4+ 24 K–R1 Q×N loses to 25 N–Q5+ K–N3 26 R–B6+ **23 Q–Q5+ B–K3 24 N–Q7+ K–N3 25 N×P+ K–N2 26 R–KN3+ Q×R** If 26 . . . K–B3 27 Q–Q8+ **27 Q×P+ N–Q2 28 P×Q R–N3 29 Q–B7 B–QB4 30 N×N B–B5+ 31 R–K2 1–0**

Velimirovic–Al Kazzaz
Nice Olympiad 1974

13 B×P!

Spassky played 13 B×N N×B 14 Q×P in the fifteenth game of the Fischer match but the text is much more to Velimirovic's enterprising taste. It may also be a stronger move.

13 ...	**P×B**
14 N/4×NP	**Q–N3**
15 P–K5	**P–Q4**

Black tries to keep the centre closed. If 15 ... P×P 16 P×P N–Q4 17 B×B N×B 18 N–Q6+ K–N1 19 N×P, with positional and material advantages.

16 P–B5!

Threatening 17 P×P P×P 18 P×N P×P 19 R×KP Q×R 20 Q–B7 mate.

16 ...	**N–R4**
17 Q–R4	**B×B+**
18 Q×B	**N×P**
19 Q×N	**P–Q5**
20 R×N	**P×N**
21 N×P	**R×R+**
22 Q×R	**R–Q1**
23 Q–K1	**P×P**
24 R×P	**Q–KR3+**
25 K–N1	**Q×P**
26 R×P	**Q×P**
27 Q–K6+	**K–N1**
28 Q–K5+	**1–0**

Black is about to lose his rook to a fork on ... QR4.

Tal–Stean
Hastings 1973/74

10 B×P!?	**P×B**
11 N/4×NP	**Q–N1**

11 ... Q–N3 is more active, and if 12 B×N then 12 ... P×B (not 12 ... N×B 13 P–K5 B–N2 14 R×P!); but possibly best of all is 11 ... Q–N2 and if 12 N×P+ B×N 13 R×B R–QN1 14 P–QN3 Q–R2 15 KR–Q1 0–0, with an unclear position.

12 P–K5   **B–N2**

12 ... R–R4! was later discovered to be an improvement, but over the board, when confronting this sacrifice for the first time, it is not at all easy to find the most accurate defence. After 12 ... R–R4 13 N–Q4 B–N2 14 Q–R3 (threat N×KP), Black can choose between 14 ... N–Q4 15 N×KP! N×N!, with immense complications, or 14 ... N×P!? 15 P×N R×KP, again with a very unclear position.

As with many of Tal's games however, it is not so much the truth that matters as the moves played by his opponent.

13 Q–K2   **P×P**
14 Q–B4!   **B–B4**

14 ... B–K2 15 N–B7+ K–B1 is hardly pleasant for Black though it does seem better than the text.

15 B×N!	P×B
16 R×N!	B–K6+
17 K–N1	K×R
18 R–Q1+	B–Q4

Unknown to Stean (at the time) his game had followed the same course as Vitolinsh–Anikayev, Riga 1973, which Tal had witnessed shortly before travelling to Hastings. That game had continued 18 ... K–K1 19 N–B7+ K–B1 20 P×P R–R4 21 P×P B–Q4 22 N/3×B P×N 23 Q–B3 R–B4 24 Q×B R×N 25 R–K1 P–R4 26 Q–R3+ 1–0

Stean's move leads to a much prettier conclusion.

19 P×P	P×P
20 N×B	P×N

21 Q×QP+	K–K2
22 Q–B5+	K–B3

Or 22 ... K–K1 23 N–N5!

23 R–B1+	K–N3
24 Q–K7	P–B4
25 Q×KP+	K–N2
26 Q–K7+	K–N3
27 P–KR4!	

Threatening mate by P–R5+ etc.

27 ...	R–R4
28 P–R5+!	K×P
29 Q–KB7+	K–R5
30 Q–B6+	K–N6
31 Q–N5+	K–R7
32 R–B2+	K–N8
33 N–K2 mate	

Bronstein–Najdorf
Argentina–USSR match 1954

1 P–K4	P–QB4
2 N–KB3	P–Q3
3 P–Q4	P × P
4 N × P	N–KB3
5 N–QB3	P–QR3

The Najdorf Variation was not so named because it was invented by the Polish/Argentinian grandmaster but because he started to popularise it shortly after the Second World War. The variation can be traced back at least as far as 1934.

6 B–KN5	P–K3
7 Q–B3	QN–Q2

Best is probably 7...B–Q2 8 0–0–0 N–B3 9 R–N1 B–K2 10 P–KN4 N × N 11 R × N Q–R4 12 B–K3 B–B3 when the chances are about even.

8 0–0–0	Q–B2
9 Q–N3	P–N4

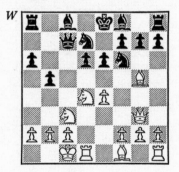

10 B × P!?
This idea was first seen in Soviet circles in 1934.

10 ...	P × B
11 N/4 × NP	

White obtains three pawns for the piece and will play to exchange material so as to be able to utilise the

strength of his connected passed pawns more easily.

Now Black must make an important decision.

11 ...	Q–N1!

Alternatives are:

a) 11 ... Q–R4 as in the game Rauser–Makogonov, p. 58;

b) 11 ... Q–B4? 12 B–K3! Q–B3 13 N × P+ B × N 14 R × B Q–N2 15 P–K5 N–R4 (or 15 ... N–K5 16 Q × P R–B1 17 R × N! B × R 18 N × N Q × N 19 B–B5 0–0–0 20 B × R B–R5 21 P–QN3 R–Q7! an ingenious attempt to obtain a perpetual check 22 K × R Q–Q5+ 23 K–K2 Q–K5+ 24 K–B1 B–N4+ —*if* 24 ... *Q × BP* 25 *P–B3!*— 25 P–QB4 B × P+ 26 P × B Q × BP+ 27 K–K1 Q–K5+ 28 K–Q2 Q–Q5+ 29 K–B2 Q–QB5+ 30 K–N2 Q–Q5+ 31 K–N3 Q–Q6+ 32 K–N4 Q–Q7+ 33 K–B4 Q–B7+ 34 K–Q4 Q–Q7+ 35 K–K4 Q–K7+ 36 K–B4 Q × BP+ 37 K–N4 Q × NP+ 38 K–R4 Q × R 39 Q–N3 1–0 Konstantinopolsky–Gerstenfeld, Lvov 1940) 16 Q–N4 P–N3 (16 ... N × P 17 Q–N5!) 17 R × P+! P × R 18 Q × KP+ K–B1 19 B–R6+ N–N2 20 N–Q5! N–QB4 21 Q–KB6+ K–K1 22 Q × N Q × Q 23 B × Q R–KN1 24 N–B7+ K–B2 25 N × R K × B 26 N–N6 and White had five!! pawns for the bishop. Verner–Belyavsky, USSR Team Ch 1969.

12 N × P+	B × N
13 Q × B	Q × Q
14 R × Q	

See diagram next page

Thus, after only fourteen moves, the game has reached an ending typical of the B × NP sacrifice.

14 ...   **P–R3!**

A fine move, particularly if followed up correctly.

15 B–Q2

A very deep move, the point of which is totally overlooked by Najdorf. Instead, 15 B×N N×B 16 R/1–Q1 B–N2 17 P–B3 K–K2 18 R–N6! is rather good for White, Fichtl–Dolezal, Czechoslovakia 1955. But Black can improve with 15 ... P×B! 16 R/1–Q1 R–KN1 with good counterplay.

| **15 ...** | **B–N2** |
| **16 P–B3** | **0–0?** |

The losing move. Black should castle Q-side and after 16 ... 0–0–0 17 B–K3 N–K4 18 R×R+ R×R 19 P–QN3 P–N4! he can follow up with ... P–N5 or ... N–R4–KB5. The text puts Black's king where it can do no good.

17 P–QN3

This move and its sequel frees White's knight from the defence of the QRP and prepares for the advance of the QBP. The point of Bronstein's fifteenth move was that had Black played 16 ... R–QB1 White's knight would still be defended after P–QN3.

| **17 ...** | **KR–B1** |

18 K–N2	**N–B4**
19 B–K3	**P–K4**
20 R/1–Q1	**N–K3**
21 R–N6	**B–B3**
22 N–Q5	**B×N**
23 P×B	

Now there are four connected pawns.

23 ...	**N–B4**
24 R–N5	**N/3–Q2**
25 P–QB4	**P–K5**
26 B×N	**N×B**
27 P×P	**N×KP**
28 P–Q6!	

White sacrifices one of his pawns to gain time. That he is only left with two pawns for the knight is unimportant—His passed pawns are very strong, his king is well placed to support their advance and Black's king is on the wrong side of the board.

28 ...	**R×RP+**
29 K×R	**N–B6+**
30 K–R3	**N×R/Q8**

Now the knight must spend three tempi to get back to home waters.

31 P–B5	**N–B6**
32 R–R5	**N–Q4**
33 P–B6	**N–B3**
34 R–R6	**K–B1**
35 P–QN4	**K–K1**
36 P–N5	**N–Q2**

The threat was 37 P–N6 R×P 38 P–N7.

37 R–R7	**R–N1**
38 R×N	**R×P**
39 R–R7	

The passed pawns are so powerful that 39 R×P also wins: 39 ... K×R 40 P–B7 R–QB4 41 P–Q7.

39 ...	**R–N1**
40 P–Q7+	**K–K2**
41 P–Q8=Q+	**K×Q**
42 P–B7+	**K–B1**

43 P×R=Q+	K×Q
44 R×P	1–0

Rauser–Makogonov
USSR Ch 1934/35

1 P–K4	P–QB4
2 N–KB3	P–Q3
3 P–Q4	P×P
4 N×P	N–KB3
5 N–QB3	P–QR3
6 B–KN5	P–K3
7 Q–B3	QN–Q2
8 0–0–0	Q–B2
9 Q–N3	P–N4
10 B×P!?	P×B
11 N/4×NP	Q–R4

W

12 N×P+

In Lilienthal–Kotov, Moscow Ch 1942, White tried 12 R×P? B×R 13 Q×B R–QN1 14 P–K5, but after 14 ... R×N 15 P×N P×P 16 N×R Q×N 17 B–K3 Q–N2 Black had the advantage.

Later, Euwe pointed out that 12 R×P? could have been refuted more convincingly: 12 ... N×P! 13 N–B7+ Q×N/2 14 R×P+ P×R 15 Q×Q N×B 16 P–KR4 B–K2 17 P×N B×P+ with a decisive advantage to Black.

Both of these refutations rely on White's QB being on KN5 so that 15 ... P×P and 12 ... N×P! respectively, attack the bishop and gain a tempo.

With this in mind Grankin, against Gutkin in the 1968 Latvian Ch, played 12 B×N! first and only after 12 ... N×B did he venture 13 R×P. The game concluded 13 ... N×P— *13 ... B×R 14 Q×B N–Q2 15 N–B7+ K–Q1 16 N×R Q×N/R1 17 R–Q1 with a winning attack, or 14 ... B–Q2 15 P–QN4!*—14 N–B7+ Q×N/2 15 R×P+ K–Q2 16 R–Q1+ N–Q3 17 N–N5 Q–B4 18 N×N K×R 19 Q–N3+ K–K4 20 P–KB4+ K×P 21 Q–N3 mate.

12 ...	B×N
13 R×B	N–R4

If 13 ... 0–0 14 R/1–Q1 ±

14 Q–R4	P–R3
15 B–K3	N/4–B3
16 P–B3	

16 R/1–Q1 and if 16 ... R–QN1 17 R/1–Q4 would have been more energetic.

16 ...	R–QN1
17 R–Q4	Q–N3
18 N–R4	Q–N4
19 P–QN3	P–K4
20 R–B4	Q–R4
21 Q–K1!	Q–R1

Black naturally rejects the exchange of queens.

22 Q–N3	B–R3
23 R–B7	B–N4
24 N–B3	Q–R4
25 N×B	Q×N
26 R–Q1	Q–R4
27 R–R7	Q–B6
28 R–Q3	Q–R8+
29 K–Q2	R–QB1
30 P–QB4	P–N4

Better 30 ... Q–N7+ 31 K–Q1
K–K2 and ... KR–Q1.

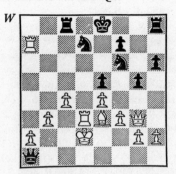

31 K–B2!
Threat 32 R–Q1

31 ...	Q–KB8
32 Q–B2	Q×Q+
33 B×Q	

At last White has succeeded in
exchanging queens. Now he advances
his passed pawns without particular
difficulty.

33 ...	N–QN1
34 K–B3	0–0

35 R–Q6 K–N2 36 P–QN4 N–K1
37 R–QN6 N–QB3 38 R–Q7 N–N1
39 R/7–N7 N–QB3 40 B–B5 R–KN1
41 P–QR4 N–Q1 42 R–N8 R×R
43 R×R N–K3 44 B–K7 P–B3
45 P–B5 K–B2 46 R–N7 K–N3
47 B–Q6 N/1–N2 48 K–B4 R–QR1
49 P–R5 N–Q5 50 R–N8 R–R2
51 R–N6 N/2–K3 52 P–R6 P–N5
53 P×P K–N4 54 P–N5 K–B5
55 R–N7 R–R1 56 R–KB7 K×KP
57 R×P 1–0

Konstantinopolsky–Ashkhanov
USSR 1934

1 P–K4	P–QB4
2 N–KB3	P–Q3

3 P–Q4	P×P
4 N×P	N–KB3
5 N–QB3	P–QR3
6 B–KN5	P–K3
7 Q–B3	B–K2
8 0–0–0	Q–B2
9 Q–N3	QN–Q2

If 9 ... P–N4 10 B×P+!

10 P–B4	P–N4

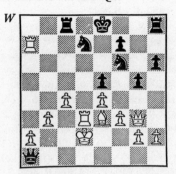

11 B×P!?
This time White does not obtain
three pawns for the piece (cf. the
Bronstein–Najdorf game), however
he counts on utilising his advantage
in development (i.e. the fact that
Black has not yet castled) and the
active positions of his pieces.

11 ...	P×B

12 KR–K1!
Having sacrificed a bishop for one
pawn White quietly brings up the
reserves. He now threatens the break-
through P–K5.

12 ...	P–N5?

12 ... P–K4? (suggested by
Aronin) is also bad for Black:
13 N–B5 (threatening 14 N×B K×N
15 N–Q5+) 13 ... P–N5 14
N×NP+ K–Q1 (or 14 ... K–B1
15 P×P P×P 16 N–Q5 N×N
17 R×N with ample compensation)
15 P×P! P×P (if 15 ... P×N

16 P×N P×P+   17 K–N1) 16
N–Q5 N×N 17 R×N, and there is
no answer to White's attack. Analysis
by Shamkovich.

Black's correct plan is first to put
his king into safety and then to
launch a counterattack: 12 ... 0–0!
13 P–K5 P×P (13 ... N–R4 at
once is bad. Mnatsakanian–Aba-
karov, Tiflis 1957 went 14 Q–B3
N×BP 15 P×P! N–Q6+ 16 K–N1!
—not 16 R×N B×B+—16 ...
N×R 17 Q×R B×P 18 N/4×NP
Q–N1 19 Q×Q B×Q 20 R×N/K1
B×P 21 B–K7 R–K1 22 B–Q6 B×B
23 N×B, and White's connected
passed pawns should have paved the
way to victory. The game continued
23 ... R–Q1   24 N×B R×N
25 R–Q1, and now Black should have
played 25 ... N–K4! 26 N–N5 K–B1
27 P–QN3 K–K2 28 P–B4 R–Q1!
and Black can rush his KNP and
KRP in answer to White's Q-side
advance. Instead the game went
25 ... N–N3?   26 N–N5 P–N4
27 P–QN3 P–R4   28 P–B4 P–R5
29 P–R4 P–K4   30 N–Q6 R–N1
31 K–B2 K–N2   32 P–R5 N–R1
33 P–R6 K–N3   34 P–R7 R–Q1
35 P–QN4 R–Q2   36 N–N5 R×R
37 K×R P–N5   38 K–K2 K–B4
39 P–B5 K–K3   40 N–B7+! N×N
41 P–N5 P–R6   42 P×P P×P
43 P–N6 P–R7 44 P×N P–R8=Q
45 P–B8=Q+ K–B3 46 P–R8=Q
Q–R7+   47 K–Q3 1–0) 14 P×P
N–R4 15 Q–R4 B×B+ 16 Q×B
P–N5! 17 N/3–N5 Q–B4 18 Q×N
R–R4!   By   counter-sacrificing
a knight, Black has seized the
initiative, e.g.
a) 19 N–Q6 Q×N/3 20 N–B5 Q–B4
21 N×P N×P!∓∓ ;

b) 19 N–N3 Q×N 20 N×R Q×N
21 K–N1 N–N3∓ ; or
c) 19 Q–K2 B–R3!

13 N/3–N5	Q–N1
14 P–K5!	P×P

14 ... R×P 15 K–N1 R–R3 was
played in Mnatsakanian–Ustinov,
USSR Team Ch 1960, and now White
should have continued with 16 B×N
P×B (if 16 ... B×B 17 P×B P×P
18 Q–N7 R–B1 19 N×KP!±±; or
16 ... N×B   17 Q×P R–N1
18 P×N!±±) 17 P×QP! (not
17 Q–N7 BP×P 18 Q×R+ B–B1
19 P×P P×P when Black gets two
pieces for a rook) 17 ... B–B1
18 N–B7+ K–Q1 19 N×R winning:
19 ... B×N 20 N–B6+.

15 P×P	R×P

If 15 ... N–R4 16 Q–R4±

16 K–N1	R–R4
17 P×N	Q×Q
18 P×P!	R–N1
19 P×Q	R×N

If 19 ... B×B 20 N–Q6+ and
21 N–B6+

20 B×B	R–N3
21 B–R4	R×P
22 N–B5	R–N5
23 N–Q6+	

Winning the exchange and the
game.

Dunhaupt–Keller
Corres 1965/66

1 P–K4	P–QB4	2 N–KB3	P–K3
3 P–Q4	P×P	4 N×P	P–QR3
5 N–QB3	P–QN4	6 B–Q3	B–N2
7 0–0	Q–B2	8 R–K1	P–Q3
9 B–N5!		P–R3	

If 9 ... B–K2 10 B×B N×B
(10 ... Q×B 11 N–B5!) 11 B×P+

P×B   12 N/4×NP Q moves 13
N×P+ K–B1   14 N×B±±; or
9 . . . N–Q2 10 P–K5 N×P (10 . . .
P×P?   11 N×KP P×N??   12
Q–R5+ and mate in two) 11 N/3×P
P×N 12 R×N!

10 B–R4	P–N4
11 B–N3	B–N2

12 B×NP+!	P×B
13 N/4×NP	Q–Q2

13 . . . Q–N3 loses to 14 N×P+
K–K2 15 Q–R5 and 16 Q×BP+,
13 . . . Q–B3 to 14 N×P+ K–K2
15 N–Q5+! and 13 . . . Q–K2 to
14 N×P+ K–B1   15 N×B Q×N
16 Q–Q8 mate

14 Q×P!	N–R3
15 Q–N6	B×N
16 P×B	K–K2
17 N–B7	N×N
18 Q×B	N–B3
19 QR–Q1	N/2–Q4

Or 19 . . . Q–B1 20 B–Q6+

20 Q–N3	1–0

Vasyukov–Averbakh
Moscow Ch 1957

1 P–K4	P–QB4
2 N–KB3	N–QB3
3 P–Q4	P×P
4 N×P	N–B3
5 N–QB3	P–Q3
6 B–KN5	P–QR3
7 Q–Q2	B–Q2
8 0–0–0	P–N4
9 B×N	NP×B
10 K–N1	P–K3

11 B×P?!   **P×B**
White has sacrificed in unfavour-
able circumstances. He has exchanged
off his active QB and queens are soon
exchanged. Without any attacking
prospects his only hope lies in the
endgame, but . . .

12 N/4×NP	Q–N1
13 N×P+	B×N
14 Q×B	Q×Q
15 R×Q	K–K2!

. . . with Black's king in the centre
and his rooks united he is well placed
to meet the advance of White's
Q-side pawns.

16 R/1–Q1	R–R2
17 N–N5	

White must play actively. Black
was intending . . . N–K4, . . . R–QB1
and . . . N–B5 threatening . . . N×P.

17 . . .	R–N2

Although White has material compensation for the piece Black has the
advantage because of his play along
the Q-side files.

18 R/6–Q2

Vacating Q6 for the knight.

18 ... R/1–QN1

If 18 ... R × N 19 R × B+ K–B1
20 R–B7 N–K4 21 P–KB4 and
Black's KR is out of play.

19 P–QN3 N–R4!

The start of Black's counter-attack.

20 N–Q6 R–B2

21 K–R1

21 N × P is met by 21 ... N–B5
22 R–Q3 B–B3 23 N–Q6 N × N
24 R × N B × P when none of White's
Q-side pawns can make a move.

21 ... B–B3

22 P–KB3?

White should not play so defen-
sively. His knight at Q6 is performing
a very useful job, keeping Black's
rooks from using the only open file
on the board. White ought to have
supported his knight by 22 P–KB4
R–Q2 23 P–K5.

22 ... R–Q2

23 P–QB4 R/1–Q1

If 23 ... R × P, not 24 P × R
N × NP+ 25 K–R2 N × R 26 R × N
R × N but 24 N–B8+! K–Q1 25
R × R+ B × R 26 P × R K × N
27 K–N2 with a clear advantage for
White in the endgame.

24 P–K5

Not 24 P–B5 because of 24 ...
N–N2 threatening both 25 ... N × P
and 25 ... N × N.

Now White gives up a pawn to
rescue his stranded knight but the
ending is quite lost.

**24 ... P × P 25 N–K4 B × N
26 R × R+ R × R 27 R × R+ K × R
28 P × B N–N2 29 K–N2 N–Q3
30 P–QR4 N × KP 31 P–QN4 P–B4
32 P–R5 K–B3 33 K–N3 P–R4
34 P–N5+ K–B4 35 K–B2 N–Q3**

**36 P–N6 N–N2 37 P–R6 K × NP
38 P × N K × P 0–1**

Dueball–Ree
Bad Pyrmont 1970

1 P–K4	**P–QB4**
2 N–QB3	**P–Q3**
3 N–B3	**P–K3**
4 P–Q4	**P × P**
5 N × P	**N–KB3**
6 P–B4	**B–K2**
7 B–K3	**P–QR3**
8 Q–B3	**Q–B2**
9 0–0–0	**P–QN4?!**

Premature. Correct is 9 ... N–B3.

10 P–K5!

10 B × P+ at once gives Black a
defensive resource denied him in the
game continuation: 10 ... P × B
11 N/4 × NP Q–N2! 12 P–K5 N–Q4
13 N × N P × N 14 Q × P Q × Q
15 R × Q (15 N–B7+ K–B1 16 N × Q
B–N5!) 15 ... B–K3! and White's
pawns are not worth Black's piece.

10 ... B–N2

Now Black no longer has this square
for his queen, and so ...

11 B × P+! P × B

12 N/4 × NP Q–B1

Best is 12 ... Q × N 13 P × Q

B×Q 14 P×B R×P (14 ... N–Q4?
15 R×N!±±) 15 P×N P×P
16 K–N1 R–R4 17 N×P+ B×N
18 R×B, when White has the more
active position and his passed QBPs
provide good endgame chances.

13 Q–N3	**P×P**
14 P×P	**N–R4**
15 Q–R3	**P–N3**
16 B–R6!	

What are you going to do with your
king mister?

16 ...	**N–QB3**
17 KR–K1	**N–N5**
18 P–R3	**N–Q4**
19 N–Q6+!	**B×N**
20 P×B	**R×P?**

Overlooking the simple refutation.
20 ... Q–B5 loses at once to 21
R×P+! and 20 ... N–N3 to 21
P–Q7+ N×P 22 R×P+! P×R
23 Q×P+ K–Q1 24 B–N5+ K–B2
25 N–N5+ and mate in two.

Relatively best is 20 ... R–R4
21 P–Q7+ Q×P 22 P–KN4
N/R4–B5 (if 22 ... N/R4–B3 23
B–N7 and 24 B×N) 23 B×N N×B
24 R×Q N×Q 25 R×B, when
White has a sound pawn more and
three connected passed pawns ready
to stride forward.

21 P–Q7+!	**Q×P**
22 P×R	**P–B4**
23 N×N	**B×N**
24 Q–QB3	**R–N1**
25 P–N4!	**P×P**
26 Q–K5	

Threatening 27 Q–N8+ Q–Q1
28 R×P+, and if 26 ... K–Q1
27 R×B! P×R 28 Q–N8+ Q–B1
29 B–N5+ K–Q2 30 Q–N5+ K–Q3
31 Q–N6+ winning the queen.
So ...

26 ...	**1–0**

Nunn–Bhend

Buenos Aires Olympiad 1978

1 P–K4 P–QB4 2 N–KB3 N–QB3 3
P–Q4 P×P 4 N×P N–B3 5 N–QB3
P–K4 6 N/4–N5 P–Q3 7 B–N5
P–QR3 8 B×N P×B 9 N–R3 P–N4 10
N–Q5 P–B4

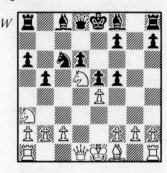

11 B×P!?

This move is more promising than 11
N×P!? (see chapter 5) because the pair
of knights combine to threaten an
unpleasant check on QB7. Black now
has a variety of moves at his disposal, of
which 12 ... R–R4 is currently
considered his best chance. Other
moves are 12 ... Q–R4+, 12 ...
Q–N4, 12 ... R–R2 (after which
White takes the exchange and tries to
win with his Q-side pawns), and the
text move.

11 ...	**P×B**
12 N×P	**R–QN1**
13 N/N–B7+	**K–Q2**
14 Q–R5	**N–Q5**

14 ... N–K2 15 Q×P/7 K–B3 16
P–QN4! forces a quick win, e.g. 16 ...
N×N 17 P–N5+ K–N2 18 Q×N+
K–R2 19 Q–B6 and mate soon follows.

15 0–0	**K–B3**

15 ... R–N2, intending to trade off
the dastardly knights, is met by 16

P–QB3 R×N 17 P×N, when White has a big advantage because Black's king is so exposed.

16 P–QN4!

Herein lies part of White's compensation for the sacrificed piece—he has two strong passed pawns.

16 ...   P×P

17 P–QB3   N–K3

If 17 ... N–N4 18 N×N R×N 19 P–QB4 R–QN1 20 P–N5+ K–N2 21 P–QR4 B–K3 22 P–R5 B×N 23 P×B, and the Q-side pawns will eventually engulf Black's king.

18 P–N5+   K–N2

Black can give up the exchange to weaken White's attack but after 18 ...

R×P 19 N×R K×NQ4 20 N–R7!, White still has a clear advantage.

19 P–N6   K–B3?

Black would have held out much longer with 19 ... Q–N4 20 Q×Q N×Q, though 21 P–QR4 and the continued advance of the pawns should still prove decisive.

20 QR–N1	**Q–N4**
21 Q–K2	**N–B4**
22 P–N7!	**N–Q6**
23 Q×KP	**N–B4**
24 Q–QB4	**R×P**
25 R×R	**1–0**

The notes to this game are mainly based on those by Nunn in *Modern Chess Theory*.

5 NxQNP (Or N-QN5)

There are, quite naturally, similarities between the sacrifice of a white knight at QN5 and that of a bishop on the same square. In some positions the sacrifice involves the capture of the QNP and later the capture of the QP, producing the same heterogeneous material balance which was discussed in the previous chapter. But in practice this theme is extremely rare. When the B×QNP sacrifice nets three pawns for the piece, White still has his QN on QB3 from where it defends his QRP (an important factor since White will have castled Q-side). In addition, the removal of White's KB speeds up the completion of his development by uniting his rooks.

The sacrifice of a knight at QN5 is purely a tactical motif aimed at installing a minor piece on that square from where it can help in the attack against Black's king. The sacrifice itself is merely a means to remove Black's QRP so that the square QN5 becomes a safe one for White to occupy.

For the sacrifice to be successful Black's queen will invariably be on QB2 so that the move N×QNP (or N-QN5) attacks the queen and calls for some immediate response from Black. If Black captures the knight White usually recaptures with the remaining knight although recapture with the KB, the queen and even the QRP are not so very uncommon.

We shall divide our study of this sacrifice according to how White recaptures on QN5 (or how he would have recaptured had Black accepted the sacrifice).

White recaptures with the knight
When White has a knight on QN5 the success of his attack normally depends on how well he can utilise Black's dark square weaknesses. An almost trivial example is Ivanovic–Nikolic, Yugoslav Ch 1969:

8 N/4–N5 P×N 9 N×P Q–N1 10 B–N6 N–Q4 Otherwise 11 B–B7 wins the queen. **11 P×N Q–K4+ 12 K–B1 R–R5 13 B–B7 Q×NP** 13...Q×QP 14 P–QB4 **14 R–QN1 Q–B3 15 P×N and White won.**

In Milic–Djurasevic (*25*) Black's Q3 square was weak for a different reason—His KB had strayed out to the K-side. This whole example is one long forced sequence. It is very exciting but the final outcome is not entirely clear.

When Black has castled Q-side, the sacrifice often opens the way for a mating attack:

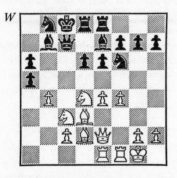

18 N/4–N5! Q–Q2 18 ... P × N comes to the same sort of thing: 19 N × P Q–Q2 20 N–R7 + K–B2 21 P–N5 (threatening 22 B × P mate) 21 ... B–QB1 22 B × P + K–N2 23 Q–K3 P–Q4 24 Q–N6 + K–R1 25 N × B Q × N 26 B–N4! followed by 27 R–R1 mating. **19 N–R7 + K–B2 20 P–N5** Threatening 21 P–N6 + K × P 22 Q–K3 + K–B2 23 N/3–N5 + P × N 24 B × RP mate. **20 ... P–Q4 21 N–R4! B–N5 22 P–K5** Threatening mate in one. **22 ... N–B3 23 P × QN B × P 24 N × B Q × N 25 P × N Q × N 26 R–R1 Q–B3 27 Q–K5 + B–Q3 28 B × P/5 + K–Q2 29 Q–R5,** and White had a winning attack as well as being a piece ahead in Ghizdavu–Ajansky, Albena 1971.

Kristinsson–Tal (*26*) is quite amus-ing. White's sacrifice should force an immediate draw (who wouldn't be satisfied with a draw against Tal?) but rather than submit to this ignom-inious end Tal actually uses the dark squares to launch a daring counter-attack, which although objectively unsound works in practice.

White recaptures with the QRP
This theme is only seen when Black has castled Q-side. White's pawn on QN5 can be a dangerous weapon in itself:

15 N–N5 P × N 16 P × P N–N1 17 N–R5 P–Q4 18 P–N6 Q–Q2 19 N × B Q × N 20 R–R7 Q–B3 21 R–B7 + Q × R 22 P × Q K × P 23 P–B5 1–0, Berzinish–Usov, Latvia 1962.

And then there is the case of the tornado on the QR-file—see the Karklins–McCormick example (*27*).

White recaptures with the KB or the queen
A check on QN5 can produce all sorts of nasty consequences for Black. Pietzsch–Bobotsov, Leipzig 1965 is not so much of a sacrifice because Black's KB7 knight is hanging in one line. Nevertheless, the idea is worth noting:

16 N/4–N5 Q–Q1 If 16 ... P×N
17 B×P+ B–Q2 18 B×B/K7 B×B
(18...K×B 19 Q×N) 19 B×P±±
17 N×P+ K–B1 17 ... Q×N
18 Q×Q B×Q 19 R×B leaves
Black two pawns down (19 ... N×R
20 R–Q8 mate). **18 B×B+ Q×B**
19 Q–B4 N×R/R8 20 Q×N P–B3
21 R–B1 K–N1 22 R×P R–KR2
23 R–N6+ 1–0 If 23 ... R–N2
24 N–B5!

The typical case is Zinser–Lombardy, Zagreb 1969, in which the
check condemns Black's king to a
painful life on the central files:

24 N–N5! P×N If 24 ... Q–B3
25 Q–N4 or 24 ... Q–K2 25 Q–R5
25 B×P+ K–K2 Or 25 ... B–Q2
26 Q–N4±± **26 P–K5** Sealing the
coffin. **26 ... N–B5** If 26 ... P–B3
27 Q–N4+ K–B2 28 P–N6+ K×P
29 R×B R×R 30 Q×R P×P
31 B–K8+ K–R2 32 B–B7 P×P
33 Q–N8+ K–R3 34 Q–R8+ K–N4
35 Q×P+ K–R5 36 N–Q4 and
Black is soon mated. **27 Q–N4+**
N–Q3 28 N–Q4 B–Q2 29 P–R4
P–QN3 30 P–B5! Q–B4 If 30 ...
P×P 31 P×N+ Q×P 32 Q–K1+
B–K3 33 N–B5+ winning the queen.
31 P×N+ K×P Or 31 ... Q×QP
32 P–B6+ P×P 33 P×P+ K×P
34 R–R6+ K–N4 35 Q–Q2+
followed by mate. **32 Q–Q2 P–K4**
33 N–N3 Q–N8+ 34 K–R2 B×B
35 Q–N4+ K–B2 36 R×B R×R
37 Q×R B–Q2 38 Q×NP Q–N5
39 Q×KP+ K–B1 40 N–Q4 Q×NP
41 Q×P Q–R4 42 Q–R8+ K–B2
43 Q–R7+ K–B1 44 Q×P and
White won.

The check at QN5 can also be a
disrupting influence if Black is driven
into a self pin, interposing on Q2. In
Koch–Simagin (*28*) Black cannot
capture on QN4 because of the effect
of the pin after White recaptures with
his queen.

Spassky–Vladimirov
29th USSR Ch 1961

Milic–Djurasevic
Belgrade 1960

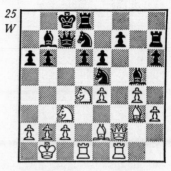

12 N/4–N5	P×N
13 N×P	Q–R4
14 N×P+	K–B1
15 B–B4	

Now the KBP is a goner.

15 ...	P×P
16 N×BP	Q–B2

If the rook moves 17 Q×BP is crushing.

17 B–QN3

Better than capturing the rook when either 17 ... B×N or 17 ... Q×B leaves Black with too much counterplay.

17 ...	N–K4?

Better defensive chances were offered by 17 ... N–B4, eliminating the light squared bishop.

18 N×N	Q×N
19 R–Q8+	N–K1
20 P–B3	P–KN4
21 Q–R5!	Q–K2
22 B–KB2	

Threatening 23 B–B5.

22 ...	B–N5
23 R×N+	

More accurate was 23 Q×N+ Q×Q 24 B–B5 mate.

23 ... R×R 24 Q×B B–K4 25 R–Q1 1–0

21 N/4–N5!	P×N
22 N×P	Q–B4
23 N×P+	K–B2
24 Q×Q+	P×Q
25 N–B4!	B–R3

If 25 ... P–B3 26 P–KR4 traps the bishop, or if 25 ... B–KB3 26 R×B! N×R 27 B×N+ etc.

26 N×N	B×B
27 N×N+	K–B1

If 27 ... P–K4 28 B×P+ K–B3 29 N–N8+ K–N2 30 R×R B×R/Q1 31 R–K1 B–QN4 32 P–B4! B–K1 33 R–Q1 ±±

28 N–N6+	K–N2
29 R×R	B×R/Q1
30 R–B2	B×P

On 30 ... B–QN4 31 P–QR4! saves the knight.

31 N–B4	B×P
32 R×P+!	R×R
33 N–Q6+	K–B3
34 N×R	B–N4

And now **35 N×B P×N 36 K–B1** would have offered White good winning chances—He can eventually create two connected passed pawns on the Q-side.

Kristinsson–Tal
Reykjavik 1964

Karklins–McCormick
US Open Ch 1971

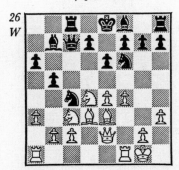

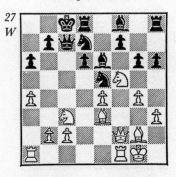

13 N/4 × NP The start of a drawing combination. **13 ... P × N 14 N × P Q–B3 15 N–R7 N × B?** Typical Tal, disdaining the draw that would come after 15 ... Q–QB2 16 N–N5 Q–B3 etc. **16 N × Q B–B4** Not 16 ... R × N 17 R–B3 when Black has nothing. **17 K–R2?** Justifying Tal's counter-sacrifice. 17 N–R5 would also be bad on account of 17 ... B × KP or 17 ... B–R1. But White has a neat resource in 17 P–QN4 B–N3 18 P–B4! N × R+ 19 P–QB5 N–N6 20 Q–K3 N/3–R4 21 P × B, when Black's knights are frozen and White's Q-side pawns will run very quickly. **17 ... N × R+ 18 R × N B × N** Now Black's minor pieces are all active and White's Q-side pawns have much further to go than in the last note. **19 P–B4 P–Q3 20 Q–QB2 B–Q5 21 P–QN4 P–K4 22 P–KB5 K–K2 23 P–QR4 P–N3 24 P–N5 B–R1 25 Q–K2 QR–KN1 26 P–R5 P–R4 27 P–N3 R–R2 28 K–N2 R/2–N2 29 P × P R × P 30 R–B3 N–R2 31 Q–K1 N–N4 32 R–B1 N × KP 33 B × N R × P+ 34 K–R2 R–N7+ 35 K–R1 R–N8+ 36 R × R R × R+ 37 Q × R B × B+ 0–1**

17 N–N5!   **RP × N**
18 P × P   **P × N**
If 18 ... P–N3 19 R–R3! threatening 20 R/1–R1 as well as 20 R–B3, or 18 ... N–B4 19 P–N4!
19 R–R8+   **N–N1**
20 KP × P   **B–B5**
21 B–N6   **Q–K2**
If 21 ... Q–Q2 22 B–R7 and the king has no escape square.
22 B × R   **Q × B**
23 B × P+!   **K–Q2**
24 Q–R7   **Q–B2**
25 R × N   **Q–B4+**
25 ... B × R loses the queen to 26 B–B8+ K–Q1 27 B–K6+ and if 25 ... B–N2 26 B–B6+ N × B 27 P × N+ K × P 28 Q–R8+ K–Q2 29 R × R with a winning material advantage.
26 Q × Q   **P × Q**
27 R–Q1+   **K–B2**
If 27 ... K–K2 28 R/1–Q8 (threatening 29 P–B6+) 28 ... P–B3 29 P–N6 and the pawn promotes.
28 R/1–Q8   **B–N2**
Or 28 ... N–Q2 29 P–N6+! N × P 30 B–N2! N–Q2 31 R/N–B8+ and 32 R × N.
29 P–N6+! K × P 30 B–N2+ 1–0

Koch–Simagin
Corres 1965/68

28
W

Rogulj–Georgiev
Varna 1977

W

18 N/4–N5!   **Q–N1**

If 18 ... P×N 19 Q×P+ R–Q2
(or 19 ... Q–Q2 20 B×B) 20 B×P
Q–B1 21 B×B Q×B 22 R–Q1 B–Q1
(or 22 ... N×KP   23 P–R5!)
23 N–K4!±±

19 B×P!	**B×B**
20 Q×B	**Q×B**
21 P–R5!	**Q–B4**
22 Q×P+	**K–Q2**
23 N–R4!	**Q×N**
24 N–N6+	**K–B3**

If 24 ... Q×N Black's three minor
pieces are insufficient against 25
P×Q KR–B1 26 R–Q1+ followed
by 27 Q×KP+ or 25 ... N–N4
26 R–Q1+ K–B3 27 Q×B N–B7+
28 K–N1 N×R 29 Q–QB7+ K–N4
30 P–B4+ K–N5 31 P–N7.

25 Q×B   **KR–K1**

25 ... Q×RP loses to 26 P–N4!
Q×N   27 Q×KP+ K–N2   28
R–B7+ winning the queen at once
and mating soon after, while on
25 ... KR–B1? 26 R×R R×R
White mates in two.

26 Q–R3   **N–N4**

Otherwise 27 R–B7, threatening
28 Q–QB3+.

27 P–R4!	**N–K5**
28 Q–KB3	**Q×KP**
29 Q×N/K4+	**Q×Q**
30 R×Q	

White is a sound pawn ahead.

13 N/3×P!

It is important here to capture with
the correct knight. 13 N/4×NP Q–N1
leaves Black with counterplay, but now
13 ... Q–N1 is met by 14 N×P! and if
14 ... BP×N 15 Q×KP+ B–K2 16
N–Q6+ etc.

13 ...	**RP×N**
14 B×P+	**K–K2**
15 P×P	**Q×KP**

A better defensive try might have
been 15 ... N–Q4, blocking one line of
attack.

16 KR–K1   **Q–B5+**

If 16 ... Q–N4+ 17 K–N1 N–N5 18
N×P! P×N 19 R–Q7+ K–B3 20
R–KB1+ winning.

17 K–N1	**B–Q4**
18 N–B6+	**B×N**

After 18 ... K–Q3 19 P–B4, Black
can exchange queens with 19 ...
Q–B4+ 20 Q×Q P×Q, but the
endgame is lost.

19 B×B   **R–QN1**

If 19 ... R–R2 20 Q–QB3 N–Q2 21
R–Q4 Q–N1 22 R/1–Q1, and Black's
extra piece is of no use against White's
onslaught.

20 Q–R3+	**Q–N5**
21 Q–R7+	**1–0**

Uhlmann–Ljubojevic
Niksic 1978

This position shows that even the world's leading players sometimes allow one of the thematic sacrifices that will bash the Sicilian flat within a few moves. Here the leading Yugoslav Grandmaster Ljubomir Ljubojevic, who many regard as an eventual challenger for the world title, has left his king in the centre and his QP poorly protected. The result is a massacre.

11 N/4–N5!	P×N
12 N×P	Q–B3
13 N×P+	K–K2

13 ... K–B1 14 Q–N4 is equally horrible, e.g. 14 ... N–K2 15 N–B5 and 16 R–Q8+ (or 15 B–B5, threatening simply 16 N×B and 17 B×N+).

14 Q–N4	K–B3

Otherwise the double check will be killing.

15 P–B4	P–KN4
16 P×N+	K–N3
17 N×BP	1–0

Because of 17 ... K×N 18 B–R5 mate.

Miagmasuren–Martens
Leningrad 1960

1 P–K4	P–QB4
2 N–KB3	P–K3
3 P–Q4	P × P
4 N × P	N–KB3
5 N–QB3	P–Q3
6 B–KN5	B–K2
7 Q–B3	

After 7 P–B4 P–KR3, White would not be able to retreat 8 B–R4 because of 8 . . . N × P.

7 . . .	QN–Q2

More flexible is 7 . . . P–QR3.

8 0–0–0	P–QR3
9 K–N1	

The alternative was 9 B–K2, preparing for P–KN4 or Q–N3. But not 9 Q–N3 at once because of 9 . . . N–R4.

9 . . .	Q–B2
10 Q–N3	N–N3

10 . . . P–QN4 allows 11 B × N B × B 12 B × P P × B 13 N/4 × NP Q–N1 14 N × P+ K–B1 (on 14 . . . K–K2 15 P–B4 is even stronger) 15 P–B4, when White has a much superior form of the Kapengut–Faibisovich example (page 44)—His QRP is defended by his king and his knights are both active.

But better than the text is simply 10 . . . 0–0.

11 P–B4	P–R3
12 B × N	

If White had not intended the coming combination he would have retreated the bishop to R4.

12 . . .	B × B

See diagram next column

13 N/4–N5!?	P × N
14 N × P	Q–N1?

On 14 . . . Q–B4 15 N × P+ K–B1

16 P–K5 B–K2 17 B–K2 Q–B2, White would have two pawns for the piece and a good position. Nevertheless, Black should have chosen this variation because after the text move White is given an additional option—which he takes.

15 P–K5!

Opening a new avenue of attack, the KB-file. 15 N × P+ etc. leads into the previous note.

15 . . .	P × P
16 N–Q6+	K–B1

Black could relieve some of the pressure by 16 . . . K–K2 17 P × P R–Q1 18 P × B+ P × P 19 N × B+ Q × N, but if you are going to be attacked you might as well be a piece ahead for your troubles.

17 P × P	Q–R2

Defending his knight with gain of tempo. If 17 . . . B–K2 18 Q–B2 B × N 19 R × B N–Q2 (on 19 . . . Q–R2 both 20 Q × N and 20 R–Q8+ are sufficient to win) 20 B–N5 Q–R2 (or 20 . . . K–K2 21 Q–R4+ P–N4 22 Q–Q4 N × P 23 R/1–Q1, and if 23 . . . P–B3 or 23 . . . N–N3 then 24 R–Q8) 21 Q × Q R × Q 22 B × N with a won ending.

18 P–QR3

Now White cannot afford to take

back the piece: 18 P × B Q × P+ 19 K–B1 Q–R8+ 20 K–Q2 Q–R4+ and 21 ... P × P when suddenly Black has the better attacking chances.

18 ...	**B–K2**
19 B–K2	**N–Q4**

19 ... B–Q2 allows a second knight sacrifice: 20 N × BP! K × N 21 KR–B1+ K–N1 22 Q–N6 R–KB1 23 R × R+ B × R 24 B–R5 and mate in two.

19 ... B × N also fails to lift the pressure from KB2 for very long: 20 R × B B–Q2 21 Q–B2 B–B3 22 R–KB1 ± ±

20 KR–B1	**B × N**

Forced.

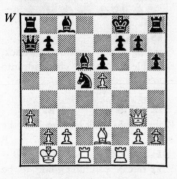

21 R × P+?

Correct was 21 R × N! P × R (there is nothing better) 22 Q–N6 P–N4 23 B–R5 etc. The text may be more aesthetically pleasing to those with sadistic tendencies but in fact it is quite unsound.

21 ...	**K × R**
22 B–R5+	**K–N1**
23 R–KB1	**N–B6+?**

Spectacular but only second best. Black's idea is to gain time for the defence by distracting White's most powerful attacking piece.

But simply 23 ... P–KN4 24

Q–Q3 P–N4 allows Black to bring his queen to the K-side where it can be sacrificed for more of White's depleted army, e.g. 25 Q–N6+ Q–KN2 26 Q–K8+ B–B1 27 R–B7 R–QR2∓ ∓

24 Q × N

If 24 K–R1 Q × P+ 25 P × Q R × P+ 26 K–N2 N–R5+ followed by 27 ... R × Q and 28 ... B × P, when Black is two pieces ahead. Or 24 K–B1 N–K7+ 25 B × N B × RP!∓ ∓.

Being a rook and two pieces ahead it is hardly surprising that Black's position is full of sacrificial resources.

24 ...   **R–R2**

Or 24 ... B–B4 25 Q–Q3 when White has a tremendous attack—He threatens both 26 B–B7+ K–B1 27 Q–Q8 mate and 26 Q–N6.

24 ... B–Q2 25 B–B7+ K–B1 26 P × B is also very good for White. e.g. 26 ... Q–R3 27 R–B3 Q × QP 28 B × P+ K–K1 29 B × B+ Q × B 30 Q–K1+ K–Q1 31 R–Q3 and after the exchange of rook for queen White will pick up one of Black's NP's by a series of checks culminating in a fork of king and pawn.

25 Q–B3?

25 P × B B–Q2 26 B–N6 wins, e.g

26 ... B–N4 (or 26 ... B–K1
27 P–Q7! B×P 28 Q–B3) 27 P–Q7
Q–N1 (if 27 ... R–Q1   28 Q–B3
Q–N1   29   Q–B7+   K–R1   30
Q–K8+ ± ±) 28 R–Q1 Q–Q1 29
Q–QN3 B–B3 30 Q×KP+ K–R1
31 Q–B5 ± ±

    25 ...   **P–KN4?**

The last mistake. After 25 ...
P–KN3! (gaining a vital tempo)
26 B×P R–N2   27 B–B7+ K–R1
28 Q–R3 K–R2 White has at least a
draw (29 Q–Q3+ K–R1   30 Q–R3
etc.) but probably no more, e.g.
29 R–B6 Q–N8+   30 K–R2 Q–QB8.

    26 P×B   **B–Q2**

Or 26 ... R–N2 27 Q–B8+ K–R2
28 B–K2 ± ±

    27 B–B7+   **K–R1**
    28 Q–KB6+   **R–N2**
    29 Q×RP+   **R–R2**
    30 Q–B6+   **R–N2**
    31 P–KR4   **Q–R5**
    32 R–R1   **1–0**

On 32 ... P–N5 comes 33 P–R5
followed by P–R6.

Keres–Ojanen
Estonia–Finland Match 1960

    1 P–K4   **P–QB4**
    2 N–KB3   **P–K3**
    3 P–Q4   **P×P**
    4 N×P   **P–QR3**
    5 N–QB3   **Q–B2**
    6 B–Q3   **P–QN4?!**

Better are the less committal
moves 6 ... N–QB3 and 6 ...
N–KB3.

    7 0–0   **B–N2**
    8 R–K1!   **B–B4**

Tal–Gipslis, Riga 1958 went 8 ...
N–QB3 9 N×N Q×N 10 P–QR4
P–N5 11 N–Q5!

    9 B–K3   **N–K2**

Better 9 ... Q–N3

    10 Q–R5!

10 B×P is also possible: 10 ...
B×N (not 10 ... P×B? 11 N/4×NP
Q–N3 12 B×B Q×B 13 N–Q6+
and Black loses back the piece)
11 Q×B P×B   12 N×P Q–B3
13 N–Q6+ with a strong attack.

    10 ...   **P–K4?**

A positional blunder of the first
magnitude. Almost anything else is
better. Now Black has two gaping
holes at Q4 and KB4 and a KP which
sticks out like a sore thumb.

    11 N/4×P   **P×N**
    12 N×P   **Q–B3**
    13 B×B!   **Q×B**
    14 P–QN4!   **Q–B3**

Or 14 ... Q×NP   15 N–B7+
K–Q1 16 KR–N1 ± ±

    15 Q×KP   **P–B3**
    16 N–Q6+   **K–B1**
    17 Q–Q4!   **N–R3**

On 17 ... N–B1 Keres had intended 18 N×B Q×N 19 P–K5!

    18 R–K3!

The threat is 19 R–B3 and 20
R×P+

    18 ...   **P–R4**
    19 P–N5!   **Q–B4**
    20 P–QB3

Had White not played 18 R–K3, Black would now have the resource 20 ... Q × Q 21 P × Q N–N5, since the white bishop would also be en prise.

20 ...	N–B3
21 N × B	N × Q
22 N × Q	N × N
23 P × N	1–0

Estrin–Abroshin
USSR Corres Ch 1959/60

1 P–K4	P–QB4
2 N–KB3	P–K3
3 P–Q4	P × P
4 N × P	P–QR3
5 N–QB3	P–QN4
6 B–K2	B–N2
7 B–B3	

Now Black must always be on the lookout for P–K5.

7 ...	Q–B2
8 0–0	N–QB3
9 R–K1	

Threatening 10 P–QR4! P–N5 11 N–Q5! P × N 12 P × P+ N/3–K2 (or 12 ... N–K4) 13 P–Q6! with a tremendous game.

9 ...	N–K4

After 9 ... N × N 10 Q × N White has a clear advantage in space and development, while 9 ... B–K2 allows 10 P–K5! N × N 11 B × B Q × B 12 Q × N when Black has no satisfactory way to complete his development.

10 B–B4	0–0–0

See diagram next column

11 N/4 × NP!	P × N
12 N × P	Q–N3
13 P–QR4	P–B3

If 13 ... N × B+ 14 Q × N P–Q3

15 Q–K2! and Black cannot meet all of White's threats: 16 P–R5, 16 R–R3 and 16 B–K3.

14 B–K2	B–B4
15 P–R5!	Q–B3

Not 15 ... B × BP+? 16 K–B1 Q–B4 17 P–QN4! regaining the piece and maintaining a strong attack against Black's king.

16 B × N	P × B
17 P–QN4!	Q × P!
18 B–B3	Q × NP
19 R–N1	

Better than 19 B × B+ K × B 20 R–N1 Q × P when Black has more chance of being able to defend himself.

19 ...	B × P+!

Not 19 ... Q × P? 20 N–Q6+ B × N 21 Q × B end of game.

20 K × B	Q–B4+
21 K–N3	P–Q4
22 R–N3	B–B3
23 Q–K2	N–K2

By returning the piece Black has managed to complete his development and set up a strong pawn centre. Nevertheless, his lack of a pawn shield on the Q-side will be the deciding factor.

24 B–N4

Black was hoping for 24 R–B3

Q–N5   25 N–R7+ K–Q2 when
suddenly he would have all sorts of
unpleasant threats.

24 ...   **B × N**

Naturally not 24 ... N–B4+
25 B × N P × B 26 R–QB3 ± ±

25 R × B   **Q–B6+**

26 Q–K3!

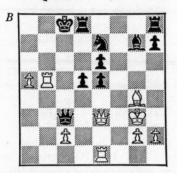

The winning move. White forces
the exchange of queens to reach an
ending in which his pieces are the
more active and his QRP threatening
to sprint to the eighth rank.

26 ...   **Q × Q+**

27 R × Q   **P–K5**

Black cannot defend both doubled
pawns.

28 B × P+   **K–B2**

29 R–N6!

Material is equal but now Black
must give up a pawn to extricate
himself from a mating net (the threat
is 30 R–QB3+ etc.)

29 ...   **P–Q5**

30 R × P   **N–B3**

31 R–N5   **P–Q6**

32 P × P   **R × P+**

33 K–R4   **R–K1**

34 P–R6   **1–0**

If 34 ... R–QR6 35 R–N7+
K–Q3 36 R–Q7+ K–B4 37 R × P
with an easy win.

Braga–Keene
Esquel 1978

1 P–K4 P–QB4 2 N–KB3 N–QB3 3
P–Q4 P×P 4 N×P N–B3 5 N–QB3
P–K4 6 N/4–N5 P–Q3 7 B–N5
P–QR3 8 B×N P×B 9 N–R3 P–N4 10
N–Q5 P–B4

This position has become one of the
most critical in Sicilian theory during
the past few years. Various ideas have
been tried for White, among them the
sacrificial continuations on White's
QN5.

11 N×P!?

For 11 B×P!? (see chapter 4, page
63).

11 ...   **P×N**

12 B×P   **B–Q2**

In order to justify his sacrifice White
must now find a method of punishing
Black's king while it is still in the centre,
or he may try to make something of his
passed QRP and QNP. Note that
whereas many of the sacrifices on QN5
net White three pawns (the QRP, QNP
and QP) and present him with three
passed pawns, both 11 N×P!? and 11
B×P!? in this variation do not pick up
the black QP and so White is normally
a little worse off when he comes to an
ending.

13 P×P	R–QN1
14 P–QR4	

Amongst other things this move introduces the possibility of R–R3, followed by the transfer of the rook to the K-side.

14 ...	Q–N4
15 P–KN4!	

Threatening 16 P–R4 and P–N5, with a total bind on the K-side.

15 ...	Q–R5
16 Q–B3	

16 Q–Q3 is an untried possibility suggested by Rossetto, but other moves allow 16 ... P–R4!, breaking up White's K-side.

16 ...	N–Q5
17 Q–B3	

It looks tempting to strand Black's king in the centre by 17 B×B+ K×B 18 Q–B3, but after 18 ... R–N2 19 P–R5 B–N2 20 P–R6 Q×NP, Black wins because of the mate threat.

17 ...	B×B
18 P×B	B–N2
19 R–Q1	0–0

Escaping from the centre. Now White must rely on his Q-side pawns.

20 Q–KN3!

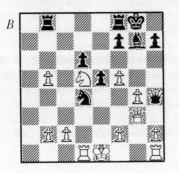

20 ...	Q×Q

Black can try for more with 20 ... N×QBP+ 21 K–Q2 N–Q5 22 Q×Q N–B6+ and 23 ... N×Q.

21 RP×Q	R×P?

Correct is 21 ... N×QBP+ 22 K–Q2 N–Q5, which offers Black slightly the better of the draw.

22 P–QB4	R×N

22 ... R×NP 23 P–B6 R–R1 might have been better, according to Keene.

23 P×R	R–N1
24 0–0	R–N4
25 R–R1	B–B3
26 K–N2	R×QP
27 KR–B1	P–K5
28 R–Q1?!	

After 28 R–K1! R–K4 29 R–R6 B–K2 30 R–R4!, Black is under pressure.

28 ...	P–R3
29 R–R6	B–K4
30 R–K1	R–N4
31 R×KP	R×P
32 R–R4	R–Q7
33 K–B1	R–Q8+
34 R–K1	R–Q7
35 R–K4	R–Q8+
36 R–K1	R–Q7
37 R–K4	½–½

The notes to this game are based on those by Keene in *Modern Chess Theory*.

6 N–Q5

The sacrifice of a white knight at Q5 is probably the most difficult to assess of all those in this volume. In return for the piece White normally gathers only one pawn as his immediate material compensation and the soundness or otherwise of White's concept must therefore lie in the evaluation of the positional compensatory factors.

Since White's QN is nearly always developed on QB3 and since Black frequently has a pawn situated at K3, the N–Q5 offer is more often a possibility than many other typical Sicilian sacrifices. For it to have most chance of success Black's king should still be on its original square and White's KR on K1, so that after ...P×N, the recapture KP×P leaves White with immediate pressure along the K-file. This pressure is often augmented by the possibility of White's other knight (at Q4) jumping into KB5 (or sometimes QB6) from where it adds force to the attack on Black's KB (developed on K2). The knight on KB5 also casts an eye on Black's KNP which is left unprotected by the move ... B–K2.

A standard feature of the aftermath of the N–Q5 sacrifice is the pawn wall on the Q-file. White has a pawn at his Q5 and Black at his Q3 (Oh to be allowed to employ algebraic notation!). This barrier divides K-side from Q-side and interferes with the co-ordination of Black's forces. In addition, the black pawn at Q3 restricts the scope of his KB without there being any real prospects of that pawn moving and allowing the bishop some freedom. Occasionally, Black's QP is still on Q2 when White offers the sacrifice—Then Black suffers from the restriction of movement of his QN and QB, either of which could be developed at Q2, as well as from serious dark square weaknesses. Ciric–Janosevic (29) is an excellent example of how White can take advantage of these weaknesses.

The easiest kind of positional sacrifice to make is the one which forces the immediate regaining of the material and yet still brings the positional advantages that usually compensate for the sacrifice. With N–Q5 this sometimes happens in one of three distinct ways:

a) Black meets the check on the K-file by interposing his QN at K4 (allowing P–KB4 by White, winning that knight). Dely–Donner (30) is an example of this and Dubinsky–Chubukov (31) carries a similar theme;

b) White picks up the pinned bishop at K7 after attacking it for the second time by N–QB6, as in Shivokhin–Ruzhentsev (32), or N–KB5; or

c) The recapture KP×P attacks a piece on QB6 and that piece cannot move. In Alexander–Lundholm (*33*) Black is compelled to return the piece because he needs a tempo to get castled.

The most serious study of N–Q5 must necessarily revolve around situations in which White cannot forcibly recapture the sacrificed material. For the purpose of this study it is convenient to consider three separate classes of position:

a) Black's king is in the centre;
b) Black has castled K-side; and
c) Black has castled Q-side.

a) Black's king is in the centre

So let's castle out of it! Certainly, if it is possible for Black to extract his king quickly and painlessly from the valley of the shadow of death, he refutes White's sacrifice. In Bilek-Golombek (*34*) the sacrifice was played in unrealistic circumstances—White's forces were not well placed to pursue the attack and Black had no real problems once he had castled.

In Seidman–Saidy (*35*) too, the speed with which Black puts his king safely on KN1 is the key to his success. But in Seidman–Fischer (*36*) Black's problems are not over once he castles because his K-side has already been ruptured. In Gheorghiu–Barczay (*37*) Black's K-side is even more vulnerable and the added presence of a white pawn at KB5 paves the way for White's remaining knight to advance to K6.

Castling Q-side may also provide the antidote. In Matanovic–Tal (*39*) for example, Black is not in any serious danger of losing until he goes

wrong in the endgame. If he does castle Q-side Black must always reckon with the possibility of a Q-side pawn storm as in Osmanovic–Cebalo (*38*) though if White has also castled Q-side the pawn storm is hardly likely to meet with much success because of the inherent danger of White exposing his own king.

If Black is unable to castle out of trouble he may try to move his king in a more sedate manner. In Bernstein–Fischer (*40*) White's attack lacks the use of one of his minor pieces, the KB, which is poorly placed on KN2. Black has time to remove his king from the line of fire to the K-side and to consolidate his material advantage. But in Nikitin–Kanko (*41*) White, with an almost identical set-up but with his KB actively placed, has a devastating attack against Black's king.

In both Estrin–Shatskes (*42*) and M. Mukhin–E. Mukhin (*43*) White's success can be traced to his great lead in development—It is unimportant in which direction Black's king chooses to run.

There are more numerous examples of the defending king fleeing to the Q-side than to the K-side. This is partly because of necessity (Black may be forced to move his king while his KB is still on KB1) and partly because it hinders Black's development less (on Q1 the king does not prevent the development of the KR to K1 nor that of the QR to QB1). Typical examples are Konstantinopolsky–Gilman (*45*), Horberg–Kotov (*46*) and Quinones–Higashi (*47*). The last two of these are identical except for the interpolation of one

K in center: Karpov-Ljubojevic 1982 (Chess at Top p.121)

pawn move on each side and I feel that both are worth including in this chapter because the difference affects White's winning procedure.

The pawn storm in Konstantino-polsky–Gilman is even more successful than in the Osmanovic–Cebalo example because Black's QNP has already moved and his Q-side is therefore more vulnerable (the QB3 square in particular). But do not be carried away by the idea that if the black king can be driven to the Q-side he will automatically be drowned in a sea of white pawns. If White has castled Q-side the pawn advance cannot be carried out with its usual ferocity because of the denuding effect that it would have on White's own king.

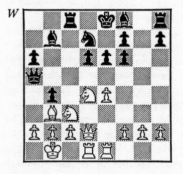

14 N–Q5 This is forced since 14 N/3–K2 leaves the KP en prise. White was wrong in allowing himself to be drawn to this sacrifice. **14 . . . P×N 15 P×P+ K–Q1 16 P–QR3 K–B2 17 P×P Q–N3 18 P–KB4** Preventing . . . N–K4 for good. **18 . . . K–N1 19 N–B5 P–KR4 20 P–N3** Already White has run out of active ideas. **20 . . . P–R5 21 P–N4**

P–R6 22 R–K3 R–N1 23 R–N1 Q–R2 24 R/1–N3 N–N3 25 R–K4 R–Q1 26 P–B4 B–B1 27 N–Q4 B–Q2 28 P–QN5 P–B4 29 P×BP R×R 30 P×R B–N2 31 N–B6+ B×N 32 NP×B R–R1 33 R–K1 N–B1 34 B–Q1 Q–B4 35 Q–QB2 N–N3 36 Q–N3 K–R1 37 B–B3 R–QN1 38 B–R1 N×BP 39 Q×R+ Clearly White's flag must have been about to fall. **39 . . . K×Q 40 R–K8+ K–B2 0–1** With only one Q-side pawn rushing up the board White's attack was doomed to fail, Bertok–Najdorf, Bled 1961.

Dimitriev–Shishov (*48*) illustrates how the underdevelopment of Black's Q-side makes it much more difficult for his king to find safety there. Ghizdavu–Ghinda (*49*) is really rather an extravagance since the N–Q5 sacrifice is unnecessary—White having another, perfectly valid winning method. Nevertheless, it is always nice to see a gory king hunt.

Hulak–Toncev (*50*) and Kuindzhi–Jansa (*51*) both rely in some way on White's remaining knight having the use of his QB6 square.

Just in case the reader has become mesmerized by the multiplicity of white wins contained in this section, let me bring him back to earth with an example of over-exuberence (or optimism).

See diagram next page
12 N–Q5? P×N 13 P×P+ K–Q1 14 N–B6+ White's QP is *en prise* and therefore he has no time for the moves 14 B–Q2 or 14 P–B3. **14 . . . B×N 15 P×B N–N3 16 B–K3 P–Q4! 17 QR–Q1 B–Q3 18 Q–B2 R–QN1 19 Q–R4 Q×P** and Black, having repulsed all threats, kept his

extra piece in Tringov–Clarke, Munich 1958. In this game White's attack went astray because his dark-squared bishop was unable to take an active part. This circumstance should have put White on his guard when he took the fatal decision on his 12th move.

b) Black has castled K-side

The sacrifice N–Q5 is rarely successful once Black has already castled. The reason for this is easy to understand—White's compensation normally depends on his pressure along the K-file and with the black king out of the way ...

Nevertheless, the sacrifice is occasionally seen under a different guise—It can be used to clear the way for another of White's pieces (usually his KB) to take part in the attack on Black's king.

See diagram next column

This position arises from some analysis by Nikitin. White continues **15 N–Q5!** and after **15 ... P×N** 15 ... B–Q1 16 Q–R5 is no less good for White: 16 ... B–N2 17 P–N6! BP×P 18 N–K7+ K–R2 19 B×KP+ K×N 20 Q×RP±± **16 B×QP R–N1 17 P–N6!** he has a terrific attack (17 ... RP×P 18 R×P).

Another example of the sacrifice helping to improve the scope of White's KB is Bogdanovic–Navarovszky, Tiflis 1965:

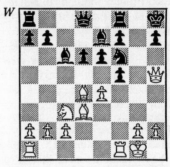

White played **15 N–Q5!** and the sacrifice cannot be accepted because of 15 ... P×N 16 P×QP B–Q2 17 R×P! (threat 18 R×N) when White forces mate. So the game continued **15 ... B×N 16 P×B R–KN1 17 P×P R–N3 18 Q–R3** 18 Q–K2! is possibly even stronger. **18 ... P×P 19 QR–K1 Q–Q2 20 R×BP!** and White won.

Ghizdavu–Buza (*52*) is only a temporary sacrifice—White regains the piece at once by a stereotyped idea and earns a pawn as interest.

In Fischer–Sofrevsky, Skopje 1967, White used the sacrifice to increase the scope of his QR:

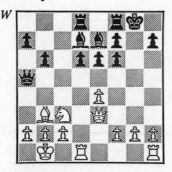

tangle quickly enough to avoid
returning the piece:

15 N–Q5! KR–K1 If 15 ... P×N
16 R×P Q–R3 17 R–KR5 (threat
18 Q–R6) 17 ... B–N5 18 R–R4
P–B4 19 P–KR3 B×R 20 P×B
B–B3 21 Q–R6 winning. **16 N×B+
R×N 17 R×P R–QB1 18 Q–Q4
B–K1 19 Q×BP 1–0**

Kim–Zhukov (*53*) is unique—
White's compensation for the sacrificed piece lies in his QP which
immediately becomes passed and
quickly rushes up the board.

c) Black has castled Q-side

Again it is rare for the N–Q5 sacrifice
to be successful once Black has
castled, but there are always exceptions. In Kolodzeichik–Yaroz, Poland
1967, Black's forces were so congested that he was unable to un-

**18 N–Q5 P×N 19 KP×P KR–K1
20 Q–B4** Hoping for 20 ... N–R2
21 B×N+ winning the queen.
**20 ... N–N3 21 B×N Q×B
22 P×N B–K3 23 Q–Q4 Q–N4
24 BP×P B×N 25 P×B Q×P/N6
26 R–R3 Q–N4 27 R–K3 B–B1
28 R/1–K1 R×R 29 R×R Q–KB4+
30 K–R2 Q–N5 31 Q–N6 1–0**

In Velimirovic–Nicevsky (*54*)
White uses the fact that Black's KB is
unprotected to gain a tempo (and a
pawn) in his attack. Thus, White's
thematic pressure along the K-file
plays its part in a game which is
decided on the Q-side.

Ciric–Janosevic
Titovo Uzice 1966

Dely–Donner
Budapest 1961

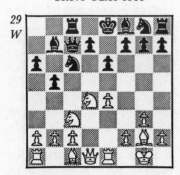

10 N–Q5!

The point of this move is that it interferes with the development of Black's K-side.

10 ...	Q–N1
11 P–QR4!	N×N?

Better is 11 ... P–N5 although after 12 N–N6 White is clearly better.

12 Q×N	R–B5
13 Q–Q3	P×N

Not 13 ... R×RP? 14 N–N6

14 KP×P+	K–Q1
15 P×P	P×P
16 P–N3	R–B4
17 B–K3!	

Taking full advantage of Black's dark square weaknesses.

17 ...	B–B1
18 P–QN4	R–B5
19 B–R7!	Q–Q3
20 Q–K3	B–K2
21 B–N6+	K–K1
22 B–B5	Q–KR3
23 Q×Q	N×Q

Or 23 ... P×Q 24 P–Q6

24 R×B+	K–Q1
25 P–Q6	1–0

12 N–Q5! P×N If 12 ... Q–B4 13 P–N3 (threatening 14 R–B4) 13 ... N×N 14 P×N B×P 15 N×P!±±, or 12 ... Q–Q1 13 N×N+ followed by 14 P–K4. **13 P×P+ N–K4** Black is forced to return the piece. If 13 ... B–K2 14 N–B5 N–KN1 15 R/4–K4 N–K4 16 R×N P×R 17 P–Q6 Q–Q2 18 B×B Q×B 19 P×B Q–B2 20 Q–Q5 R–B1 21 R×P, and there is no defence to 22 N–Q6+.

13 ... K–Q1 is also useless: 14 B–Q2! K–B1 (or 14 ... P–QR4 15 Q–R1!) 15 B–R5 Q–B4 16 N–N3 Q–R2 17 R–QB4+ N–B4 18 B–R3+ K–N1 19 N×N P×N 20 P–Q6 etc. **14 P–KB4 0–0–0** If 14 ... N/3–Q2 15 P×N N×P 16 B–B4± **15 P×N P×P 16 R×KP! B–Q3** If 16 ... Q×R 17 R–B4+ K–Q2 18 B–B4 Q–R4 19 R–B7+ K–K1 20 Q–K1+ followed by mate. Again the QR comes into its own. **17 R–K3 K–N1 18 R–QB3 Q–Q2 19 N–B6+ B×N 20 R×P!** And not 20 R×B? Q×R! 21 P×Q B–B4+ when Black wins. **20 ... B×QP 21 R–N6+ B–N2 22 Q×B+! Q×Q 23 R×B+ K–R1 24 R–N4+ 1–0.**

Dubinsky–Chubukov
Student Tournament, Moscow 1964

31
W

13 N–Q5!   **P×N**
14 P×P   **Q–N3**

The worst possible way to try for
the exchange of queens (and to
defend the QNP) because it over-
works the knight at Q2. But in any
event Black's problems are severe:
14 ... Q–N1 15 KR–K1+ B–K2
16 N–R5 and 14 ... Q–R2 15
KR–K1+ B–K2 16 Q×P are both
very unpleasant.

15 KR–K1+   **K–Q1**

If 15 ... B–K2 16 B×N P×B
17 Q–K4 N–K4 (17 ... Q–Q1 18
N–Q4) 18 P×N BP×P 19 N–
Q4!± (19 ... Q×N?? 20 B–N5+)

16 B×N+   **P×B**
17 Q–K4   **N–K4!?**

An unusual defensive idea.
Although not forced to do so, Black
returns the piece so as to block the
K-file and to deprive White's knight
of the Q4 square. Chubukov obviously
considered that if he permitted the
invasion of his position by White's
queen (18 Q–K8+, 19 Q×BP,

20 B–B5) the future would hold few
prospects. But now White has a
tremendous game because of Black's
vulnerable king.

18 P×N   **BP×P**
19 Q–B3   **B–K2**
20 B–B5

20 Q×P? allows 20 ... B–N5
21 B–K2 (21 R–Q2 B–N4) 21 ...
Q–K6+ 22 R–Q2 R–KB1 23 Q–N7
B×B when Black should win.

20 ...   **P–QR4**
21 K–N1 P–R5   **22 N–B1 R–B1**
23 R–B1 B–R3   **24 B–Q3 P–B4**
25 B×B Q×B   **26 Q–KR3 Q–B1**
27 Q×RP P–R6   **28 R–B3 P×P**
29 K×P P–K5   **30 R–QN3 B–B3+**
31 K–N1 K–K2   **32 P–N4 R–R6**
33 Q–R7+ R–B2   **34 Q×P R×R+**
35 N×R Q–B6   **36 Q×P+ B–K4**

W

37 N–Q4 R–B5   **38 Q–R7+ K–B1**
39 N–K6+ K–K1   **40 Q–N8+ K–K2**
41 Q–Q8+ K–B2   **42 Q–KB8+**
K–N3 43 N×R+ K–R2 44 Q–B5+
K–N1   **45 Q–K6+ K–R2**   **46**
Q–B7+ B–N2   **47 Q–R5+ K–N1**
48 Q–K8+ K–R2 49 Q–K4+ K–N1
50 K–B1 1–0

Shivokhin–Ruzhentsev
RSFSR 1961

32
W

15 N–Q5!

An unusual feature of this position is the situation on the QN-file. That Black's QB is pinned against his queen adds force to the thematic move N–B6.

15 ...   **P×N**
16 P×P   **0–0**

There is nothing else. If 16 ... Q–B2 17 N–B5 N×P 18 R×B Q×R 19 B×N winning.

17 N–B6

Not 17 Q×B? R–K1 when Black wins a rook.

17 ...   **Q–B2**
18 N×B+   **K–R1**

Now White is a pawn ahead with a strong attack.

19 B–N5   **N/4–Q2**
20 R–KR4   **KR–K1**
21 P–QB4   **P–R3**
22 Q–Q2   **N–KN1**

There is no defence to the threatened sacrifice.

23 B×P   **P×B**
24 R×P+   **K–N2**
25 Q–N5+   **1–0**

Alexander–Lundholm
Corres 1969–70

33
W

Black's counter-attack was premature.
15 N–Q5! P×N Possibly better is 15 ... 0–0–0 16 N–N6+! N×N 17 B–Q2 and now: not
a) 17 ... P–N5 18 B×P Q–N4 19 Q–K1 N–B5 20 P–N3 P–Q4 21 P×N P×BP 22 R×R+ K×R 23 B×B R×B 24 Q–B3, when Black's position falls apart; but
b) 17 ... Q–R5! 18 B–N4! P–Q4! 19 P–N3 B×B 20 P×Q B×P+ 21 K–N1 N×P 22 R–R3 B–N5 23 P×P B×P 24 Q–K5, when White is certainly better but there is no clear winning line. **16 P×P 0–0–0 17 P×B P–Q4** Threatening 18 ... N×RP 19 P×N B×P+ 20 K–N1 Q–N5+ and mate next move. **18 B–Q4 B×P 19 Q–N4+** 19 P×B Q×P+ gives Black a perpetual check. **19 ... K–B2 20 B×N NP×B** 20 ... QP×B loses to 21 B–K5+ K–N3 22 P×B P–B6 23 Q–N1+ K×P 24 Q–N2+ K–N3 25 Q–B2+ K–N2 26 Q–B3+ and 27 Q×P. **21 P×B P–B6 22 QR–K1 Q×P+ 23 K–Q1 Q–N5 24 B–K5+ K×P 25 Q–B3 1–0** After 25 ... Q–N8+ 26 K–K2 Q×P+ 27 K–B1 the black QBP is a goner.

Bilek–Golombek
Kecskemet 1968

Seidman–Saidy
USA Ch 1961

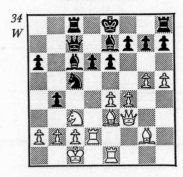

18 N–Q5

Doomed to failure but nevertheless the only consistent continuation since other knight moves leave the KP *en prise*. White had reached the diagrammed position by mixing two strategies. Firstly he had advanced on the K-side while Black developed along normal Sicilian lines. Then, instead of persevering with his K-side attack by P–N6, White brought his KR to the centre in preparation for the knight sacrifice on Q5.

18 ... P×N   19 P×P B–N4
Threatening 20 ... N–Q6+ **20 K–N1**
If 20 B×N Q×B 21 Q–K4 0–0 22 Q×B KR–K1 and Black wins.
20 ... 0–0   21 P–B5 KR–K1 22 Q–N4 B–B1 23 Q×P What else? There is nothing to do on the K-side. **23 ... N–Q6!** A fine counter-sacrifice. **24 P×N B×P+   25 R×B Q–B7+ 26 K–R1 R×B!** Decisive. **27 R/3–Q1** R×R   **28 Q×R Q×B   29 P–N6 R–B2** Avoiding White's only hope of salvation: 29 ... RP×P 30 RP×P P×P?? 31 Q–K6+ **30 P–R3 Q–B6 31 Q–N1 Q×BP 32 Q–N6 Q–QB7 33 R–KB1 P–B3   34 R–K1 P×P 35 P×P R–K2 36 R–KN1 Q–QB4 0–1**

13 N–Q5 White's attack lacks the one tempo that would make this sacrifice sound. Were his KR on K1 White would have excellent winning prospects. Yet it is not the text move which deserves a question mark because 13 N/3–K2 would lose a pawn to 13 ... N×KP. White was at fault earlier in the game for allowing himself to reach this position. **13 ... P×N 14 P×P** With his KR on K1 White would be threatening to win back the piece by 15 N–B5, and 14 ... P–N3 would lose to 15 N–B6 B×N 16 P×B N–K4 17 P–KB4 etc. **14 ... 0–0   15 N–B5 KR–K1   16 B×N B×B** Not 16 ... N×B? 17 Q–N5 B–KB1 18 N–R6+ K–R1 19 N×P+ with an immediate draw. **17 N×QP KR–N1 18 P–QR3 Q–B2! 19 N×P N–B4   20 P–Q6 N×B   21 P×Q N×Q+   22 R×N R–QB1 23 N–Q6 R×P   24 P×P R–Q1   25 P–QB4 B–B3   26 K–R2** Otherwise 26 ... R–N1. **26 ... R/2–Q2   27 P–B5 B–K4 28 R/1–Q1 B×RP 29 K–N3 B–B5   30 R–Q3 P–KR4 31 R–Q4 B–K4 32 R/4–Q2 P–R5 33 R–KR1 B×N 34 P×B R×P 35 R×R R×R 36 R×P R–N3 and Black won**

Seidman–Fischer
USA Ch 1957/58

Gheorghiu–Barczay
Vrnjacka Banja 1967

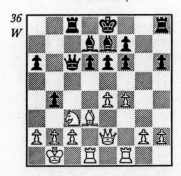

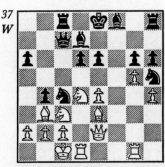

17 N–Q5 Naturally this sacrifice would be much more dangerous if White's KR were on K1 instead of KB1 as it could have been when it was moved from R1 two moves earlier. **17 ... P×N 18 P×P Q–B2** The QP is poisoned: 18 ... Q×QP? 19 B×P Q–K3 20 Q–Q3 and 21 KR–K1 with a tremendous position. **19 B×P R–QN1 20 KR–K1 B–QB1 21 B×B** 21 B–Q3 is met by 21 ... R–R2 followed by ... Q–R4. **21 ... R×B 22 R–Q4!** Threatening both 23 R–K4 and 23 R–B4. **22 ... 0–0!** The only move, taking advantage of the defensive role of White's queen which must guard QB2. **23 R–K4 KR–K1 24 P–B5 K–R2! 25 P–B3** White would do better to keep up the pressure by 25 P–KN4 followed by P–KR4 and P–N5; Black is tied to the defence of his bishop and, if the bishop moves, to the defence of the rook on K1. Now Black can force a draw at once. **25 ... P×P 26 R×B Q–N3 27 R×P+** Not 27 P–QN3 P–B7+ 28 K–B1 Q–Q5! 29 R×P+ K–N1 and White is lost. Analysis by Fischer. **27 ... K–N1 28 Q–N4+ K×R ½–½**

19 N–Q5! This sacrifice is particularly effective because Black's K-side is so wide open. **19 ... P×N 20 KP×P N–K4** If 20 ... N×B 21 Q×N/3+ K–Q1 22 B–R4!; or 20 ... B–K2 21 P×P when White still has excellent attacking chances as well as two pawns for the piece. **21 N–K6 B×N 22 P×B B–N2** If 22 ... B–K2 simply 23 P×P! B×P 24 R×NP! N×R 25 Q×N with a devastating attack. 22 ... Q–B3 fails to 23 R–Q5! P×P (or 23 ... B–N2 24 R/1–Q1) 24 R–R5! Q–K5 25 R×N! Q×R 26 B–R4+ **23 Q×P! P×P 24 R×QP 0–0** Black cannot save himself: 24 ... K–K2 25 R/1–Q1 KR–Q1 26 R×R R×R 27 R×R! Q×R (27 ... K×R 28 B–N6) 28 B–B5+ K–B3 29 P–K7+ **25 P–K7+ K–R2** If 25 ... R–B2 26 Q×R+ Q×Q 27 R–Q8+ ±± **26 P×R=Q B×Q 27 R–N6 B–B4 28 B×B** Not 28 R–N7 B×B+ 29 K–N1 B×R 30 R×Q+ R×R with an unclear position. **28 ... Q×B 29 R–N7+ K–R1 30 R–Q1 P–N5 31 Q–K6! R–B1 32 R–K7 N–B6 33 Q×P/N6! Q×R 34 Q–KR6+ 1–0**

Osmanovic–Cebalo
Cateske Toplice 1968

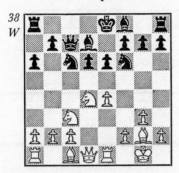

38
W

10 N–Q5!?

An interesting alternative to the normal continuation 10 N×N B×N (or 10 ... P×N 11 P–N3 ± Fischer–Nicevski, Rovinj/Zagreb 1970) 11 P–QR4, which offers White few real prospects of a lasting advantage.

10 ...	P×N
11 P×P+	N–K2
12 B–N5!	B–N5

In his notes to the game in *Informator 5*, Milic suggests 12 ... P–R3. Then, after 13 B×N P×B 14 Q–Q3 0–0–0 15 P–QB4, White still has good attacking prospects on the Q-side.

13 Q–Q2	0–0–0
14 P–QB4	P–R3
15 B×N	P×B
16 P–N4	

Like so many of the positional piece sacrifices in this volume, this particular one is difficult to assess. Black certainly has very little counterplay to balance White's Q-side pawn rush but whether or not White's attack gives full compensation for the piece is another matter. But the practical problems that face Black are certainly not to be sneezed at.

16 ...	P–KR4

Not 16 ... N–B4? 17 Q–B4 winning a piece.

17 QR–N1	B–R3
18 Q–B3	KR–K1
19 P–N5	Q–N3
20 P×P	Q×P
21 P–B5	B–Q7!

Returning the piece is the only defence. If 21 ... K–N1 22 R×N! R×R 23 N–B6+

22 Q×B	P×P
23 Q–B3	P–N3
24 N–N5	N×P
25 B×N	R×R+
26 Q×R	R×B
27 Q–K8+	K–N2
28 Q–K4!	

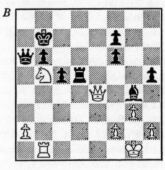

B

28 ...	Q×P?

A blunder in time trouble. Better is 28 ... B–K3 but after 29 P–QR4 K–B1 30 Q–KB4 White has too many threats.

29 N–B3 B–B4	30 Q×B R×Q
31 N×Q K–B3	32 N–B3 R–B6
33 N–N5 R–Q6	34 K–B1 P–B5
35 K–K2 R–Q4	36 N–B3 R–Q6
37 N–K4 P–B4	38 N–Q2 P–N4
39 N–B3 Black lost on time	

Matanovic–Tal
Portoroz 1958

39
W

13 N–Q5 P×N 14 N–B5 B–KB1 15 P×P 0–0–0 It is even possible for Black to castle 'by hand' so as to preserve the option of keeping his rook on QR1 where it can support the possible advance of the QRP: 15 ... Q–N3 16 KR–K1+ K–Q1 17 R–K2 (17 R–K4 gains a tempo by attacking the QNP but then 17 ... P–QR4 ought to be adequate) 17 ... R–B1 18 R/1–K1 K–B2 19 B–K3 N–B4 20 B–Q4 K–N1 21 N–K3 N×B 22 RP×N Q–N4 23 N–B4 N×P 24 B–B2 B–B3 25 Q–Q4 R–B2 26 B–N3 K–R1 and White has run out of play, Lokvenc–Tal, Munich 1958. Presumably Tal considers 15 ... 0–0–0 inferior to 15 ... Q–N3 since the Munich game was played after the Portoroz Interzonal. But after the text Black is surely better. White has no play on the K-file and with his king on the Q-side a pawn rush is unthinkable. **16 P–QR3 P–R3 17 P×P Q–B2 18 B–KB4 P–N3** Giving up a third pawn to tie up White's pieces on the wrong side of the board. **19 N×RP N–K4 20 B–N5 B×N 21 B×B N–B5?** Better was 21 ... N/3–Q2 or even 21 ...

N–R2. Now Matanovic can equalize! **22 B×N Q×B 23 B–N7 N×P 24 P–QN3! Q×P/N5 25 Q×Q N×Q 26 B×R R×B 27 R×P N–Q4 28 P–QB4 N–K6 29 R–KB6 N×NP?!** Correct is 29 ... R–R2, e.g. 30 P–N3 N–N5! 31 R–B4 R×P 32 R–K1 N–R3, or 30 R–K1 N×P 31 R–K7 N–R5, and in each case the result should be a draw. After the text Black's task is more difficult. **30 R×BP R–Q1 31 K–B2 N–R5 32 R–K1 R–Q2** 32 ... N–B4 would seem more natural. **33 R–K8+ K–B2 34 R/8–K7 R×R 35 R×R+ K–N3 36 P–B4 N–N7** And here 36 ... B–B1 was better, followed by ... B–B4+ and maybe then ... N–N7. The point of playing ... B–B1 first is to keep White's rook out of the sixth rank for as long as possible. **37 R–K6+ K–R2 38 R–KB6 B–K5+ 39 K–B3 P–R4** Now 39 ... B–B4 fails to 40 K–N4 N×P 41 K–R5 and 42 R×RP+ when the united passed pawns will prove decisive. **40 K–N2 P–R5!** If 40 ... B–B4 41 K–R3, 42 K–R4 and 43 K×P etc. **41 P–N4?** 41 P×P would have preserved some winning chances. **41 ... N–K6 42 R–K6 N×P+ 43 K–B3 B–Q4 44 R×P N–N3 45 P–R4 P–R6 46 P–N5 B–B2 47 R–N1** If 47 R–N7 N–R5+ 48 K–B2 P–R7 49 R–N1 B–N3+ and 50 ... B–N8 **47 ... P–R7??** 47 ... N–Q4+ 48 K–N3 K–N3 draws. **48 K–N2 K–N1 49 R–N7 B–N6 50 R–N1 B–B2 51 K–R1 K–B1 52 R–N7 B–K1 53 R–N5 N–Q2 54 P–R5 N–B3 55 P–R6 K–B2 56 R–N7+ K–N3 57 R–K7 1–0**

Bernstein–Fischer
USA Ch 1957/58

Nikitin–Kanko
Leningrad 1957

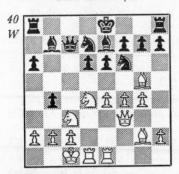

13 N–Q5? This sacrifice fails because White's KB is inactively placed and plays no part in the coming attack. Compare example *41*. **13...P×N** Not 13 ... N×N 14 P×N B×P? (14 ... B×B 15 P×B N–K4 16 Q–QN3±) 15 Q×B! P×Q 16 R×B+ K–Q1 (16 ... K–B1 17 B×P) 17 R/1–K1 K–B1 18 B×P K–N1 19 N–B6+ and White wins. Analysis by Fischer. **14 P×P K–B1** If 14 ... K–Q1? 15 N–B5 R–K1 16 Q–K3 N–B4 17 N×NP R–KN1 18 N–B5 R–K1 19 N×B±± **15 N–B5 R–K1 16 Q–K3 B–Q1 17 Q–Q4 B–B1! 18 B–R4** Threatening 19 P–N5. **18 ... N–B4** Just in time. Now we see the point of Black's 17th move—White's attack is one tempo short of success. **19 N×NP K×N 20 P–N5 B–B4!** Threatening 21 ... N–N6+ 22 RP×N Q×P mate. **21 P×N+ K–R3 22 Q–B4** The only defence. If 22 K–N1 B×QBP+ winning the queen. **22 ... N–Q2 23 Q×Q** Otherwise the advanced KBP falls. **23 ... B×Q 24 B–B3 B–Q1! 25 B–N5+ K–N3 26 R–N1 B×KBP and Black won**

13 N–Q5!   P×N
If 13 ... N×N 14 P×N B×B (or 14 ... B×P 15 B×B K×B 16 B–K4 when Black has no good move) 15 P×B B B×P 16 P–N6!
14 P×P
Threatening 15 N–B5 as usual.
14 ...   K–B1
If 14 ... K–Q1 15 R×B! (not 15 N–B5 B–KB1 16 Q–K3 Q–B4!) 15 ... K×R 16 N–B5+ K–Q1 (or 16 ... K–B1 17 N×NP K×N 18 B–R6+ followed by mate) 17 N×NP and 18 N–R5.
15 N–B5   B–Q1
If 15 ... R–K1 16 N×NP R–KN1 17 N–B5 R–N3 18 B–R6+ K–N1 19 N×B+ winning.
16 B–R6!
After 16 N×NP R–KN1 17 N–B5 R–N3 18 B–R6+ K–N1, White has nothing. Now White restores the material equilibrium and maintains his enormous positional advantage.
16 ... R–KN1 17 B×NP+ R×B 18 Q–R6 N–R4 19 P–N4! B–KB3 20 P×N Q–R4 21 N×R B×N 22 Q×QP+ K–N1 23 R–N1 Q×RP 24 R×B+ K×R 25 R–N1+ K–R1 26 Q–R6 1–0

Estrin–Shatskes
Central Chess Club Ch 1967

42
W

8 N–Q5

White is so far ahead in development that this sacrifice offers excellent practical chances. A more cautious plan which nonetheless gives White the advantage is 8 N–R4 N–KB3 9 R–K1. Bikhovsky–Suetin, USSR 1966 continued 9 ... P–Q4 10 P–K5 N–K5 11 P–QB4 N–B4 12 N×N B×N 13 B–K3 N–Q2 14 Q–N4 Q–N3 15 QR–B1 0–0 16 Q–R4 P–N3 17 N–B3, and White had a winning K-side attack.

| 8 ... | P×N |
| 9 P×P | B×P |

The loss of this pawn is of no great importance to White because with Black's QP still on its original square White is not likely to be able to contemplate N–B6 or N–K6 (for either of which the pawn at Q5 is a necessary support). The only significant factor about the capture of the QP is that Black can now use his QB to block the K-file but as is shown in the next note this is not a serious drawback from White's point of view.

| 10 R–K1+ | B–K2 |

If 10 ... B–K3 11 Q–B3 R–R2 12 B–K3 R–B2 13 B–KB4 R–B1

(a novel way for Black to get his QR to QB1!) 14 QR–Q1 with dangerous threats—Moiseyev.

| 11 N–B5 | N–QB3 |

If 11 ... K–B1 12 Q–N4! B–KB3 13 B–KB4 with a tremendous bind.

| 12 N×P+ | K–B1 |
| 13 N–R5! | |

B

In the actual game Estrin played the inferior 13 N–B5 which gave Black the opportunity to consolidate his K-side: 13 ... B–K3 14 Q–N4 B–B3 15 B–KB4 P–Q4 16 Q–R5 and now 16 ... B×N would have left White with almost nothing to show for the sacrificed piece.

The text is an improvement suggested by Moiseyev.

| 13 ... | B–K3 |
| 14 Q–B3 | |

Threatening 15 R×B QP×R 16 Q×N.

14 ...	B–B3
15 B–K3	P–R3
16 B–QB5+	B–K2
17 R×B!	B×B
18 B–N6 and White wins	

M. Mukhin–E. Mukhin
USSR Student Team Ch 1970

43
W

Savon–Liberzon
37th USSR Ch 1969

44
W

9 N–Q5! As in the Estrin–Shatskes example White's substantial lead in development is the key to his success here. **9 ... P×N 10 P×P K–Q1** Naturally not 10 ... B×P 11 B–B3+ **11 B–B3 B–Q3?!** Too ambitious. Black should have tried 11 ... P–Q3 followed by ... N–Q2 though his position would remain very cramped. **12 N–B5 P–B3** The continuation of Black's peculiar idea. By establishing his bishop at K4 he thinks that he will solve his problems on the K-file. If 12 ... N–K2 13 N×N B×N 14 P–Q6, White wins back the piece with much the better game. **13 Q–Q4 B×RP+ 14 K–R1 B–K4 15 Q×P P–Q3 16 R×B!** So much for the blockade on the K-file. 16 ... QP×R loses to 17 Q–B8+ K–Q2 18 Q×NP+ etc. and 16 ... BP×R to 17 N×QP R–R2 18 N×B+ and 19 Q–B8+ etc. Now Black's days are over. **16 ... P–QR4 17 Q×QP+ Q×Q 18 N×Q P×R 19 N×B+ K–Q2 20 N–B5+ K–Q3 21 N–K4+ K–Q2 22 B–N4+ K–K1 23 B–N5 R–R3 24 B–K6 R–N3 25 P–QN3 N–Q2 26 B–K3 R–N5 27 N–Q6+ K–K2 28 N–B7 1–0**

13 N–Q5!   **P×N**
14 P×P   **B–N5**

If 14 ... N–QN1 15 B×N P×B 16 Q–R5 (to prevent castling) followed by R–B3 and R/3–K3.

14 ... N×P is impossible because of 15 B–K4!

15 Q–K3   **N×P**

Not 15 ... N–QN1 16 B×N P×B 17 P–B5 trapping the light squared bishop.

16 Q–K4   **N–N3**
17 B×B   **N×B**
18 P–B5!   **P–KR4**

Forced. If 18 ... B–R4 19 P–N4.

19 P–KR3   **B×RP**
20 P×B   **P–Q4**
21 Q–R4   **K–B1**
22 N–Q4   **R–R3**

Has Black weathered the storm? **23 P–B6!** No. His king is still under fire. **23 ... P×P 24 K–R1 N/3–B1 25 R–K3 Q–Q3 26 R/3–B3 K–K1 27 R×P R×R 28 R×R Q–K4 29 R–B1 N–Q3 30 N–B3 Q×P 31 R–K1 R–R2 32 Q–KB4 R–Q2 33 N–K5 Q–B6 34 R–KB1 R–B2 35 Q–B6 N/2–B1 36 R–KN1 K–B1 37 K–R2 Q–Q7+ 38 R–N2 Q–K6 39 B–R7 1–0** (time).

Konstantinopolsky–Gilman
USSR Corres Ch 1949/50

10 N–Q5!   **P×N**
11 P×P+   **K–Q1**
12 B–N5   **N/1–Q2**

A typical position. White controls the K-file and the square QB6 for his knight and his pieces are better disposed. Moreover the black king is exposed. However, finding the correct plan of attack is not easy. For instance 13 N–B6+ yields nothing in view of 13 ... B×N 14 P×B N–K4.

13 Q–K2   **K–B1**

Not 13 ... Q–B4 because of 14 N–B6+ K–B2 15 B–K3. Now, if 14 Q–K8+ Q–Q1 15 Q×P N–K4, Black's pieces revive. 14 P–QR4 looks strong, with P–R5 and R–R3–QB3 to follow. One possible continuation might be 14 ... B×P 15 B×B N×B 16 Q–B3 Q–B5 17 Q×P Q×N 18 R–K8+ K–B2 19 R×R and White should win. Or alternatively 14 ... P–R3 15 B×N N×B 16 R–R3 K–N1 17 R–QB3 Q–Q2 18 N–B6+ B×N 19 P×B Q–B2 20 P–R5! P–QN4 21 Q–K3 R–R2 22 Q–N6+! K–R1 23 R/3–K3 and again Black is hopelessly placed.

The plan adopted by Konstan-
tinopolsky, a pawn advance on the Q-side, is also most effective.

14 P–QB4   **K–N1**
15 P–QN4!   **K–R2**
16 P–QR4!   **R–K1**
17 B–K3   **N–K4**
18 N–B6+   **N×N**

If 18 ... B×N then 19 P–R5!

19 P×N   **B×P**
20 P–R5   **R×B**
21 Q×R   **B×B**
22 K×B   **P–Q4**
23 P–N5!

23 ...   **B–B4**
24 RP×P+   **B×P**

Not 24 ... Q×QNP 25 R×P+ Q×R because of 26 Q×B+!

25 R×P+   **K–N2**
26 Q–R3   **R–Q1**

Or 26 ... P×P 27 Q–KB3+; or 26 ... Q×BP 27 R–K7+

27 R–K7   **N–Q2**
28 P×P   **Q–B4**
29 Q–KB3   **Q×NP**

Naturally, not 29 ... Q×R?? 30 P–Q6+

30 R–R3 K–B2 31 R×P K–Q3 32 R×P N–K4 Not only is Black's king terribly exposed but White is now even ahead on material. **33 Q–B6+ K×P 34 Q×N+ 1–0**

Very nice attack complex

Horberg–Kotov
Telegraph game, USSR 1959

46
W

Quinones–Higashi
Siegen 1970

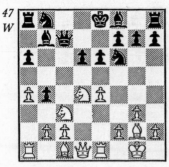

47
W

10 N–Q5

It would have been more precise to play 10 P–QR4 P–N5 first (thereby leading to the position of Quinones–Higashi, example 47).

10 ...	**P×N**
11 P×P+	**K–Q1**
12 B–N5	**N/1–Q2**
13 P–QB4	

Here 13 P–QR4 was also possible, but on 13 Q–K2 Black has the answer 13 ... Q–B5 which is not at his disposal if the moves P–QR4 P–N5 have been interpolated.

13 ...   **P–R3**

13 ... P–N5, a move suggested by Kotov, comes to nothing after 14 Q–K2.

14 B×N+ N×B 15 P×P P×P 16 Q–N3 Q–B4 If 16 ... Q–B5 then 17 Q–K3! threatening 18 QR–B1 as well as 18 N–B6+ B×N 19 Q–N6+ **17 N–B6+ B×N 18 P×B R–R2 19 R/K–QB1 Q–N3 20 P–QR4 P–Q4 21 P–R5 Q–N1 22 B×P B–Q3 23 B×P R–B1 24 B–N6** and after a stubborn resistance Kotov, with his king exposed and no compensating advantage in material, was forced to capitulate.

11 N–Q5! P×N   11 ... N×N 12 P×N P–K4 13 P–R5 leaves Black in terrible straits because as well as being behind in development he is certain to lose his QNP before very long. **12 P×P+ K–Q1 13 B–N5** With the threat of 14 Q–K2 and 15 Q–K8 mate. **13 ... B–B1** If 13 ... B–K2 (not 13 ... N/1–Q2 14 Q–K2! nor 13 ... Q–Q2 14 B×N+ P×B 15 Q–R5 with a bind) 14 N–B5 R–K1 15 N×NP R–N1 16 Q–Q4! with an overwhelming bind. **14 B×N+ P×B 15 Q–R5** Preparing to double rooks. **15 ... R–R2 16 R–K4 B–KN2 17 R/1–K1 Q–B4** If 17 ... P–B4 18 Q–R4+ P–B3 19 R–K6 R–B1 20 Q×RP, and Black is still completely tied up. **18 Q–K2 B–Q2 19 N–N3 Q–N3 20 P–R5 Q–N4 21 Q–K3 R–B2** 21 ... Q–N2 loses to 22 Q–B4 Q–B2 23 R–B4 when Black loses two more pawns at once. **22 Q–B4 R–K1 23 Q×QP R×R 24 R×R K–B1 25 B–B1 Q–R5** If 25 ... Q–N2 26 R×P Q–R2 27 P–QB4! **26 R×P Q–R7 27 N–B5 Q–R8 28 R×N+ K×R 29 N×P+ 1–0**

Dimitriev–Shishov
Dubna 1971

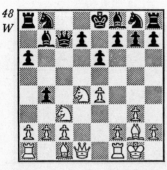

Ghizdavu–Ghinda
Bucharest 1971

9 N–Q5! This position is almost identical with the Osmanovic–Cebalo (example *38*). Here Black's QN is still on QN1 and White's KR on KB1. These differences favour White because his rook can come to the K-file in one move whereas Black's QN has no moves after White's recapture on move 10. White is therefore able to attack Black's king in the centre, where it is more vulnerable, rather than on the Q-side. **9 ... P×N 10 P×P K–Q1 11 R–K1 N–KB3 12 B–N5** Threatening 13 Q–K2 (and 14 Q–K8 mate) and if 13 ... B–B4 (or 13 ... B–Q3) 14 N–B5± **12 ... Q–N3 13 P–QB3 P–R3 14 B×N+ Q×B 15 Q–K2 B–Q3** Or 15 ... B–B4 16 QR–Q1, threatening 17 N–B6+ and 18 P×P (or 18 N×P). **16 QR–Q1 P–KR4** Black cannot develop his knight by 16 ... P–QR4 and 17 ... N–R3 because White can reply 18 N–B6+ and 19 N×P. **17 P–QR3 P×RP** Better was 17 ... P–R4. **18 P×P P–R5 19 Q–N2 P×P 20 RP×P K–B1 21 R–N1 R–QR2 22 Q–N6** Regaining the sacrificed material and leaving White with an overwhelming position.

19 N–Q5 White can also win by 19 R–R1! P–Q4 20 P×P Q–Q3 21 N–N5!! P×N 22 R×R N–N3 (22 ... Q–B2 23 Q×P!) 23 B×N P×Q 24 R×B+ K–Q2 25 R–Q8 mate. But the text move presents us with a typical example of Black's king being hounded into the open while his undeveloped army lies dormant. **19 ... P×N 20 P×P N–B4 21 KR–K1! K–Q2** If 21 ... N–N6+ 22 K–K2! B–N5+ 23 K–B1 K–Q2 24 N–K5+ P×N 25 Q–B6+ K–K2 26 B–B5+! Q×B 27 R×P+ B–K3 28 P–Q6+ finito. **22 R–QR1! Q–N7** 22 ... N–N6+ still does not work: 23 K–K2! N×R 24 N–K5+! P×N 25 Q–B6+ K–Q1 26 B–N6+ K–K2 27 B–B5+ winning the queen. **23 R/K1–QN1 N–N6+ 24 K–Q1 Q×R/R8 25 R×Q N×R 26 N–K5+! P×N 27 Q–B6+ K–Q1 28 B–N6+ K–K2 29 P–Q6+ K–K3 30 P–Q7+ B–Q3 31 P–B5+! K×BP** Or 31 ... K–K2 32 P–B6+ P×P 33 P×P+ K–K3 34 P–Q8=Q R×Q 35 B×R R–N1 36 B–B7±± **32 Q×R B×P 33 Q×R B–R5 34 Q×RP+ K–K3 35 Q–R3+ K–K2 36 Q–B8! B×P+ 37 K–K2 B–N5 38 Q–B7+ 1–0**

Hulak–Toncev
Lake Balaton 1970

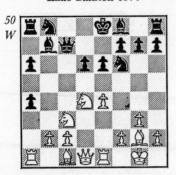

Kuindzhi–Jansa
Lvov 1961

11 N–Q5!

Similar to examples 46 and 47. But here White has played P–QR4 and Black has captured, thereby allowing White quickly to bring his QR into the attack.

| **11 ...** | **P×N** |
| **12 P×P+** | **K–Q1** |

If 12 ... B–K2 13 N–B5 N–N1 14 B–N5 P–B3 15 N×NP+ K–B2 16 N–K6 ± ±

13 R×P

With the simple threat of 14 B–Q2 and 15 B–R5.

| **13 ...** | **QN–Q2** |

13 ... N×P is met by 14 Q–B3 followed by 15 P–B4. 13 ... B×P loses to 14 B×B N×B 15 Q–B3 N–N3 16 B–N5+

| **14 P–QB4** | **N–K4** |
| **15 B–Q2** | **N×BP?** |

Relatively best is 15 ... Q–Q2. The text loses Black a piece.

16 N–B6+ B×N 17 R×N B–K2 18 R×B/6 Q–N1 19 B–R5+ K–K1 20 R–B7 N–N1 21 R/1×B+ N×R 22 Q–K1 Q–Q1 23 R–N7 R–QN1 24 R–R7 R–R1 25 B×Q R×R 26 B–R5 1–0

17 N–Q5!

An ideal situation. White's pieces are all active and Black has no Q-side counterplay. In addition, Black's queen is most unfortunately placed.

| **17 ...** | **P×N** |

If 17 ... Q–R4 18 N×B K×N 19 N–B5+! P×N 20 P×P+ and 21 Q×B ± ±

| **18 P×P** | **N–N3?** |

Black would do better to give back the piece by 18 ... N–B4 19 N–B5 0–0 20 N×B+ K–R1 21 R–K3 (so that 21 ... N–R5 can be met by 22 R–N3) when he is a pawn down with the worse game.

19 R×B+!

Forcing a quick win.

19 ...	**K×R**
20 Q–K4+	**K–Q1**
21 N–B6+	**B×N**
22 Q×Q	**B–N4**
23 Q×P+	**N–Q2**
24 K–N1	**R–QB1**
25 B×N	**B×B**
26 Q–QN6+	**1–0**

Ghizdavu–Buza
Romania 1971

52
W

Kim–Zhukov
USSR Armed Forces Ch 1968

53
W

| 13 N–Q5! | P×N |
| 14 N×N | N–K4 |

14 ... Q×N 15 B×P costs Black
the exchange without his even having
the active square QR5 for his queen
(compare the Ostapenko–Zhartsev
game, page 121, in which Black
played ... P–QN5 before White's
sacrifice).

15 N×B+	Q×N
16 B×P	B–N2
17 B×B	Q×B
18 R–Q5!	KR–K1
19 R/1–Q1	QR–B1
20 K–N1!	N–B3
21 R×QP	N–N5

If 21 ... R×P 22 Q–B3! wins in
all variations, e.g. 22 ... R–K2
23 Q×N!

22 Q–B3!

Threatening 23 R–Q7.

22 ...	Q×P
23 Q×Q	R×Q
24 P–QB3	N–B3
25 R×N	1–0

13 N–Q5! An unusual idea. In
return for the piece White gets a very
strong passed pawn. **13 ... P×N
14 P×P N–K4 15 N×N P×N
16 B×P B–Q3** If 16 ... Q–R2
17 P–Q6 B–Q1 18 B×N B×B
19 P–Q7, when Black must give back
the piece and leave White with a
very active game. **17 B×N P×B
18 Q–R5** Threatening simply R–Q4–
KR4 etc. **18 ... B–B5 19 R×B!**
Q×R Not 19 ... R×B 20 P–Q6.
20 P–Q6 K–R1 The threat was
21 P–Q7 Q–B1 22 P–Q8=Q R×Q
23 Q×BP+ and 24 Q×BP mate.
**21 P–N3 R–KN1 22 Q×BP R–B1
23 P–Q7!** Q–Q1 Or 23 ... R×Q 24
P×Q=Q+ R×Q 25 B×R B–K4
26 P–N3±± **24 Q–K6 B–K4 25
R–Q5 P–N4** If 25 ... B×QNP, 26
R–KR5 followed by 27 B–B2 leads to
mate. **26 B–B2 R–R2 27 B–B5
R–QB2** If 27 ... B×QNP 28 B×P
28 P–B4! B×NP 29 B×P! P–B4 Or
29 ... K×B 30 R–R5+ K–N2 31
Q–N4+ K–B2 32 R–R7 mate. **30
Q–R6 R–KB3 31 B–N6+ K–N1 32
Q–R7+ K–B1 33 Q–R8+ K–K2
34 Q–K8+ Q×Q 35 P×Q=Q
mate**

Velimirovic–Nicevski
Skopje 1971

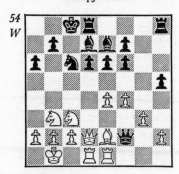

54
W

16 N–Q5!

Black is very vulnerable on the K-file even though he has castled.

16 ...   **P×N**
17 P×P   **N–R2**

Forced if he is to keep his extra piece.

18 Q–B3+   **K–N1**
19 B×QRP   **KR–K1**

If 19 ... P×B 20 R×B N–N4 (or 20 ... Q–N3 21 Q×P when White already has three pawns for the piece and another one is ripe to fall) 21 Q–N4 with too many threats.

20 Q–N4   **B–QB1**
21 R–K2   **Q–B6**
22 R/1–K1   **R–Q2**
23 B–B4

White's only weak spot is protected and Black is so tied down that he is helpless against White's simple Q-side onslaught. **23 ... R–B2 24 N–Q4 Q–N5 25 P–QR4! R–Q1 26 N–N5** 26 R×B? R×R 27 R×R fails to 27 ... Q–Q8+ 28 K–R2 Q×N and Black should win. **26 ... N×N 27 P×N P–N3** If 27 ... R–K1 28 P–N6 R–Q2 29 B–N5. **28 R×B R×R 29 R×R Q–Q8+ 30 K–R2 Q×BP 31 B–N3 Q×RP 32 Q–Q4 1–0**

Ghizdavu–Covaci
Romania 1970

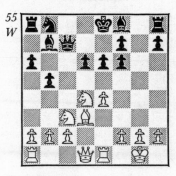

55
W

11 N–Q5!   **P×N**
12 P×P+   **K–Q1**
13 Q–B3   **P–B4**

If 13 ... N–Q2 14 N–B6+ B×N 15 P×B and 16 Q×P+, or 13 ... B–K2 14 N–B5 R–K1 15 N×B R×N 16 Q×P B×P 17 B–B5 (threatening mate in two) 17 ... B–K3 18 B×B P×B 19 R×P±±

14 Q×P   **B–N2**

Both 14 ... N–Q2 and 14 ... B–K2 allow 15 Q×BP.

15 Q–N5+   **P–B3**
16 N–K6+   **K–B1**
17 Q–N4!   **P–KR4**
18 Q–R3   **Q–B2**
19 N×B+

The game actually continued 19 N–N5+ Q–Q2! 20 B–B5 P×N 21 B×Q+ N×B 22 R–K7 and White eventually won. The text wins by force.

19 ... N–Q2 20 N–B5! K–B2 21 R–K7 Q–B1 22 R×N+! K×R 23 N–N7+ P–B4 24 B×BP+ K–K2 25 Q–K3+ K–B3 26 Q–K6+ K–N4   27 P–KR4+ K×P   28 P–KN3+ K–N4 29 P–KB4 mate

Tal–Mukhin
USSR Ch 1972

56
W

13 N–Q5! **P×N**
14 P×P+

White can also play 14 P–K5 P×P
15 R×P+ K–Q2 16 P–QB4±±
14 ... **K–Q2**
15 P–QB3!

If 15 N–B6 then not 15 ... Q–N3
16 B×N P×B 17 Q–B3 Q–B4
18 QR–Q1 R–KN1 19 Q×P R–N2
20 R–K7+ B×R 21 Q×B+ K–B1
22 Q–B8+ K–B2 23 Q×R/8 and
White won, I. Zaitsev–Savon, USSR
Ch ½-final 1969, but 15 ... Q–B1
and after 16 B×N P×B 17 Q–R5
K–B2 18 Q×BP+ K–N3 the
position, though probably good for
White, is not clearly untenable.
15 ... **P–N6**

If 15 ... P×P 16 Q–R4+ wins.
16 Q×P **N–B4**
17 Q–B4 **Q–B1**

Or 17 ... R–B1 18 P–QN4
N/4–K5 19 N–B6 N×B (19 ...
Q–N3 20 R×N±±) 20 N–N8+!!
R×N 21 Q–B6 mate.

18 N–B6 P–R3 19 B×N P×B
20 R–K3 K–B2 If 20 ... P–QR4
then 21 P–QN4±± **21 P–QN4**
R–KN1 1–0

Hubner–Visier
Maspalomas 1974

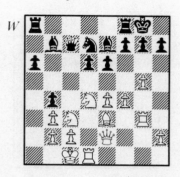

W

17 N–Q5! **P×N**

17 ... B×N 18 P×B N–B4 19 Q–B4
P×P 20 Q×QP, also leaves White in
command because of his control over
KB5.
18 N–B5 **N–B4**

18 ... KR–K1 19 B–Q4 B–KB1 is
met by 20 N–R6+ K–R1 21 Q–R5,
with an irresistible attack.
19 B–Q4! **N×KP**

If 19 ... N–K3 20 P×P B×QP 21
B×P KR–B1 22 N×B+ Q×N 23 R×B
K×B 24 P–B5, with an overwhelming
attack.
20 N×NP **P–B3**

The only move, hoping to creep out
via KB2. If 20 ... N×R 21 P×N P–B3
22 N–B5, or 20 ... B–B1 21 Q–R5 and
22 P–B5, in both cases with a crushing
advantage.
21 P×P **N×R**
22 Q–N4! **N–K7+**
23 K–N1 **B–B1**
24 N–B5+ **K–B2**
25 Q–R5+ **K–K3**
26 P×B **B–Q2**
27 P×R=N+ **1–0**

27 ... R×N 28 N–N7+ K–K2 29
Q×N+, and White is a piece ahead.

Bellon–Larsen
Las Palmas 1977

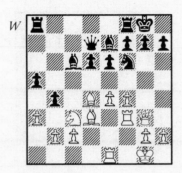

17 N–Q5!?

Most Grandmasters tremble when a speculative continuation is played against them, but not Bent—he has nerves of steel.

17 ...   **P×N**
18 P×P   **B×P**
19 R×B!?

19 B×P+ K×B 20 Q–R4+ K–N1 21 R×B Q–N5 is also unclear. The idea of the text move is to deprive Black of the opportunity of exchanging queens with ... Q–N5.

19 ...   **Q×R**
20 R–K3

Now 20 B×P+ must be met by 20 ... K–R1 (20 ... K×B?? 21 Q–R4+ and 22 R–R3 wins for White, since Black can no longer play ... Q×R now that his queen has been decoyed of ... Q2) 21 Q–R4 (if 21 R–K3 Q×R! kills the attack) 21 ... B×R 22 B–N6+ K–N1 23 B×N Q–K6+ winning for Black.

20 ...   **B–K3**
21 B×P+   **K×B**

21 ... K–R1 would now be wrong on account of 22 B–K4, with a very strong attack.

22 Q–N5?

Much too slow. White should have been content with 22 Q–R4+ K–N1 23 R–KN3 B–N5! 24 R×N KR–K1 25 R×P!, forcing a draw.

22 ...   **R–R1!**

This simple move refutes White's attack and leaves Black a rook ahead for nothing: **23 P–B5 K–N1 24 R–KN3 R–KR2 25 P×B Q×P 26 Q×N Q–K8+ 27 Q–B1 Q×Q+ 28 K×Q P×P 29 P×P R–QB1,** and Black's extra material was decisive.

Voitsekh–Zelinsky
USSR Corres Ch ½-final 1969–70

1 P–K4	P–QB4
2 N–KB3	P–Q3
3 P–Q4	P × P
4 N × P	N–KB3
5 N–QB3	P–QR3
6 B–KN5	P–K3
7 P–B4	B–K2
8 Q–B3	Q–B2
9 0–0–0	QN–Q2
10 P–KN4	P–N4
11 B × N	N × B
12 P–N5	N–Q2
13 P–B5	N–B4!

13 ... B × P+ 14 K–N1 N–B4 has been shown to be too risky on account of 15 B × P+ P × B 16 N/4 × NP, e.g.

a) 16 ... Q–R4? 17 N × P+ K–K2 18 Q–R5! P–N3 19 Q × B+ P–B3 20 Q–R6 1–0 Seuss-Beni, Austria 1965; or

b) 16 ... Q–K2 17 N × P+ K–B1 18 P–KR4 B × P (If 18 ... B–B3 19 P–K5 ±; or 18 ... B–R3 19 N × P! ±) 19 N × P! Q × N (19 ... K × N 20 P × P+ K–N1 21 R–Q8+ followed by mate) 20 R × B B–N2 21 Q–B2 '... and it is not easy for Black to free himself because of his unfortunately placed king'—O'Kelly.

After 13 ... B × P+ 14 K–N1, 14 ... P–K4 provides no joy for Black because of the thematic 15 N–K6! P × N 16 Q–R5+ etc., while 14 ... N–K4 fails to 15 Q–R5 B–B3 16 P × P ±.

14 P–B6!

This is the only way for White to continue his attack. All of the alternatives allow Black's Q-side counterplay to get moving too fast:

a) 14 R–N1 P–N5 15 N/3–K2 P–K4 16 P–B6 P × N 17 P × B P–Q6! ∓ Boleslavsky–Aronin, USSR Ch 1956;

b) 14 P–N6 RP × P 15 P × NP B–N4+! 16 K–N1 P–N5 17 N/3–K2 P × P 18 Q–N4 B–B3 19 Q × NP+ Q–B2 ∓ —Gutman;

c) 14 P–QR3?! B × P+ 15 K–N1 0–0! ∓ Pietzsch–Bogdanovic, Sarajevo 1966;

d) 14 P × P P × P 15 B–R3 P–N5 16 N/3–K2 B × P+ 17 K–N1 (so far we have followed Mukhin–Danov, Irkutsk 1966) 17 ... B–B3! ∓; or

e) 14 P–N4?! N–R5! 15 N × N P × N 16 P × P B B × NP+ 17 K–N1 0–0! ∓ Matulovic–Masic, Yugoslav Ch 1969.

14 ...	P × P
15 P × P	B–B1

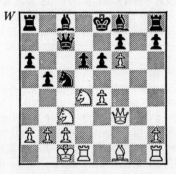

16 B–R3?!

We must regard the text as dubious because it commits White to the knight sacrifice that follows and on the basis of the games and analyses at our disposal the sacrifice would appear to fall short of soundness.

16 Q–R5 is now regarded as the correct continuation, and if 16 ... P–N5?, 17 N–Q5! works because White's queen soon comes into the mêlée. Scholl–Donner, Amsterdam

1970 concluded 16 Q–R5! P–N5?
17 N–Q5! P×N 18 P×P B–Q2
19 R–K1+ K–Q1 20 Q×BP
(Krnic recommends 20 K–N1 as
being stronger. After 20 Q×BP he
gives 20 ... B–R3+ 21 K–N1
B–K1!) 20...K–B1 21 R–N1 K–N2
22 N–K6! Q–B1 (Or 22 ... B×N
23 Q×Q+ K×Q 24 P×B±±)
23 N×N P×N 24 B–R3 K–B2
25 R–K6! Q–N2 26 Q×B/7+!
K×Q 27 R–K7++ K–Q3 28
R×Q K×P 29 R–K1 B–R3+
30 K–N1 KR–K1 31 R/7–K7 1–0.

After 16 Q–R5, Black's best seems
to be 16 ... B–Q2 when 17 B–R3
P–N5 18 N/3–K2 0–0–0 19 Q×BP
B–R3+ 20 K–N1 QR–B1 21 Q–R5
R×P 22 KR–B1 R/1–B1 23 R×R
R×R 24 Q–R4 R–N3 25 N–KB3
produces a very complex position as
in Parma–Zuckerman, Netanya 1971
and Browne–Mecking, San Antonio
1972.

16 ...　　　　**P–N5!**

If Black falters with 16 ... B–Q2,
White again has the possibility of
17 Q–R5 when 17 ... P–N5 still
fails to 18 N–Q5! e.g. 18 ... P×N
19 P×P 0–0–0 20 N–B6 R–K1
21 KR–K1 K–N2 22 B×B Q×B
23 Q–R4! K–B2 24 Q×NP B–R3+
25 K–N1 R×R 26 R×R R–K1
27 R–K7! Zhuravlev–Gutman, Latvian Ch 1967. Indeed, from White's
sixteenth move onwards, this system
could well be named the Latvian
Variation since most of the explora-
tory work has been performed by
Latvian analysts and players.

In the above line, 18 ... Q–N2?!
(instead of 18 ... P×N) is no better.
Martinovic–Buljovcic, Yugoslav Ch
1965 continued 19 KR–K1! 0–0–0

20 N–K7+ K–N1 21 K–N1 B–K1
22 Q–R4±.

17 N–Q5

White has no choice. After 17
N/3–K2? B–QN2 18 N–N3, both
18 ... P–Q4 19 Q–R5 Q–B5+
20 K–N1 Q×BP (Tatai) and 18 ...
0–0–0 (Gutman) give Black excellent
chances.

17 ...　　　　**P×N**
18 P×P　　　　**B×B**
19 KR–K1+

Udovcic has recommended 19
Q×B, but this presents Black with a
free tempo since after 19 ... Q–Q2
20 KR–K1+ K–Q1 21 N–B6+
K–B2, his king has reached QB2
without first visiting QB1. Ree-
Bouwmeester, Dutch Ch play-off
1967 continued 22 Q–R4 P–QR4
(Gufeld suggests 22 ... P–KR4
23 Q×NP P–R4!) 23 K–N1 R–KN1!
with advantage to Black. Not 23 ...
P–R4 24 Q–QB4! K–N3 25 P–QR3!
P×P?! 26 P×P Q–N5 27 R–Q4
Q–B1 28 K–R2, when Black's king
is too exposed, Poulsson–George,
Ybbs 1968.

19 ...　　　　**K–Q1**
20 N–B6+　　　　**K–B1**
21 Q×B+

21 ...　　　　**Q–Q2!**

This move seems to be the key to the refutation of White's sacrificial variation. The point is that Black's king gets to QB2 in one tempo whereas in the alternative line (21 ... K–N2) it takes two tempi. The result of this gain of tempo is that White's initiative is rapidly apprehended and Black's forces quickly become coordinated.

22 Q–R4

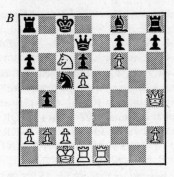

In an article in the 1969 bulletin of the Latvian Chess Club, Boleslavsky suggested 22 Q–R5 but it would appear that Black has at least two good lines against this try:

a) 22 ... K–B2 23 N–K7 R–K1 24 Q × BP B–R3 + 25 K–N1 KR–B1 and 26 ... R × P∓ ∓;

b) 22 ... P–R4 23 R–K3 K–B2 24 R/1–K1 K–N3 25 K–N1 R–KN1 26 Q × RP R–N3 27 Q–R4 Q–N5 28 Q × Q R × Q, and with the exchange of queens Black has consolidated his material advantage. Gurevich–Shershnev, ½-final Latvian Corres Ch 1969–70.

22 ...	P–QR4
23 R–K2	

23 K–N1 has been tried with the idea of continuing with 24 Q–QB4 without fear of the reply ... B–R3 + followed by ... KR–K1. Oskengoyt–Shershev, ½-final USSR Corres Ch 1969–70 continued 23 ... P–R4 24 Q–QB4 Q–N2 25 R–K8 + K–B2 26 R × R Q × R 27 R–K1 K–N3 28 P–QR3 Q–R3 29 N × RP Q × Q 30 N × Q + K–N4 31 P–N3 N–Q2 and Black soon won.

23 R–K3 K–B2 24 K–N1 R–KN1 is also good for Black. Sorokin–Zelinsky, USSR Corres Ch 1971–72.

The text prepares to double rooks on the K-file which would threaten R–K8 + followed by R/8–K7.

23 ...	K–B2
24 R/1–K1	K–N3

Preventing 25 R–K7.

25 K–N1

A necessary prophylactic move, for if 25 Q–QB4 at once, 25 ... B–R3 +26 K–N1 KR–K1 and Black has finally managed to develop his K-side (27 R–K7 fails to 27 ... B–B1!).

25 ...	R–KN1
26 P–KR3	

Again White must defend—the threat was 26 ... R–N5 or 26 ... Q–N5 and in either case Black's game becomes active.

26 ... R–N3

As well as keeping White's KBP under observation the text threatens 27 ... R–KR3 winning the KRP.

27 Q–QB4	Q–B1!
28 P–QR4	Q–R3

28 ... P × Pep 29 P–N4 P–R7 + 30 K–R1 P × P 31 Q × NP + K–B2 would allow White to introduce fresh problems with 32 N–K7.

29 Q–Q4	R–N6

With the idea of 30 ... P–N6 (not to mention 30 ... R × P).

30 Q–KB4	R–N8!

A neat simplifying shot. The threat
is 31 ... Q×R.

31 K–R2	**R×R**
32 R×R	**N×P**
33 R–K7	

The last try!

33 ...	**B×R**
34 P×B	**R–KN1!**

So that 35 Q×BP is met by 35 ...
Q–B5+ with mate to follow. Now the
game is over.

**35 Q–K3+ N–B4   36 P–K8=Q
R×Q 37 Q×R Q–B5+ 38 K–N1
Q×QP 39 N–K7 Q–Q8+ 40 K–R2
P–N6+ 41 P×P Q×P+ 42 K–N1
Q–Q8+ 43 K–R2 Q–R5+ 44 Q×Q
N×Q 45 K–R3 N–B4 46 P–N4
N–K5 47 K–N3 P×P 48 K×P
K–B2 49 K–B4 K–Q2 50 N–Q5
K–K3 51 K–Q4 N–N4 0–1**

Kopylov–Danov
Irkutsk 1966

**1 P–K4 P–QB4   2 N–KB3 P–Q3
3 P–Q4 P×P   4 N×P N–KB3
5 N–QB3 P–QR3 6 B–KN5 P–K3
7 P–B4 B–K2   8 Q–B3 Q–B2
9 O–O–O QN–Q2 10 P–KN4 P–N4
11 B×N N×B   12 P–N5 N–Q2
13 P–B5 N–B4! 14 P–B6! P×P
15 P×P B–B1 16 B–R3?! P–N5!
17 N–Q5 P×N 18 P×P B×B
19 KR–K1+ K–Q1 20 N–B6+
K–B1 21 Q×B+ K–N2**

See diagram next column

22 R–Q4

White has two other serious
possibilities:
a) 22 N×P—see the game V.
Zhuravlev–Zaklauskis, p. 105.
b) 22 R–K2 R–KN1! (Probably the

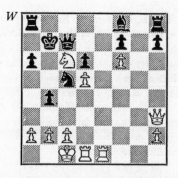

only move. Boersma–Maeder, Groningen 1967/68 went instead 22 ...
P–KR4 23 R/1–K1 K–N3 24 Q–R4
P–QR4, and with 25 Q–QB4!! White
could have maintained a very strong
attack. 22 ... Q–Q2 has also been
tried without success. N. Zhuravlev–
Prieditis, Latvian Corres Ch 1967–69
continued 23 Q–R4 P–QR4 24
R/1–K1 Q–B4 25 Q–QB4! Q×KBP
26 Q–N5+ K–B2 27 N×NP!±±.)
23 R/1–K1 K–N3 24 Q–R4 P–QR4
25 K–N1 Q–Q2∓. This continuation
has been suggested by the Latvian
master Gutman.

22 ...	**P–QR4!**
23 N×NP	**Q–Q2!**

Not 23 ... P×N? 24 R×P+
K–R2 25 R–K3 N–R3 26 R–QR3
B–R3+   27 K–Q1! Q–B1 28
R×N+! 1–0 Minic–Tringov, Bel-
grade 1965.

24 Q–QB3

Or 24 Q–R4 P×N 25 R×P+
K–B2 26 K–N1 R–K1 27 R–QB4
R–KN1   28 P–R4 R–N5! 0–1
Rajkovic–Masic, Yugoslav Ch 1968.

24 ...	**P×N**
25 R×P+	**K–B2**
26 R/4–K4	**R–KN1**
27 R–K7	**B×R**
28 R×B	**R–N8+**

29 K–Q2　　　K–N3!
0–1

V. Zhuravlev–Zaklauskis
Latvian Corres Ch 1967–69

The first 21 moves are the same as in the last game. See diagram p. 104

22 N×P

At one time this was the main line of the whole variation starting with 13 P–B5 and it was thought that White's chances were better. After a while Black started to win most of the games but now it appears that with accurate play White can force a draw.

22 ...　　　Q–Q2
23 Q–R4

23 Q–R5 R–KN1 24 N–B6 has twice been shown to be of no use to White because he can never win the KBP (the aim of Q–R5). V. Zhuravlev–Petkevich, Latvian Ch 1967 went 24 ... R–N3　25 K–N1 R–K1 26 Q–R4 R–N5　27 Q–B2 R/5–K5 28 R×R　R×R　29 Q–Q2 (Or 29 P–N4 Q–N5) 29 ... Q–B2　30 K–R1 Q–N3 and Black won. Fischer (against Ciocaltea, Netanya 1968) was equally successful with 24 ... P–QR4　25 Q×RP R–N3　26 K–N1

R–KR3　27 Q–N8 R×BP　28 Q–N2 (If 28 R–KB1 N–K5　29 K–R1 P–R5∓—Aronin)　28 ... K–N3 29 R–Q4 Q–B4　30 P–N4 P×P 31 R×P+ K–B2 0–1.

The text prepares for the possibilities of Q–QN4+ or Q–QB4.

23 ...　　　R–KN1
Threatening 24 ... R–N5.
24 P–KR3　　R–N3
25 N–B6　　　P–QR4
Preventing 26 Q–QN4+.
26 K–N1　　　R–KR3
27 Q–QB4　　R×BP
28 R–K3　　　R–N3
29 Q–N5+

After 29 R/1–K1 P–B4 30 Q–N5+ (Not 30 R–K7? B×R　31 R×B R–N8+) 30 ... K–B2 31 P–N4 P×P 32 R–K7 B×R　33 R×B R–N8+ 34 K–N2 N–R5+　35 K–N3 R–N8+ 36 K–B4 N–N7+　37 K–Q4 (Or 37 K–N3 R–R6+ 38 K×P N–Q8+) 37 ... R–Q8+　38 K–K3 R–K8+ Black stands better.

29 ...　　　K–B2
30 R–QR3　　Q–B1
31 R×P　　　Q–N2

Not 31 ... R×R　32 Q×R+ K–Q2 33 Q–N5±; nor 31 ... P–B4 32 N–K7! Q–N2　33 N×R Q×Q 34 R×Q P×N　35 R–N1 when White should win the ending.

32 Q–B1　　　P–B3
33 R–N5　　　Q–R3
34 P–R3　　　P–B4
35 P–B4　　　R–B3
36 R–K1　　　P–B5
37 Q–B3　　　Q–B1
38 K–R2　　　R–B2
39 P–N4　　　N–R5

Returning the piece by 39 ... R–N2 40 P×N R–N6 looks tempting, but after 41 Q–R5 R/6×QRP+

42 K–N2 B–N2+ 43 K–B2 Black soon runs out of checks, e.g. 43 ... R–QB6+ 44 K–N1 R–R8+ 45 K×R R×RP+ 46 K–N1 R×Q 47 R–K7+ Q–Q2 48 R×Q+ K×R 49 R–N7+±±; or 43 ... R–R7+ 44 K–Q3! R/1–R6+ 45 K–K4 Q–B1 46 P×P+ K×P 47 P–B5+ K–B2 48 P–Q6+ K×N 49 R–N6+ K–Q2 50 Q–N4+±±.

40 N–Q4 B–N2!

This simple developing move is very strong! If 40 ... Q–Q2 with the idea of putting the king on the safe square QB1, White can continue forcefully with 41 P–B5! (threatening 42 P–B6! or 42 R–N7+!) 41 ... K–Q1 (If 41 ... K–B1 42 P–B6 Q–R2 43 Q–N4+, or 41 ... P×P? 42 P–Q6+) 42 P–B6 Q–R2 (Or 42 ... Q–B1 43 N–K6+ K–K1 44 N–N7++ K–Q1 45 R–K8+ K–B2 46 N–K6+ Q×N 47 R–N7 mate) 43 N–K6+ K–B1 44 N×B R×N 45 R–R5 Q–N1 46 Q–N4+ K–B2 47 R–K7+ K–N3 48 Q–N1+ followed by mate.

41 N–K6+ K–Q2

42 K–N3

42 R–QB1 is also possible, e.g. 42 ... N–B6+ 43 R×N B×R 44 Q×B P–B6 45 P–B5 R–N1 46 P–B6+ K–K2 47 R×R Q×R 48 P–B7 Q–QB1 49 Q–B1 P–B7 50 Q–N5+ R–B3 51 Q–N7+ R–B2 52 Q–N5+ with a draw by repetition.

42 ... N–B6

43 N×B?

A fatal error. White has two reasonable moves:

a) 43 R–N6 R×P+ 44 K×R Q–QR1+ 45 K–N2 Q–R7+ 46 K–B1 N–R5 47 R–N7+ K–B1 48 R×R Q–QN7+ 49 K–Q1

N–B6+ 50 Q×N B×Q 51 R–B8+ K–Q2 52 N–B5+ P×N 53 R–B7+ K–Q1 54 R–B8+ with perpetual check. The analysis of this variation is by Kirillov.

b) 43 N–B5+ also draws: 43 ... P×N (Or 43 ... K–B2 or Q1 44 N–K6+ etc.) 44 Q–N4+ K–Q1 (Not 44 ... K–B2 45 R×P+ nor 44 ... K–Q3 45 R–K6+) 45 Q–N5+ K–Q2 46 Q–N4+ (Unclear is 46 R×P!? Q–B1) 46 ... K–Q1 47 Q–N5+ etc.

43 ... N×R

44 Q–N4+ K–B2

45 N–K6+ K–N3

46 P×N R×P+!

0–1

It's mate in three.

Zhdanov–Zelinsky
Latvian Ch 1970

1 P–K4	**P–QB4**
2 N–KB3	**P–Q3**
3 P–Q4	**P×P**
4 N×P	**N–KB3**
5 N–QB3	**P–QR3**
6 B–QB4	**P–K3**
7 B–N3	**P–QN4**
8 0–0	**QN–Q2**

For a study of the pawn grab 8 ... P–N5 9 N–R4 N×P see page 27.

9 R–K1	**N–B4**
10 B–N5	

For 10 B–Q5! see the game Belyavsky–Marjanovic, page 130.

10 ... B–N2

11 P–QR4!?

Inviting a move which in turn invites the (probably unsound) sacrifice that follows. Better is still 11 B–Q5 for which see page 113.

| 11 ... | **P–N5** |

11 ... P×P is also possible, e.g. 12 B×RP+ N×B 13 R×N B–K2 or 12 N×RP N×B 13 N×N B–K2, and in each case Black probably has a slight edge because of his bishop pair and better pawn centre.

12 N–Q5!?

The logical follow up to his previous move. 12 N–R2 would be more prudent but less consistent with White's active plan of development.

12 ...	**P×N**
13 P×P+	**K–Q2**
14 N–B6	**B×N**

Forced, since 14 ... Q–B2 loses to 15 B×N P×B 16 Q–N4+, while 14...Q–N3 15 B×N P×B 16 Q–B3 is equally pleasant for White.

| **15 P×B+** | **K–B2** |

It is best not to capture the pawn because White would then be able to make good use of the long diagonal: 15 ... K×P 16 B×N P×B 17 B–Q5+ and now 17 ... K–N3 18 B×R Q×B 19 Q–Q4± or 17 ... K–B2 18 B×R Q×B 19 Q–R5±.

| **16 B×P** |

So now White has two pawns for the piece but Black's king is not really so insecure and it cannot be argued objectively that White has sufficient compensation.

| 16 ... | **P–R3** |

Bad would be 16 ... B–K2 on account of 17 Q–K2, e.g. 17 ... N/3–K5 18 B×B Q×B 19 B–Q5 followed by 20 P–KB3.

17 B–R4

After 17 R–K8 White wins Black's queen but the heterogenous material balance of rook and two pieces for queen and two pawns would certainly favour Black. In addition, White would lose any initiative that he might have in the present position.

| 17 ... | **P–N4** |
| **18 B–KN3** | **N/4–K5** |

If Black wishes to exchange off White's bishop then this is certainly the correct knight with which to accomplish the task, viz. 18 ... N/3–K5 19 Q–Q4 Q–B3 20 R×N N×R 21 Q×NP R–QN1 22 Q×N Q×B 23 Q–Q4 R–R2 24 Q–R7+ K–B1 25 Q×P+ K–Q1 26 P–N4, when White has four pawns for the piece and Black's king will soon feel the effect of White's advancing Q-side army, e.g. 26 ... Q–B3 27 R–KB1 Q–QB6 28 P–N5 and although White's queen is temporarily incarcerated, Black has no good defence to the threat of 29 P–B3 followed by B–B2.

Much stronger than the text however, is 18 ... K×P! when White does not have at his disposal the refutation mentioned in the note to Black's fifteenth move.

| **19 Q–Q4** | **N×B** |
| **20 RP×N** | **R–KR2** |

Not 20 . . . P–QR4 21 R–K6 B–N2 22 R/1–K1.

21 Q × NP

21 . . .   Q–N1?

21 . . . R–N1 would be considerably stronger. If then 22 Q–R5+ R–N3 23 B–N3 (On 23 B–B4 P–Q4 is even more effective) 23 . . . P–Q4, Black threatens 24 . . . B–N5. 22 Q–B4 is also strongly met by 22 . . . R–N3.

But now Black's QR is shut out of play and his queen is soon shown to be offside.

22 Q–QB4   P–Q4

Black gives up another pawn in order to force the exchange of queens. If 22 . . . Q–N3 23 R–K3 is strong, with the threat of 24 R–N3 Q × QBP 25 Q–K6.

23 B × P   Q–N5
24 R–K6!?

24 P–QB3 Q × Q 25 B × Q is stronger—Black would not be able to capture the pawn because of 25 . . . K × P? 26 R–K6+ K–B4 27 B–R2 threatening mate in one. And if Black cannot capture the pawn, what then? White's R–K6 is still a possibility and with his QBP at QB3 White can advance P–QN4–N5 etc.

24 . . .   Q × Q

After 24 . . . Q × NP 25 R/1–K1

White's Q-side pawns are no longer of value but in contrast he has acquired dangerous threats against Black's king, particularly on the QN-file, e.g.

a) 25 . . . Q–N5 26 Q–Q3 followed by P–QB3 (if necessary) and R–N1;
b) 25 . . . R–Q1 26 Q × P R × B (If 26 . . . N × B 27 Q–R7+ ± ±, or 26 . . . Q–N3 27 Q × Q+ K × Q 28 R × N ± ±) 27 Q–R7+ K–B1 28 R–K8+ N × R 29 R × N + ± ±;
c) 25 . . . N × B 26 Q × N R–Q1 27 Q–B4 Q–N3 28 R/1–K3 B–Q3 29 Q–K4 R–N2 (Or 29 . . . R–B2 30 Q–N6) 30 R–N3 Q × QBP 31 Q–Q4 ± ±.

25 B × Q   N–N1?

A time trouble error. 25 . . . N–K1 followed by 26 . . . N–Q3 was a better plan, though White could keep the forward QBP supported by his bishop while the other Q-side pawns advanced methodically.

26 R–Q1   R–N2

What else? 26 . . . N–K2, the idea behind Black's last move, is met by 27 R–Q7+ K–B1 28 R–B6 R–R1 29 B–K6.

27 P–QB3   P–QR4

Otherwise P–QN4–N5 is killing.

28 B–N5   R–B2
29 R–Q7+   R × R
30 P × R   N–K2
31 P–QB4

Preventing 31 . . . N–Q4.

31 . . .   N–B4

If 31 . . . R–Q1 32 P–KN4 and Black has no moves.

32 R–QB6+   K–N2

Or 32 . . . K–Q1 33 R–B6.

33 R–B8   1–0

Because of 33 . . . R × R 34 B–R6+.

Tal–Larsen
10th Match Game, Candidates 1965

1 P–K4	P–QB4
2 N–KB3	N–QB3
3 P–Q4	P×P
4 N×P	P–K3
5 N–QB3	P–Q3
6 B–K3	N–B3
7 P–B4	B–K2
8 Q–B3	0–0
9 0–0–0	Q–B2

9 ... P–QR3 allows 10 P–K5!

10 N/4–N5	Q–N1
11 P–KN4	P–QR3
12 N–Q4	N×N
13 B×N	P–QN4?!

More active (and correct) would have been 13 .. P–K4! 14 P–N5 B–N5!, e.g. 15 Q–N2 P×B 16 P×N P×N 17 P×B P×P+ 18 K–N1 B×R 19 P×R=Q+ Q×Q 20 B–B4 B–R4 21 Q–R3 P–KN3 22 Q–Q7, when White should probably regain most of the sacrificed material but he cannot hope for any advantage—Nikitin.

14 P–N5	N–Q2
15 B–Q3	P–N5

15 ... B–N2 would be too slow—White replies 16 P–QR3! and Black has little counterplay.

16 N–Q5

Assessments of the merit of this sacrifice have varied between !? (Nikitin), ! (Shamkovich) and !! (Chess Review). Three years after the game was played there was still some controversy over what should have been the correct result. Now it appears that Tal's idea qualifies for a half point at the very least but of course in a variation as complex as this it is necessary to take into consideration the immense practical difficulties facing the defending player.

16 ...   **P×N**

Acceptance is obligatory because 16 ... B–Q1 is refuted by 17 N–B6 +!, e.g. 17 ... P×N 18 P×P B×P 19 KR–N1 + K–R1 20 P–K5 B–KN2 21 R×B! K×R 22 Q–N4 + K–R1 23 R–N1 and mate next move.

17 P×P

The Q3–KR7 diagonal has now been opened up for White's bishop (and queen). The immediate threat is 18 Q–K4 winning a piece. Black cannot play 17 ... B–Q1 because of 18 B×KRP+! K×B 19 Q–R5+ K–N1 20 B×P! K×B 21 Q–R6+ K–N1 22 P–N6 N–B3 23 KR–N1 B–B4 24 P–N7! winning.

17 ...   **P–B4**

Considerable controversy centred around the question of whether 17 ... P–N3 would have been a better defensive move as was claimed by Larsen after the game. In his original notes to the game in *Shakhmatny Bulletin* (number 6, 1966) Shamkovich 'refuted' 17 ... P–N3. Almost two years later however, Nikitin (*SB* number 3, 1968) retaliated with some analysis that 'refuted' the refutation. Not to be deterred, Shamkovich came back two months later in the same learned journal presenting the refutation of the refutation of the refutation. This last refutation was deemed to be a good thing and the correspondence was closed! Let us see what all the fuss was about.

After 17 ... P-N3, White has two likely looking continuations.

A 18 P-KR4
B 18 QR-K1!

Tal's suggestion of 18 Q-R3 (to which he appended an exclamation mark) is met by 18 ... N-B3 19 Q-R6 N-R4, and if 20 B-K2 R-K1! 21 B×N B-B1∓∓, or 20 P-B5 B×BP 21 B×B R-K1∓∓.

A 18 P-KR4

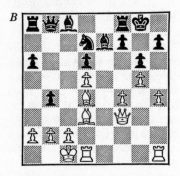

18 ...   N-B4
19 B-B4!

Suggested by Shamkovich in the refutation of the refutation of the refutation. Larsen had given 19 P-R5 (not 19 B×N P×B 20 P-R5 R-R2!) 19 ... N×B+ 20 R×N B-B4 when 21 P×P is met by 21 ... BP×P! (not 21 ... B×P/3 22 R×P! B×R 23 Q-R5±±) 22 R×P K×R 23 R-K3 Q-B2 24 Q-K2 R-R2!!

(An amazing way to gain a tempo. Not 24 ... Q×P+? 25 Q×Q B×Q 26 R×B+ K-N1 27 R-KN7+ K-R1 28 R×P+ K-R2 29 R-N7+ K-R1 30 K×B±) 25 B×R B-Q1! 26 B-Q4 K-N1 27 Q-R2 Q-KR2∓∓.

19 ...   B-B4
20 P-R5!   Q-B2

After 20 ... B-K5 21 Q-K3 B×R (or 21 ... R-K1 22 P×P B×P/3 23 P-B5 B×BP 24 P-N6! B×P/3 25 R×P!), Shamkovich's 22 Q×B doesn't seem to work after 22 ... Q-Q1! 23 Q-K1 B-B6 24 P×P BP×P, but 22 P×P BP×P 23 B×N looks convincing enough.

21 P-N3

White has good attacking chances, e.g. 21 ... B-K5? 22 Q-R3 B×R 23 R×B±±.

B 18 QR-K1!

18 ...   B-Q1

Not 18 ... R-K1? 19 B-B6 when White regains the piece and keeps his initiative.

19 Q-R3!   N-K4!

If 19 ... N-B3 20 Q-R6 N-R4 21 B-K2 and Black no longer has the resource ... R-K1 followed by ... B-B1 which was mentioned in the note to Tal's 18 Q–R3 (see previous page).

The immediate 19 ... B–N3? loses to 20 B×NP! and now 20 ... BP×B 21 R–K7 R–B2 22 Q–K6 N–K4 23 Q×R+! N×Q 24 R–K8 mate, or 20 ... N–B3 21 Q–R6! BP×B (or 21 ... B×B 22 P×N) 22 P×N±±

20 Q–R6   B–N3!

20 ... N×B+ 21 P×N Q–B2+ 22 K–N1 P–B3 23 P×P (threatening 24 R–K7) 23 ... Q–B2 fails to 24 R–K6! B×R (or 24 ... B–N2 25 P–B5 B×QP 26 R–N1!) 25 P×B Q–QN2 26 P–B7+ R×P 27 P×R+ Q×P 28 P–B5! opening up all the lines in the vicinity of Black's king.

The text is Nikitin's refutation of the refutation.

21 P×N

If 21 R×N B×B 22 P–KR4 P×R 23 P–R5 Q–R2 24 RP×P BP×P 25 B×NP B–B4∓∓; or 21 B×N P×B 22 P–KR4 P–K5! 23 P–R5 (if 23 R×P B–KB4 followed by ... Q–Q3 consolidating, or 23 B×KP B–Q5! winning White's queen) 23 ... Q×P+ 24 K–N1 B–KB4 25 P×P B×P∓∓

21 ...   B×B

22 R–K4!

The usual method of attack comes to nothing: 22 P–KR4 B×KP 23 R×B P×R 24 P–R5 Q–R2! 25 P×P BP×P 26 B×NP B–B4! 27 B×B R×B 28 P–N6 Q–KN2! 29 P×P+ K–R1.

The text is a quicker way of creating mating threats on the KR-file.

22 ...   B–B7!

22 ... Q–R2 23 R–R4 P–B4 24 KP×Pep B–K6+ 25 K–N1 R×P loses to 26 R–K1!, and 22 ... B×KP

to 23 R–R4 R–K1 24 Q×RP+ K–B1 25 B×NP! P×B (or 25 ... R–R2 26 R–B1 R/1–K2 27 R–B6!) 26 R–B1+ B–B4 27 Q×P.

23 P–K6!

Nikitin only considered 23 R–B1 Q–R2! 24 P–K6 B–N2. The text is Shamkovich's coup de grace, cutting Black's QB out of the game and threatening to win in a prosaic manner by P–KR4–R5 etc.

23 ...   R–R2

Shamkovich examines two alternatives:

a) 23 ... Q–R2 24 K–N1 P×P (if 24 ... B–Q5 25 P×P+) 25 P×P Q–KN2 26 P–K7 Q×Q 27 B–B4+ K–R1 28 P×Q R–K1 29 R–KB4! B–KB4 30 R×B/2 R×P 31 P–N3±; and

b) 23 ... P×P 24 P×P P–Q4 25 R–K2 Q–B5+ 26 K–N1 Q–R5 27 B×NP! Q×Q (or 27 ... P×B 28 Q×P+ K–R1 29 P–K7 B–KB4 30 P×R=Q+±) 28 B–B7+ K–R1 29 P×Q B×P 30 B×B 'with a roughly equal ending'.

This last variation seems to be crucial for the objective merit of Tal's sacrifice at move sixteen. Unless some improvement can be found for White the best that he can hope for is a marginally better ending.

24 P–KR4   R–K2

24 ... P×P 25 P×P P–Q4 26 P–K7 R–K1 loses to 27 P–R5! B–KB4 (or 27 ... P×R 28 B–B4+) 28 P×P B×P 29 R–K6 Q–B5+ 30 K–N1 B×B 31 P×B Q–B4 (if 31 ... Q–KB2 32 P–N6 Q–N2 33 P×P+ K–R1 34 Q×Q+ K×Q 35 P–R8=Q+) 32 P–N6! R/1×P (or 32 ... R/2×P 33 Q×P+ R×Q 34 R×R/8+ K–N2 35 P×R±±)

33 P×P+ K–R1 (or 33 ... Q×RP
34 R–KN6+) 34 R–KB6 Q×QP+
35 K–R1 R–KB2 36 Q–B8+!

25 P–R5   Q–R2
26 KP×P+   R/2×P

If 26 ... R/1×P 27 P×P R–KN2
28 P×P+ K–R1   29 Q×R+!±±

27 P×P   R–KN2
28 R×P

White has a dangerous initiative—
Shamkovich.

Now let us return to the game.

18 QR–K1   R–B2

Black must defend the second rank
as well as his bishop. On 18 ... B–Q1
Tal had intended 19 Q–R5 N–B4
20 B×NP N×B+ 21 K–N1 N×R
22 P–N6!! K×B 23 Q×RP+ K–B3
24 P–N7 R–K1 (24 ... R–B2?
25 P–N8=N mate!) 25 R–N1!
N–N7! 26 P–N8=Q R×Q 27
Q×R±±, but this line is not so
clear after 21 ... Q–B2! (instead of
21 ... N×R), e.g. 22 B×R N×R
23 R×N Q–B2! 24 Q×Q+ K×Q
25 B×P P–QR4.

True Tal could have played 18
KR–K1 (instead of QR–K1) and if
18 ... B–Q1   19 Q–R5 N–B4
20 B×NP! N×B+ 21 R×N when
he can transfer his QR to KR3, but
after 18 KR–K1 Black can adopt the

same defence as in the game (18 ...
R–B2) and the advance of White's
KRP is therefore not so dangerous.

But worry not dear reader! Shamkovich has examined the continuation
18 QR–K1 B–Q1 under his micro-
scope and discovered that White can
play 19 B×NP! K×B (not 19 ...
N–K4 20 P×N B×P+ 21 K–N1
K×B 22 R/K1–N1±) 20 Q–R5!
and now Black has no defence to the
threat of 21 Q–R6+ K–N1 22 P–N6:
a) 20 ... K–R1 21 R–K8! (or
21 P–N6 N–B3 22 Q–R6);
b) 20 ... N–B4 21 Q–R6+ K–N1
22 P–N6 N×B+ 23 K–N1 Q–B2
24 KR–N1±±;
c) 20 ... Q–B2 21 Q–R6+ K–N1
22 P–N6 N–B3 23 KR–N1 N–N5
24 R×N!±±; or
d) 20 ... N–K4! (clearing the second
rank for his rook) 21 P×N R–R2
(not 21 ... P×P?   22 Q–R6+
K–N1 23 KR–N1±±, nor 21 ...
Q–B2 22 KR–N1 K–R1 23 P–N6
Q–KN2—*23 ... R–KN1 24 P–N7+*
—24 NP×P Q×RP 25 Q×Q+
K×Q 26 R–K3!, and Black is helpless against the mate threat.) 22
Q–R6+ K–N1 23 KR–N1 R–KN2
24 P–N6 Q–R2 (defending the rook
and keeping control of K6 and KN8)
25 P–K6 P×P 26 R×P R×R
27 Q×R/6+ Q–KN2 28 Q×Q+
K×Q 29 P–K7 and White reaches
the ending with a good extra pawn.

19 P–KR4   B–N2!

19 ... N–B4 20 P–R5 N×B+
21 Q×N B–B1 allows 22 P–N6 R–K2
(22 ... P×P??   23 P×P R–K2
24 R–R8+!±±) 23 R×R B×R
24 P–R6!!

19 ... N–B1 is too passive: 20 P–R5
Q–B2 (not 20 ... P–N3? 21 R/K1–

N1! Q–B2 22 P×P N×P 23 Q–R5 N×P 24 P–N6!) 21 P–N6 R–B3 22 P–R6! and Black's king's defences are blasted open, e.g. 22 ... R×P 23 P×P R×P 24 B×R K×B 25 R/K1–N1+ N–N3 26 R×N+!, or 22 ... RP×P 23 P×P K×P 24 Q–R3 K–B2 25 Q–R8 B–Q1 26 R–R7+! N×R 27 Q×N+ K–B1 28 Q–R8+ K–B2 29 R–K8 ± ±

The text prepares to switch the queen to the K-side where it is needed to help stem the flow of White's advancing pieces

20 B×BP?

20 P–R5 underprotects the KNP and allows 20 .. N–K4! 21 P×N B×NP+ 22 K–N1 P×P when Black has good play. But more in the spirit of the position is 20 P–N6 P×P 21 P–R5! P–N4! 22 B×BP B–KB3! 23 P×P! B×NP+ (23 ... B×B? 24 B–K6 N–K4 25 R×N) 24 K–N1 Q–KB1 (or 24 ... N–B1 25 P–R6! P×P 26 R/K1–N1 ± ±) 25 B–K6 and Black is helpless, e.g. 25 ... B–KB3 26 P–R6! B×B 27 B×R+, 25 ... R–K1 26 Q–N4! or 25 ... N–K4 26 Q–B5! B–KB3 27 P–R6!

20 ...   **R×B**

Larsen rejected the passive defence 20 ... N–B1 because of 21 Q–K4!

Q–K1 (or 21 ... P–N3 22 B–N4 followed by P–KR4–R5) 22 B×RP+ N×B 23 P–N6 N–B3 24 P×R+ K×P 25 Q–B5! when White's attack is crushing, e.g. 25 ... B–QB1 26 Q–N5 Q–R1 27 KR–N1 Q–R2 28 R×B+! K×R 29 Q×P+ Q×Q 30 R×Q+ and 31 B×N.

21 R×B   **N–K4!**

If 21 ... R–B2 22 R×R K×R 23 R–K1 Q–Q1 24 Q–K4 N–B1 25 P–R5 and Black is defenceless.

22 Q–K4   **Q–KB1**
23 P×N!   **R–B5**
24 Q–K3   **R–B6**

A few swindling chances were offered by 24 ... B×P 25 P×P R×B 26 Q×R B×R 27 P–N3 B–B6, preventing the advance of the KRP, but after 28 Q–QB4+ K–R1 29 R–KB7 Q×P 30 R×B, White would have a pawn more and a dominating position.

25 Q–K2   **Q×R**
If 25 ... B×P 26 P×P!
26 Q×R   **P×P**
27 R–K1!

With the complications over White is about to win a pawn and unleash an attack made possible by the presence of opposite coloured bishops.

27 ...   **R–Q1**

28 R×P	Q–Q3
29 Q–B4!	

Threatening 30 R–K8+

29 ...	R–KB1
30 Q–K4	P–N6
31 RP×P	R–B8+
32 K–Q2	Q–N5+
33 P–B3	Q–Q3
34 B–B5!	

One last combination to end the game.

34 ...	Q×B
35 R–K8+	R–B1
36 Q–K6+	K–R1
37 Q–B7!	1–0

A fitting end to a Candidates match.

Velimirovic–Ljubojevic
Yugoslav Ch 1972

This game, which deservedly won the brilliancy prize, was played in one of the early rounds of the championship. For the remaining three weeks of the tournament most of the contestants were more interested in analyzing the soundness of Veli-mirovic's concept than with their own results. Months later the game was still the subject of much controversy in the chess world. When Parma visited England for the Tees-side tournament in April 1972 (the game had been played in February) he assured me that the sacrifice was unsound, an opinion which he later expressed in print when annotating the game for *Informator 13*. In October of that year, at the Skopje Olympiad, Parma confessed that his earlier idea was wrong and that the sacrifice was indeed sound.

Whatever the truth of the matter, the game is very exciting. The notes here are based on Velimirovic's own analysis in *Makedonski Shakh*.

1 P–K4	P–QB4	2 N–KB3	P–Q3
3 P–Q4	P×P	4 N×P	N–KB3
5 N–QB3	P–QR3	6 B–KN5	P–K3
7 P–B4	B–K2	8 Q–B3	Q–B2
9 0–0–0	QN–Q2	10 B–Q3	P–QN4
11 KR–K1	B–N2		

By omitting the move 7 ... B–K2 and proceeding instead with his Q-side development, Black could reach a position almost identical to that in the diagram but with the difference that the extra black move would have been 11 ... P–N5 (and Black's KB would still be on KB1). White can then sacrifice on Q5 under circumstances that are one tempo more favourable than those in the present game. Kavalek–Gheorghiu, Skopje 1972 went: 12 N–Q5! P×N 13 P×P+ K–Q1 14 B–B5! (an echo of the note to Ljubojevic's 13th move) 14 ... B–K2? (it was essential to move the queen somewhere; but not to B4 because of 15 B–K6! with the same idea as in the game) 15 B–K6! R–KB1 (or 15 ... Q–R4 16 B×P Q×RP 17 N–K6+ K–B1 18 N×P Q–R8+ 19 K–Q2 Q×P 20

R×B± ±) 16 B×P R×B 17 N–K6+ K–B1 18 N×Q and White won.

12 N–Q5!

Presented with the diagrammed position in the fifteenth game of his match with Fischer, Spassky disdained the text sacrifice in favour of 12 Q–N3 which also gave him the advantage. It would have been interesting to see Fischer's inevitable improvement on Ljubojevic's play.

12 ...   N×N

12 ... P×N 13 N–B5 is also critical, e.g.:

a) 13 ... B–KB1? 14 P–K5! P×P 15 P×P N×P (or 15 ... N–K5 16 B×N P×B 17 R×P Q–B4— *17...N–B4 18 N–Q6+!—*18 P–K6! P×P 19 N×P+!—Larsen) 16 N×P+! B×N 17 B×N B×B 18 Q×B winning Enevoldsen–Hamann, Danish Ch 1972;

b) 13 ... P×P? 14 B×KP B×B 15 R×B with a clear advantage to White—Larsen;

c) 13 ... P–R3!? 14 P–K5 (14 P×P P×B 15 R×B+ K–B1 16 P×P N×P 17 Q–K2 is very unclear—Parma) 14 ... P×P 15 P×P N×P 16 R×N? (16 Q–N3!) 16 ... Q×R 17 B–KB4 P–Q5 18 B×Q B×Q 19 P×B K–B1 20 N×B K×N 21 B×QP KR–QB1 and Black's material advantage is sufficient to win. Boey–Hamann, Skopje 1972; or

d) 13 ... K–B1 which is an untried suggestion of Larsen's.

13 P×N   B×B

On 13 ... B×P Velimirovic had intended 14 Q×B! P×Q 15 R×B+ K–B1 16 B–B5 R–Q1 17 B–K6!! winning.

14 R×P+!

It is rumoured in master circles in Yugoslavia that 14 N×KP is also good for White.

14 ...   P×R

Velimirovic considers 14 ... B–K2! to offer Black the best chances of defending his position: 15 N–B5! (if 15 R/1–K1 N–K4! 16 R×B+—*or 16 P×N P×R!*—16 ... Q×R 17 P×N P–N3 and Black is better) 15 ... P×R 16 N×NP+ K–Q1! (not 16 ... K–B2 17 N×P Q–R4 18 Q–R5+ K–N1 19 Q–N4+ K–B2 20 Q–N7+ K–K1 21 B–N6+ P×B 22 Q×P mate) 17 N×P+ K–B1 18 N×Q K×N 19 B–B5 with an unclear position.

15 N×KP!

15 Q–R5+ looks tempting but it doesn't work: 15 ... P–N3! (not 15 ... K–Q1 16 N×KP+ K–B1 17 Q×B! Q–R4 18 Q×P R–K1 19 B–B5 followed by 20 N–B5± ±) 16 B×KNP+ K–K2 17 Q×B+ N–B3 18 N×KP Q–R4 19 B moves QR–KN1, and White has nothing to show for the sacrificed rook.

15 ...   Q–R4

Capturing the KBP costs Black a tempo because after 15 ... B×BP+ 16 Q×B Q–N3 17 Q–N5! he must defend his KNP.

Parma's 'refutation' of the whole idea was 15 ... Q–N3 16 Q–R5+ P–N3 17 Q×B (17 B×KNP+ K–K2 18 Q×B+ N–B3 19 B moves QR–KN1 is winning for Black as in the last note) 17 ... Q–K6+ 18 K–N1 K–B2 (18 ... N–K4?! 19 Q–B6 N–B2 forces White to take a perpetual check) and White has nothing for the rook. But this is not correct. Now, however, Parma is no longer convinced that his 'refutation' can, strictly speaking, be called a refutation.

16 Q–R5+   P–N3
17 Q×B

17 B×KNP+ K–K2! 18 Q×B+ N–B3 19 B–B7 still does not prevent 19 ... QR–KN1!∓ ∓

Now White threatens 18 B×KNP+ P×B 19 Q×P+ K–K2 20 Q–N7+ K–K1 21 Q×R+, when he has four pawns for the piece and Black's king is still faced with grave difficulties.

17 ...   R–KN1

Most of the post-mortem analysis (as opposed to Parma's post-post-mortem analysis in *Informator 13* and his post-post-post-mortem analysis which reversed that assessment) revolved around Black's last move. For a time it was thought that 17 ... N–B1 might hold Black's position together but Velimirovic dismisses that suggestion with 18 Q–B6! and now:
a) 18 ... R–KN1 19 N×N R×N 20 Q–K6+ K–Q1 21 Q×QP+ K–K1 22 Q–K6+ K–Q1 23 R–K1 K–B2 (or 23 ... Q–B2 24 P–Q6 and 25 Q–K7+) 24 Q–K7+ K–N3 25 Q–K3+ K–B2 26 Q–B5+ ± ±;
b) 18 ... B×P 19 B–K4!! and Black

has no moves—19 ... B×B loses to 20 Q×R K–K2 21 N–N5 when White wins back the piece, while 19 ... B×N   20 B×R R–N1 21 B–B6+ is equally fatal; or
c) 18 ... N×N 19 P×N R–KB1 20 B×KNP+! P×B 21 Q×P+ K–K2 (21 ... K–Q1 22 P–K7+ K×P 23 Q–N7+ ± ±) 22 P–B5 Q–Q1 23 R–K1! when, despite being a rook and a bishop ahead, Black's position is hopeless.

18 R–Q2

Intending to bring his rook to the K-file with devastating results. 18 P–B3 (the same idea—White plans 19 R–K1) allows the counter-sacrifices 18 ... R–QB1 19 R–K1 R×P+! 20 K–N1 N–K4! 21 P×N B×P.

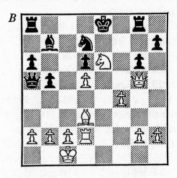

18 ...   N–B1

The last (forlorn) hope was 18 ... N–B4 which loses to 19 N×N P×N 20 P–Q6 Q–Q1 (or 20 ... R–N2 21 Q–B6) 21 R–K2+ K–Q2 (if 21 ... K–B1   22 Q–R6+ K–B2 23 Q×RP+ R–N2 24 B×KNP+ K–B3 25 Q–R5 R×B 26 Q–R4+ K–N2 27 R–K7+ followed by mate) 22 R–K7+ K–B1 23 Q×BP+ K–N1 24 R–QB7! (threat 25 Q–N6 R–R2 26 B–K4) 24 ... R–R2 25 B–K4!

(not 25 Q–N6 Q–B3! followed by
26 ... R–N2 *26 B–K4?? Q×BP+*)
25 ... R–K1 (if 25 ... Q–B3
26 Q×R+! K×Q 27 R×B+ etc.)
26 Q–N6! R×B 27 R×B+ R×R
28 Q×Q+ K–R2 29 Q–QB8 and
Black has no way to prevent the
promotion of White's QP.

19 N×N   Q–Q1

Naturally 19 ... K×N fails to
20 Q–B6+ K–K1 21 R–K2+ K–Q2
22 Q–B7+ etc. and 19 ... R×N to
20 R–K2+ K–Q2 21 Q–K7+ etc.
Black could prolong the game by
giving up his queen (19 ... Q×R+
20 K×Q R×N) but his pieces would
remain unco-ordinated and there
would be nothing to do against the
advance of White's K-side pawns
(21 P–B5 is probably one way of
winning rapidly).

Now Black's position is in ruins.

20 N×RP	**Q×Q**
21 P×Q	**K–B2**
22 N–B6	**R–R1**
23 P–KN3	**B–B1**

After 23 moves Black's three
remaining fighting units are all on
their original squares!

24 P–KR4	**B–B4**
25 B×B	**P×B**
26 P–R5	**R–QR2**
27 R–B2	**1–0**

Andersson–Kuijpers
Wijk aan Zee 1971

1 P–K4 P–QB4		2 N–KB3 P–K3
3 P–Q4 P×P		4 N×P N–KB3
5 N–QB3 P–Q3		6 P–KN4 P–QR3
7 P–N5 KN–Q2		8 B–N2 N–QB3
9 P–B4 Q–N3		10 N–N3 B–K2
11 Q–K2 Q–B2		12 B–K3 P–N4

13 0–0–0   B–N2

13 ... P–N5 at once might be
stronger.

14 P–KR4   P–N5

If 14 ... N–R4 15 P–R5 followed
by P–N6.

15 N–Q5

15 N–R4 is met by 15 ... N–R2
followed by 16 ... B–QB3 and
15 N–N1 doesn't look very exciting.

15 ...	**P×N**
16 P×P	**N–R4**
17 N×N	

The only way to keep the initiative.
If 17 N–Q4 Black can safely castle
Q-side.

17 ...	**Q×N**
18 B–Q4	**K–Q1**

But not 18 ... K–B1 because of
19 P–R5 followed by P–R6.

19 KR–K1	**R–K1**
20 R–Q3!	

Not 20 B×P K–B2 threatening
21 ... B×NP.

20 ...   Q–N4

It is logical for Black to play for the
exchange of queens though as we
shall see White still maintains his
pressure in the queenless middle-
game. But is there anything better for
Black? 20 ... N–B4? loses to 21 R–K3
Q–B2 22 B×N and 23 P–Q6.

20 ... Q×RP? also loses: 21 R–K3 B×QP 22 R×B! R×R 23 Q×R+ K–B2 24 B–R3 (not 24 B–N6+ K–B3!) 24 ... B–K3 25 B×B P×B 26 R×P etc. A tempting defensive try is 20 ... B×QP!? 21 B×B Q×B 22 B–N6+ N×B 23 R×Q N×R, but after 24 Q–B4, even though White is behind in material, he has excellent winning prospects because of the wave of K-side pawns that will rush down the board once his queen has swept through the seventh rank.

21 B×P!

This move is the key to White's victory. With the KNP gone Black cannot prevent White from establishing a strong pawn at KB6. Once this has been accomplished Black's whole army has about as much freedom as an inhabitant of Devil's Island.

21 ...   N–B4

21 ... K–B2 fails to achieve anything: 22 R–K3 Q×Q 23 R/1×Q R–KN1 24 R×B R×B 25 B–R3 R–Q1 26 B–K6! with good winning chances for White.

22 R–K3   Q×Q
23 R/1×Q   B–QB1

On 23 ... R–QB1 24 P–B5 is very strong.

24 B–Q4!

After the obvious 24 B–B6, Black can survive by 24 ... R–R2 followed by 25 ... P–QR4, 26 ... B–R3 and 27 ... B–N4 (defending the K1 square and thereby threatening simply 28 ... B×B).

Now White threatens 25 B×N P×B 26 P–Q6.

24 ...   B–N5
25 R–K1   R–QB1

Not 25 ... K–Q2 26 B×N P×B

27 R×B+! R×R 28 R×R+ K×R 29 P–Q6+ picking up the rook.

26 B–B6   R–B2
27 K–Q2

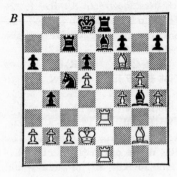

27 ...   N–R5?

Immediately fatal. The best defence was 27 ... B–B4! and now:

a) 28 B–Q4 R–N1! 29 B–R3 B×B 30 R×B/3 K–Q2 followed by some regrouping manoeuvre;

b) 28 P–R5? N–R5 29 R×B R/1×R 30 B–K4 B×B 31 R×B P–R4 32 P–B5 K–K1 winning;

c) 28 P–N3! N–K3! 29 P×N P×P! (not 29 ... R×P+? 30 K–Q1 P×P 31 B–R3! when White has an easy win) and White's task is not so simple although the extra pawn should be sufficient for eventual victory.

After the text Black is unable to untangle his pieces and save his K-side pawns.

28 B–Q4   B–B4
29 B–K4   B×B
30 R×B   N–B4
31 R/4–K3   R–N1
32 P–B5   R–Q2
33 P–R3!

Opening up another file for the entry of a white rook into the Q-side.

33 ...   P–QR4

34 P×P	P×P
35 P–B6	

The culmination of White's positional ambitions on the K-side—Black must now wait for the death sentence to be carried out.

35 ...	B–B1
36 R–K8+	K–B2
37 R–QR1	R–Q1
38 R–R7+	K–N1
39 R×R+	K×R
40 R–Q7+	K–R3
41 R×BP	1–0

Since on 41 ... P–R3 or 41 ... R–R1 White can win by marching his king to KB5 and promoting the KNP.

Stein–Tal
USSR Team Ch 1961

1 P–K4	P–QB4	2 N–KB3	P–Q3
3 P–Q4	P×P	4 N×P	N–KB3
5 N–QB3	P–QR3	6 B–KN5	QN–Q2
7 B–QB4	Q–R4	8 Q–Q2	P–K3
9 0–0–0	P–N4	10 B–N3	B–N2
11 KR–K1	N–B4	12 B×N	

For 12 P–K5! see the game Matsukevich–Vooremaa, page 138.

12 ...	P×B
13 Q–B4	B–K2
14 Q–N4!	

A move recommended by Tal himself. 14 N–Q5? has been tried instead but it seems that by capturing the knight on White's Q4 instead of the one on Q5, Black can avoid the usual perils of accepting the N–Q5 sacrifice—White having no quick way of opening up the K-file: 14 ... P–K4! 15 N×BP+ K–Q1 16 Q–B5 P×N 17 B–Q5 B–QB1! 18 Q–B3 R–R2 19 P–K5 N–Q2 20 N×N R×N

21 K–N1 P×P 22 R×KP Q–B2 (Black's king is surprisingly well protected) 23 R–R5 Q–N3 24 B×P B–N2 25 Q–KN3 Q–Q3 26 Q–KR3 B–KB3 27 B–N3 Q–K2 28 P–R4 R–K1 29 P×P P×P 30 Q–N3?? (Black was clearly better in any event) 30 ... Q–K7 0–1 Arsenev–Asaturian, Trud TU Ch 1961.

14 ...	0–0–0
15 B–Q5!	

The main point of White's previous move. White exchanges off a relatively useless bishop for one that helps protect Black's king. 15 N–Q5 was also possible: 15 ... KR–K1 (not 15 ... N×B+?? 16 N×N Q×P 17 N–B3 winning the queen) 16 N×B+ R×N 17 K–N1 with a slight advantage to White.

The text is stronger.

15 ...	P–N5?

Better is 15 ... R–Q2.

16 B×B+	K×B

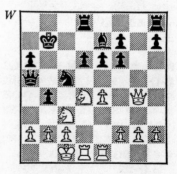

17 N–Q5!	P×N

Forced. If 17 ... KR–N1 18 N–B6!!±±; 17 ... B–B1 18 Q–R5! P×N 19 Q×BP+ Q–B2 20 Q×QP+ with a persistent attack; 17 ... P–R4 18 Q–N7 P×N 19 P×P KR–K1 20 Q×P/B7 Q–B2 21 N–B6 B–B1 22 R×R±±; or

17 ... P–N6   18 RP×P Q–R8+
19 K–Q2 Q×P   20 N–QB3 P–Q4
21 P×P P–B4   22 Q–B3 N×P+
23 N×N and Black has a terrible
game.

18 P×P	R–Q2
19 N–B6	

Now it becomes clear why Black's
best 15th move was ... R–Q2—he
would now have an extra tempo to
save him from losing back his extra
piece.

19 ...	Q×P
20 Q×P+	K–B2
21 N×B	

The rest is easy.

21 ...	R–QN1
22 Q–R3 Q–B5	23 N–B6 R–N6
24 Q–R5+ R–N3	25 K–N1 N–R5
26 R–Q4 N×P	27 K–B1 Q–B4
28 R–K3 K–N2	29 R–QB3 R–N4
30 Q–R3 Q×Q	31 R×Q R×P
32 N–R5+ 1–0	

Kupreichik–Tal
Sochi 1970

1 P–K4 P–QB4	2 N–KB3 P–Q3
3 P–Q4 P×P	4 N×P N–QB3
5 N–QB3 N–B3	6 B–QB4 Q–N3
7 N–N3 P–K3	8 B–K3 Q–B2
9 P–B4 P–QR3	10 B–Q3 P–QN4
11 P–QR3 B–K2	12 Q–B3 B–N2
13 0–0 R–QB1	14 QR–K1 0–0
15 Q–R3	P–N5

See diagram next column

The positions that arise after
16 P×P N×NP are known to offer
Black the better prospects, e.g.
17 P–K5? P×P   18 P×P Q×P
19 R×N N×B and White is lost.

So Kupreichik makes his opponent
an offer he can't refuse.

16 N–Q5!?	P×N
17 KP×P	

The first point. White's KB is now
glaring at KR7.

17 ...	N–N1
18 B–Q4	

The second point. With Black
having no control over his Q5 square
White threatens simply 19 B×N and
20 Q×P mate.

18 ...	P–N3

18 ... P–R3 loses to 19 B×N B×B
20 Q–B5 etc.

19 R–B3?

Better is 19 R–K3! so that 19 ...
B×P can be met by 20 Q–R4. But
if White plays to regain some of the
sacrificed material he relinquishes the
initiative to his opponent: 19 P–B5
B×P 20 R×B Q×R 21 P×P BP×P
22 B×N Q–K3 and Black should win.

19 ...	B×P
20 R/3–K3	

The third point. White's control of
the K-file acts like a razor, cutting
Black's forces in two.

20 ...	B–Q1
21 Q–R4	

Forcing Black to defend his KN
and thereby preventing ... N–QB3
which would dislodge the powerful
white bishop from Q4.

21 ...	QN–Q2
22 Q–R6	Q–N2

Intending 23 ... B–N3 so as to exchange off one of White's key active pieces.

After the game Tal suggested that this task might be accomplished by the Tal-like move 22 ... Q–N3?! when 23 B×Q B×B leaves Black threatening both 24 ... R–K1 and 24 ... N–N5. But even Tal didn't take his suggestion seriously.

23 R–N3

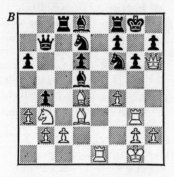

23 ...	N–B4?

Inconsistent and the losing move. After 23 ... B–N3! the exchange of White's QB results in the almost immediate collapse of his attack: 24 B×NP B×B+ 25 N×B BP×B 26 R–K7 (26 R×P+ P×R 27 Q×P+ leads to nothing) 26 ... R–KB2; or 24 R–K7 B×B+ 25 N×B Q–N3 26 B×NP Q×N+ 27 K–B1 K–R1.

Tal had been under the hallucination that after 23 ... B–N3 24 R–K7 B×N 25 B×NP B×B+ 26 K–R1 K–R1, White could win by 27 B×BP because 27 ... N–K5 fails to 28 Q×P+!! K×Q 29 B–N8++ and 30 R–R7 mate. But instead of 27 ... N–K5 Black can play 27 ...

N–N5! when White must take a draw by 28 B–N6 N–B7+ (28 ... N×Q?? 29 R×P+ K–N1 30 B–K4+ and mate in two) 29 K–N1 N–N5+ etc. (30 K–B1? B–B5+ 31 K–K1 B–B7+ 32 K–Q1 N×Q 33 R×P+ K–N1 34 B–K4+ B×R∓∓).

24 N×N	P×N
25 P–B5!	P×B
26 BP×P	BP×P
27 B×NP	K–R1

White was threatening both 28 B–B7++ and 28 B×P++.

28 Q×R+	N–N1
29 B–B5!	

Not 29 B–K4 B–N3 30 B×B R×Q 31 B×Q P–Q6+ 32 K–R1 B–B7 33 R–KB1 P×P! and Black threatens 34 ... B×R and 34 ... B–K6.

29 ...	R–N1
30 R–K8	Q–KB2
31 R–R3!	1–0

Ostapenko–Zhartsev
USSR 1969

1 P–K4 P–QB4 2 N–KB3 N–QB3
3 P–Q4 P×P 4 N×P N–KB3
5 N–QB3 P–Q3 6 B–QB4 P–K3
7 B–K3 B–K2 8 Q–K2 0–0 9 B–N3
Q–B2 10 0–0–0 P–QR3 11 KR–N1
P–QN4 12 P–N4 P–N5 13 N×N
Q×N

See diagram next page
14 N–Q5

A well known move in this popular variation. White clears the way for the occupation of Q5 by his bishop.

14 ...	P×N
15 P–N5	P×P

Naturally not 15 ... N×P 16 B×P.

| 16 P×N | B×P |

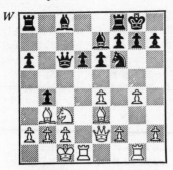

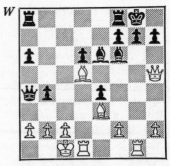

17 B–Q5   Q–R5
18 Q–R5!

After 18 B×R, Black quickly develops a very strong attack against White's king: 18 . . . B–K3! 19 B×P B×NP+! 20 K×B Q–R6+ 21 K–N1 B×P+ 22 K–R1 B–B5+ picking up the queen.

18 B–Q4 looks strong because it neutralises Black's play along the long diagonal but in practice this move also fails to give White any advantage: 18 . . . B×B   19 R×B B–K3! 20 Q×KP QR–B1 (not 20 . . . QR–K1 21 Q–B4!) 21 B×B P×B 22 R×QP Q×RP   23 R×NP+! K×R   24 R–Q7+ R–KB2   25 R×R+ K×R   26 Q–N7+ K–B3 27 Q×R ½–½ Gipslis–Tal, Moscow 1967.

The text is an important improvement on existing theory.

18 . . .   B–K3
See diagram next column
19 R×P+!!

A devastating sacrifice. Black's apparently secure king position is breached and he is forced onto the defensive for the remainder of the game. Without this move White would be in grave difficulties because his own king is poorly defended.

19 . . .   B×R

19 . . . K×R allows mate in four by 20 Q–R6+ etc.

20 R–N1   KR–B1

Black tries to clear an escape route for his king. If 20 . . . QR–B1 (20 . . . K–R1 loses at once to 21 R×B K×R   22 Q–R6+ and 23 B–Q4) 21 R×B+ K×R   22 B–Q4+ P–B3   23 Q–N5+ K–B2 24 Q×P+ K–K1 25 Q×B+ K–Q1 26 B–N6+ R–B2 27 Q×QP+ K–K1 28 Q–K5+ R–K2 29 Q–N8+ K–Q2 30 Q–B7+ and mate next move.

21 R×B+!   K×R

Of course not 21 . . . K–B1   22 R×BP+ etc.

22 Q–R6+   K–N1
23 B×P

Guarding against the threat of mate at QB2 and threatening mate in three by 24 B×P+ etc.

23 . . .   P–N6

Black has three inadequate swindling attempts:

a) 23 . . . Q×BP+   24 B×Q B–B4 25 B–Q4 R×B+   26 K–Q1 P–B3 27 Q×BP followed by mate;

b) 23 . . . R–B5   24 B×P+ K–R1 25 B–N5 R–B5 26 B–B5+ and mate in two;

c) 23 . . . R×P+   24 B×R R–QB1 25 Q×P+ K–B1 26 Q–R8+ K–K2 27 B–N5+ K–Q2 28 Q×R+ K×Q

29 B×Q when White is a piece ahead.

The best chance is 23 ... R–B4! 24 B×P+ K–R1 25 B–B5+ K–N1 26 B–Q4 R–K4 27 B×R P×B 28 Q–R7+ K–B1 29 B×B P×B 30 Q–R8+ K–B2 31 Q×R Q×RP 32 Q–N7+ K–B3 33 Q×NP, when White should win the ending.

24 B×P+	K–R1
25 B–KB5+	K–N1
26 Q–R7+	K–B1
27 B–R6+	K–K1
28 Q–N8+	K–K2
29 B–N5+	K–Q2
30 Q×P+	K–B3
31 B×B	

Black suffers badly from his king, queen and rooks all being on white squares, not to mention the fact that he is being mated.

31 ...	K–N3

If 31 ... Q×P 32 Q–Q7+ K–N3 33 B–K3+ K–R4 34 B–Q2+ K–N3 35 Q×P+ R–B3 36 B–K3+ K–N2 37 Q–Q7+ R–B2 38 B–Q5+ K–N1 39 Q–Q8+ R–B1 40 Q–N6 mate, while 31 ... R–B2 loses to 32 B–Q5+ K–N3 33 B–K3+ R–B4 34 Q–QN7+ K–R4 35 B–Q2+ and mate in two.

32 B–K3+	K–R4

32 ... R–B4 33 B×P Q–K1 34 Q–QB4 is equally hopeless.

33 B×R	R×B
34 Q–B5+	R–B4

Or 34 ... Q–N4 35 Q×R P×RP 36 Q–B7+ K–R5 37 P–N3+ K–R6 38 Q×P+ Q–N5 39 Q×Q+ K×Q 40 K–N2 etc.

35 B×R Q–N4	36 B–N4+ K×B
37 P–QR3+ K–B5	38 Q×Q+
P×Q 39 P×P+ K–Q6	40 K–Q1

1–0

And lastly, a comedy of errors.

Zhdanov–Tukmakov
Riga 1968

1 P–K4	P–QB4
2 N–KB3	P–Q3
3 P–Q4	P×P
4 N×P	N–KB3
5 N–QB3	P–QR3
6 B–QB4	P–K3
7 B–N3	P–QN4
8 0–0	B–N2
9 R–K1	QN–Q2

9 ... P–N5 10 N–Q5! P×N 11 B–R4+ QN–Q2 12 P×P+ B–K2 13 N–B5 is crushing for White.

10 N–Q5!

The sacrifice 10 B×P P×B 11 N×KP is also playable, e.g. 11 ... Q–R4? 12 N–Q5 R–B1 13 B–Q2 winning the queen, or 11 ... Q–N1 12 N–Q5 K–B2 with an unclear position.

10 ...	N–B4

If 10 ... P×N 11 P×P+ B–K2 12 N–B5 N–K4 13 N×NP+ White has a very strong attack in return for his material investment.

11 N×N+?!

The correct way to pursue the attack was 11 B–N5! and if 11 ... P×N 12 P–K5! P×P 13 R×P+ B–K2 (or 13 ... N–K3 14 N×N

P×N 15 R×KP+ K–B2 16 B×N
P×B 17 R–K3 P–KR4 18 R–Q3)
14 N–B5 N–K3 15 N×P+ K–B1
16 R×N K×N 17 R–K3, and again
Black's king is dangerously exposed.

11 ...   **P×N??**

A terrible positional blunder. After
11 ... Q×N the chances would be
about equal.

12 Q–R5

Threatening to capture on K6.

12 ...   **Q–Q2**

13 P–KB3?

The KP does not need protecting
in this way. 13 B–Q2 was considerably
stronger and if 13 ... N×P??
14 B×P or 13 ... B×P 14 R×B
N×R 15 B×P.

13 ...   **R–B1**

Black must leave his king in the
centre: 13 ... 0–0–0 14 B–K3 gives
White excellent Q-side attacking
prospects.

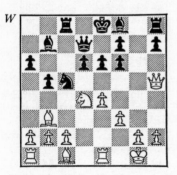

14 B–Q5??

This must be unsound—White has
insufficient minor pieces to join in the
attack and Black's king can find a
haven on the Q-side. Better would
have been 14 B–K3 or 14 B–Q2.

14 ...   **P×B**

15 P×P+   **K–Q1**

16 B–Q2   **K–B2**

17 P–QN3

Intending 18 P–QR4 or 18 P–QB4.

17 ...   **K–N1?!**

Better was 17 ... P–B4 followed
by ... B–N2 so as to take immediate
advantage of the newly opened long
diagonal.

18 P–QR4   **P×P?**

18 ... P–B4 was still better though
after 19 P×P P×P (19 ... B–N2?
20 N–B6+) 20 R–R5, Black's use
of the long diagonal is more limited
than in the last note.

19 P–QN4   **R–N1**

20 P×N   **P×P**

20 ... R×BP 21 P–QB4 R×BP
22 N–B6+ also exposes Black's king
to danger.

21 B–B4+   **K–R1**

22 N–B6   **P–B5**

If 22 ... B×N 23 P×B Q×P
24 R–K4 P–B5 25 Q×BP and
Black's position is in ruins. The text
threatens 23 ... P–R6.

23 R×P   **P–B4?**

A serious inaccuracy. Better was
23 ... B–B4+ 24 K–R1 and then
24 ... P–B4 because ...

24 R–R5!

... now Black's KB is deprived of
its best diagonal.

24 ...   **R–N3**

25 R/1–R1

Threatening 26 R×P+ B×R
27 R×B+ K–N2 28 R–R7+
winning the queen.

25 ...   **B–B4+!**

The only move.

26 R×B   **R/1×N!**

27 R×R

See diagram next page

27 ...   **R×R?**

After 27 ... Q×P 28 R×R

Q–Q5+ 29 B–K3 Q×R+ 30 K–B2
RP×R 31 Q–R4 Q–K4 32 Q–Q8+
Q–N1 33 Q–N6 B–B1 34 Q–QB6+
Q–N2 35 Q×BP B–K3, the chances
are roughly equal. In the game
continuation White's queen penetrates Black's position before the
defending queen has time to return
home to guard her husband.

28 P×R	Q–Q5+
29 B–K3!	Q×R+
30 K–B2	B×P
31 Q×P/B5	

This is the crucial tempo that Black
lost when making his 27th move.
Now there is no way to guard both
the back rank and the QR2 square.

31 ...	Q–R1
32 Q–B5	K–N2
33 Q–N6+	1–0

Karpov–Dorfman
USSR Championship 1976

1 P–K4 P–QB4 2 N–KB3 P–Q3 3
P–Q4 P×P 4 N×P N–KB3 5 N–QB3
P–K3 6 P–KN4 B–K2 7 P–N5 KN–Q2
8 P–KR4 N–QB3 9 B–K3 P–QR3 10
Q–K2! Q–B2 11 0–0–0 P–N4 12 N×N
Q×N 13 B–Q4! P–N5

| 14 N–Q5! | P×N |
| 15 B×P | |

The immediate 15 P×P would be a
serious error because after the forced
continuation 15 ... Q×QP 16 B×P
Q×KR 17 R–K1 N–K4 18 B×N P×B
19 Q×KP, Black can simply castle long
and White's position is resignable.

15 ...	R–KN1
16 P×P	Q–B2
17 B–B6	

White must be careful over the order
in which he plays his moves. The point
behind leaving the rook on Q1 for the
time being is that if 17 R–K1 N–K4 18
B×N P×B 19 P–KB4 P×P, White can
no longer play 20 P–Q6.

| 17 ... | N–K4 |

Black must block the K-file at once.
e.g. if 17 ... N–B4 18 R–K1 R–R2 19
B–R3 B×B 20 R×B and 21 R–K3.

18 B×N	P×B
19 P–KB4	B–KB4
20 B–R3	

Karpov was widely criticized for this
move, and it was suggested that 20 P×P
R–QB1 21 R–R2 was stronger,
however the World Champion decided
against this continuation on the
grounds that after 21 ∴ Q–R4 both
the endgame (22 Q×P Q×Q 23 B×Q)
and the middle-game (22 Q–B3 P–N6!)
would pose problems.

20 . . .	**B×B**
21 R×B	**R–QB1**
22 P×P	

Possibly 22 P–N3 is objectively stronger, to avoid Black's next move.

22 . . .	**Q–B5!**
23 R /1–Q3	**Q–B5+!**

The best move in a very tricky position. 23 . . . Q×QRP is refuted by 24 P–Q6, but 23 . . . R×P!? 24 P×R Q×RP is far more complex. Karpov gives as one possibility 25 P–Q6 B×Pch 26 R /R–K3 R–B5 27 Q–N2, with multiple threats.

24 K–N1	**R–B5!**
25 P–Q6	**R–K5**
26 R /R–K3	**R×R**

And not 26 . . . R×NP 27 P×R B×P 28 P–Q7+ K–Q1 29 R–Q1!! R×R 30 Q×P followed by mate.

27 R×R	**Q×RP**
28 Q–B3!	

On 28 P×B?? Q–R8+ 29 Q–K1 Q×Q+ 30 R×Q K×P, White loses the end game because of the black KRP.

28 . . .	**Q×P**

28 . . . B×NP 29 P–K6 P×P 30 R×P+ K–Q1 31 Q–QB6! and Black is totally lost.

29 R–K1?!

29 Q–QB6+ K–B1 30 P×B+ Q×P 31 Q–R6+ R–N2 leaves Black tied up. The text only wins when followed up with super-accurate play by White.

29 . . .	**Q–N7**
30 Q–B5	**R–N3**
31 R–KB1	**Q–Q4**
32 P×B	**K×P**

At last material equilibrium has been restored, but of course White still preserves a big initiative because Black's king is exposed in the centre of the board.

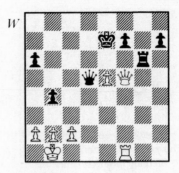

33 Q–B4	**P–QR4**
34 Q–R4+	**K–K1**
35 Q×RP	**Q–B6**
36 Q–R8+	**K–K2**
37 Q–R4+	**K–K1**
38 Q–QB4!	**Q–N2**
39 P–N3	**R–K3**
40 R–N1	

Giving back the extra pawn in the interests of prosecuting his attack.

40 . . .	**R×P**
41 R–N8+	**K–K2**
42 Q–R4+	**K–Q2**
43 Q–B6	

More accurate than 43 R–Q8+ K–B2 44 Q–Q4 R–K8+ 45 K–N2 Q–B3 46 R–Q5, when 46 . . . P–R5! forces White to go into an ending with only two pawns against one: 47 P–R3 Q–B6+ or 47 Q×NP Q×R 48 Q×R P×P.

43 . . .	**R–K2**
44 Q–B5+	**K–Q3**
45 Q×RP	**R–K4**
46 Q–Q8+	**K–K3**
47 K–N2	**P–B3**
48 R–KB8	**Q–N2**
49 Q–QB8+	**K–Q4**
50 Q–B4+	**1–0**

Certainly one of the most interesting struggles of the 1970s.

7 B–Q5

This sacrifice occurs in only one type of Sicilian position and is, consequently, rare in master chess. For the sacrifice to have any point Black's QNP must have moved so that B–Q5 carries a threat (B×R). If the sacrifice is declined Black must either move his rook (usually allowing White's Q4 knight to jump into QB6 with great effect) or interpose his QB on QN2 (which permits the exchange of light squared bishops).

White's compensation typically stems from his pressure along the K-file, much the same as with the N–Q5 sacrifice. Occasionally, however, White uses the sacrifice as a means to insinuate his QB3 knight to Q5:

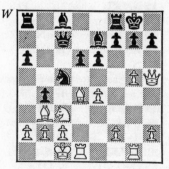

16 B–Q5! P×N 16 ... P×B loses to 17 N×P (the point—now Black gets mated) 17 ... Q–N2 18 B×N P×B 19 N–B6+ and 16 ... R–N1 or 16 ... B–N2 to 17 P–N6! etc. **17 Q–R6! P–B3 18 KNP×P B×P 19 B×R P×P+ 20 K–N1 B×B 21 R×B R×P 22 Q–K3 R–B2 23 Q–KN3 R–Q2 24 R/1–Q1 Q–N1 25 B–B6 R–QB2 26 R×P P–R3 27 Q–N6 Q–N3** Interesting, but Black was totally lost in any case—To stave off mate he had to give up a piece on Q2. **1–0** Yoffe–Lyubin, Leningrad Ch ½-final 1969.

... P–QN5 can sometimes be an awkward reply to the B–Q5 sacrifice because if White moves the attacked QB3 knight his position is not so active after Black accepts the sacrifice: Strekalovsky–Polugayevsky, 1958.

14 B–Q5! P–N5! 15 B×B P×N 16 B–B6+ K–B1 17 Q–K3 Q×P 18 Q×P? Better 18 P×P. **18 ... R–QN1.** Black has the more active position. If 19 P–QN3 P–K4 20 N–B5 R×P!∓ ∓

Fischer–Rubinetti
Palma 1970

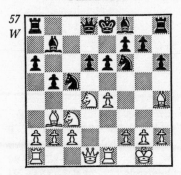

57
W

Honfi–Tatai
Monaco 1968

58
W

12 B–Q5!　　　**P × B**

Alternatives are 12 ... Q–N3
13 B × N NP × B　14 Q–R5 0–0–0
15 B × B+ N × B　16 QR–Q1 R–Q2
17 R–K3 R–N1　18 P–KR4! K–N1
19 P–QN4! with an excellent game
for White, Polgar–Filep, Hungarian
Ch 1969; and 12 ... Q–B1　13 B × N
NP × B　14 P–QN4! N–Q2　15 B × B
Q × B　16 Q–R5 R–B1　17 R–K3
K–K2　18 R–Q1 again with a clear
advantage to White, Ribli–Szekely,
Hungarian Ch 1969.

13 P × P+　　　**K–Q2**
14 P–QN4　　　**N–R5**
15 N × N　　　**P × N**
16 P–QB4　　　**K–B1**

17 Q × P Q–Q2　18 Q–N3 P–N4
19 B–N3 N–R4　20 P–B5! P × P
21 P × P Q × P　22 R–K8+ K–Q2
23 Q–R4+ B–B3　24 N × B 1–0.

11 B–Q5　　　**P–R3**

Black's alternatives amount to:

a) 11 ... P × B　12 P × P+ K–Q2
13 P–QN4 N–R5　14 N × N P × N
15 P–QB4! with play similar to the
Fischer–Rubinetti example.

b) for 11 ... P–N5　12 B × B N × B
13 N–Q5! see the example Tal–
Mukhin, p. 86.

c) for 11 ... Q–B2 see the notes to
Belyavsky–Marjanovic, p. 114.

12 B × B　　　**N × B**
13 B–R4　　　**R–B1**
14 P–R4　　　**P–N5**
15 N–Q5!

Again!

15 ...　　　**P × N**
16 P × P+　　　**K–Q2**
17 N–B6

and White has a tremendous attack,
the game continuing 17 ... R × N
18 P × R+ K × P　19 P–QB3 (19
Q–Q3 N–B4　20 Q–B4 is also strong)
19 ... P–Q4　20 P × P B × P　21
R–QB1+ N–B4　22 Q–Q4 with a
great game for White.

Fatalibekova–Baumstark
Ladies Interzonal, Tbilisi 1976

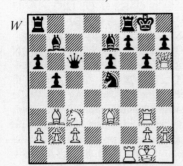

18 B–Q5!

A typical interference sacrifice in this type of position. White's mating attack along the KR-file is being held back by Black's counter threat of ... Q×P mate. With the text move White blocks the long diagonal for just one move, thereby buying time to shift her rook from KN3 to KR3. No matter whether Black moves her queen or captures the bishop there is no defence to 19 R–R3 and so ...

18 ...   1–0

Belyavsky–Marjanovic
USSR–Yugoslavia, Erevan 1971

1 P–K4	P–QB4
2 N–KB3	P–Q3
3 P–Q4	P×P
4 N×P	N–KB3
5 N–QB3	P–QR3
6 B–QB4	P–K3
7 B–N3	P–QN4
8 0–0	QN–Q2?!

Until the end of 1970 the usual continuation was 8 . . . B–N2 9 R–K1 QN–Q2 10 B–N5 (for 10 N–Q5 see the game Zhdanov–Tukmakov, page 109) 10 . . . P–R3 11 B–R4 (Ivkov suggests 11 B×N! N×B 12 P–QR4 P–N5 13 N–R2 N×P 14 N×NP P–Q4 15 N/N4–B6 Q–N3 16 P–QB4!!±) 11 . . . N–B4? (better 11 . . . P–N4 12 B–N3 N–K4— Ivkov. Hence his suggested improvement.) 12 B–Q5! reaching the same position which was discussed in the last two examples.

If, instead of 10 . . . P–R3, Black tries 10 . . . N–B4, 11 B–Q5! is still strong: e.g. 11 . . . Q–B2 12 B×N NP×B 13 P–QN4 N–Q2 14 B×B Q×B 15 Q–R5 (now the position is almost identical to that in the Ribli–Szekely game after sixteen moves with the relatively unimportant difference that here Black's KRP has not moved) 15 . . . Q–B1 16 R–K3 N–K4 (with Black's rook on QB1 instead of his queen this move would not be possible on account of 17 N×KP). So far we have followed the game Palermo–Najdorf, Mar del Plata 1965, in which White now opened up the Q-side to his disadvantage (17 P–QR4 P×P 18 N×RP R–QN1) and Black eventually won. Instead

White might try 17 N–Q5!? P×N 18 P×P, e.g. 18 . . . B–K2 19 R/1–K1 R–R2 20 Q–K2 Q–Q2 (20 . . . 0–0? 21 Q–R5! or 20 . . . Q–B2 21 P–KB4 N–N3—*21 . . . N–B5 22 R–K4—* 22 N–B6 R–N2 23 N×B N×N 24 R×N+ Q×R 25 Q–B2 Q×R+ 26 Q×Q+ K–Q2 27 Q–B3 with good winning chances for White because of Black's many weak pawns and the time it takes him to get his rooks working properly.) 21 N–B6 N×N 22 P×N Q–B2 23 R×B+ Q×R 24 Q–Q2 Q×R+ 25 Q×Q+ K–Q1 26 Q–B3 ± ±

9 R–K1!	N–B4
10 B–Q5	

Even more effective when Black has not played . . . B–N2 because he is now forced to accept the sacrifice— . . . P–N5 no longer comes into consideration as a possible resource.

10 . . .	P×B
11 P×P+	K–Q2
12 P–QN4!	N–R5

After 12 . . . N–N2 13 N–B6 Q–B2 (or 13 . . . Q–N3 14 B–K3) 14 Q–B3, White threatens a killing check on the KR3–QB8 diagonal.

13 N×N	P×N
14 P–QB4	B–N2
15 Q×P+	K–B2
16 B–N5!	Q–Q2
17 Q–R5+	K–B1
18 B×N	

Unthematic. The natural plan is to prepare for P–B5 by 18 QR–B1. But 18 P–B5 at once would be a mistake: 18 . . . P×P 19 P×P Q×P 20 N–B3 B–Q3! followed by 21 . . . B–B2 consolidating.

18 . . .	P×B
19 N–B6!?	

The idea is to prevent Black from

moving both his QR and his KB. A better continuation however was 19 R–K2 and 20 R/1–K1.

19 ...   **R–KN1**

Not 19 ... Q–B2 20 Q–R4 B×N 21 P×B B–K2 22 P–N5 with ample compensation for the piece, nor 19 ... B×N 20 P×B Q×P 21 Q–KB5+ K–N1 22 P–N5 etc.

20 Q–N6?

Necessary was 20 P–N5! maintaining the pressure and keeping the QB6 square well protected.

20 ...   **P–B4?**

Black rejected 20 ... Q–B2 because after 21 R–K8+ K–Q2 22 Q–K3 he saw only 22 ... B×N which loses to 23 R/1–K1! Instead he could play 22 ... R×R and on 23 Q–KR3+ simply 23 ... R–K3.

White would therefore answer 20 ... Q–B2 with 21 N–R7+ K–Q2 22 Q–Q4 with an unclear position.

21 P–N5!

Now Black's position is very difficult to defend. On 21 ... Q–B2 White can safely retreat his queen to the centre without having to fear the capture on QB6.

21 ...   **P–B5?**

22 QR–N1

Threatening 23 P×P B×P 24 N–R7+!

22 ... P–QR4   23 R–K4 P–B4 24 R–K6 R–N3 25 R/1–K1 R×R 26 P×R Q–QB2 27 P–K7 B×P 28 N×B+ K–Q1 If 28 ... K–Q2 29 N–Q5! B×N 30 R–K7+ **29 Q–Q4 Q–B4 30 Q–N7 B–K5 31 N–Q5 R–R2 32 Q–B8+ K–Q2 33 P–N6 R–N2 34 Q–K7+ 1–0**

White sometimes advances his KBP to B5 in order to undermine Black's KP which is on K3. Often, it does not suit Black to exchange pawns on KB4 either because White recaptures with his KP and then utilizes the K-file for an attack against Black's uncastled king, or because White recaptures with the knight, at once introducing pressure against the points K7 and KN7. If Black decides against this exchange of pawns he has little option but to advance his KP to K4, hoping to keep the centre closed until such time as he can force the thematic break . . . P–Q4.

The alternative would be to permit White to exchange pawns on K6 which would leave the first player with some of the advantages that he gets after the N–K6 sacrifice (use of the KB-file and the KR5–K8 diagonal) but without his having given up any material. Thus we arrive at the skeleton position for the sacrifice N–K6; Black has pawns at KB2, K4 and Q3, White has a knight at Q4 and a pawn at KB5. Black has not yet castled and, for the sacrifice to have any real chance of success, Black's Q2 square should be occupied by a knight.

After Black's capture . . . BP×N he is weak along both the K1–KR4 diagonal and the KB-file, and to justify his sacrifice White must be able to take immediate advantage of the weakness of Black's king and possibly of the gaping hole at Q5 that was created by Black's . . . P–K4. If Black has a knight on Q2, White's recapture BP×P will attack this knight and leave White with the initiative. The viability or otherwise of White's sacrifice depends entirely on how he is able to use this initiative.

The following example is ideal in many respects, White extracting full compensation for the piece by initiating a decisive king hunt:

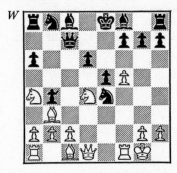

12 B–Q5 B–N2 13 N–K6! P×N
14 Q–R5+ K–Q1 15 B–K3 N–B4
16 B×B Q×B 17 N×N P×N
18 QR–Q1+ K–B2 19 P×P K–N3
20 B–N5! P–N3 21 B–Q8+ K–N4
22 P–B4+ P×Pep 23 P–R4+ 1–0
Levy–McCague, London 1965.

Even if White's Q–R5+ is prevented, Black's king may still be subjected to a similar thrashing as in Levy–Tan (*59*).

Under some, very favourable, circumstances the sacrificed material is regained almost at once leaving White with an overwhelming advantage because of the aforementioned weaknesses in Black's position as in Spassov–Antunac (*60*).

Ghinda–Mobius (*62*) is unusual in that Black is unable to accept the sacrifice immediately. Instead, he must first move his queen thereby giving White a breathing space which is used to introduce another piece into the attack.

There is one important variation on the main theme of this sacrifice. If Black has already castled and he has played . . . P–KN3, the sacrifice may be played with the idea of weakening Black's KNP by distracting the KBP.

Here is one such example in which the sacrifice is the prelude to a mating attack:

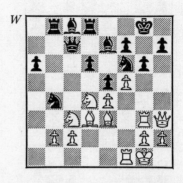

20 N–K6! P×N   21 P×NP N×B
22 P×P++ K–R1   23 Q–R6 N–R4
24 R–B7 B–N4   25 Q×N B×B+
26 K–B1 Q×R+   27 Q×Q and
Black lost on time just as he was about to be mated, Berzin–Peterson, USSR 1965.

Levy–Tan
Training Game 1965

**59
W**

Spassov–Antunac
Dresden 1969

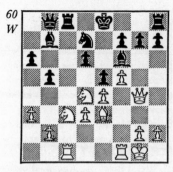

**60
W**

12 N–K6! **P×N**
13 P×P **B–K2**

Not 13 ... B–B1 14 R×N! P×R
15 Q–R5+ K–Q1 16 N–Q5 Q moves
17 B–N6+±±

14 R×N!!

Much stronger than 14 P×B+
Q×P.

14 ... **B×R**

If 14 ... P×R 15 N–Q5 Q–N2
16 P×B+ K×P 17 N–N6+
regaining the sacrificed material with
an immense positional plus for
interest.

**15 N–Q5 Q–N2 16 Q–R5+ K–Q1
17 B–N6+ K–B1 18 P×B+ Q×P
19 N–B7!**

Threatening 20 B–K6.

**19 ... K–N2 20 N×R R×N 21
B–K3** Having restored the material
equilibrium White can now afford the
time to prise open the Q-side at his
leisure. **21 ... N–K2 22 P–QR4**
More to the point than 22 Q×RP.
**22 ... P–R3 23 Q–Q1 B–N4 24
B×B P×B 25 P×P Q×P 26 Q×P
Q–N3+ 27 Q×Q+ K×Q 28 R–Q1
N–B3??** He was lost anyway. This
just gives him an excuse for resigning.
29 R–Q6 1–0

19 N–K6! P×N 20 P×P R–B2
20 ... N–B4 allows 21 R×B! P×R
22 B×N followed by 23 Q–N7
winning. **21 P×N+ R×P 22 N–Q5
B×N 23 P×B Q–Q1** If 23 ... Q–N2
24 Q–K6+ K–B1 (or 24 ... K–Q1
25 R×B) 25 R×B+ P×R 26
B–R6+. **24 Q–R5+?!**

Missing a forced win in 24 R–B8!!
Q×R 25 Q–K6+, e.g.

a) 25 ... K–Q1 26 B–N6+ R–B2
27 Q×QP+ Q–Q2 28 R×B!;

b) 25 ... B–K2 26 Q–B7+ K–Q1
27 B–N6+ R–B2 28 Q×P! followed
by 29 R–B1; or

c) 25 ... K–B1 26 R×B+! P×R
27 B–R6+.

Nevertheless, White's position still
has much to offer because of his
control of the QB-file. **24 ... R–KB2
25 R–B6 0–0!** **26 R/1–B1** And not
26 R×RP?? B–N4! when suddenly
it is Black who wins. **26 ... Q–Q2**
26 ... P–K5 at once would offer
better hopes of counterplay. **27
R×RP** White's immediate threat is
28 R–R7. **27 ... Q–N2 28 R×P
P–K5 29 P–Q4 Q–R2 30 Q–Q1
B–K4 31 R–K6 and White won.**

Schrancz–Kuhne
Corres 1964

Ghinda–Mobius
Zinnowitz 1970

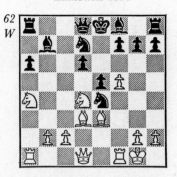

12 N–K6! **P×N**
13 P×P **N–B4**

After 13 ... N–QN1 14 B–N5 B–
K2 15 B×N B×B 16 Q–R5+ P–
N3 17 Q–R6 Black's king would
soon suffer from its precarious situation in the centre, e.g. 17 ... B×P
18 R×B! Q×R 19 R–KB1 B–B4
(19 ... Q–Q1 20 Q–N7±±) 20 N–
R6 R–R2 21 N–B8 Q–N2 (21 ...
R–QB2?? 22 R×B) 22 Q–N5 with
overwhelming threats.

13 ... N–N3 is no better because
of 14 R×N! Q×R 15 N×N etc.

14 R×N! **Q×R**
15 N×N **B–B3**

Since 15 ... P×N allows 16 Q–Q7
mate.

16 B–Q5 R–B1 17 N–Q7! B×N
On 17 ... Q–R5, simply 18
P–KN3, while 17 ... Q–K2 fails to
18 B×B R×B 19 Q–Q5 R–B2
20 B–K3 with the decisive threat of
B–N6 followed by Q–N7.

18 P×B+ K×P 19 Q–N4+ K–B2
20 B–N5 P–KR4

20 ... Q–N3 loses to 21 R–KB1
B–K2 22 R–B7 QR–K1 23 Q–R4.

21 Q–R4 Q–N3 22 R–KB1 K–N1
23 R–B7 R–B3 24 B–K3 1–0

13 N–K6! **Q–B1**
Black must make room for his king
to move. If 13 ... P×N 14 Q–R5+
K–K2 15 P×P Q–K1 16 R–B7+
etc.

14 N–N6! **Q–B3**
14 ... N×N 15 B×N/6 P×N
loses to 16 Q–R5+ K–Q2 17 P×P+
K–B3 18 B–R5! N–B4 19 R–B7.

15 N×R **P×N**
16 Q–B3! **P×P**
17 Q×P **N/5–B3!**
18 Q–R3 **B×N**

18 ... B–K2 allows White to win
elegantly by 19 B×QRP!! B×N
20 B–QN5! Q–B1 21 R×N!

19 R×P **Q–Q4**
20 P–B4 **Q×B**
Or 20 ... Q–N2 21 R/1–R1±±

21 Q–K6+ **K–Q1**
22 R×B+ **K–B2**
23 B–B2 **P–N3**
24 P–QN4 **B–N2**
25 R–R7+ **K–N1**
26 R/1–R1 **Q–K5**
27 Q×QP+ **1–0**

Soloviev–Gratvol
USSR 1968

13 N–K6?

This sacrifice is unsound because White's forces are not sufficiently active for him to have a sustained attack. In particular, the white KB would be much better placed on QN3.

13 ...   **P×N**
14 P×P   **N–N3**

If 14 ... N–B4, Black succumbs to 15 B×N followed by 16 N–Q5 and 17 Q–R5+ when White has a tremendous attack. But an earlier game suggests that provided Black can guard his K1–KR4 diagonal he may concede the Q4 square without suffering too many ill effects: 14 ... N–B1 15 B×N B×B 16 N–Q5 Q–Q1 17 Q–KN3 (17 Q–B3 N×P) 17 ... B×P (not 17 ... N×P 18 Q–N6+ K–B1 19 B–R5 Q–Q2 20 P–KN3! followed by 21 KR–B1 etc.) 18 B–R5+ B–B2 19 N×B+ P×N 20 Q–N7 (There is nothing better) 20 ... B×B 21 Q×R B×R 22 R×B Q–K2 23 R–B1 K–Q2 24 R×P R–K1 25 Q×P N–K3 26 P–KN4 R–KB1 27 P–N5 R×R 28 P×R Q–B2 29 P–KR4 N–B5 30 Q–N5 N–R4 31 Q–B5+ K–B2

0–1 Gheorgescu–Drozd, Bucharest 1962.

15 B×N   **0–0?**

15 ... B×B 16 Q–R5+ K–Q1 (16 ... K–B1 17 R×P! threatening both 18 R×N and 18 R–Q7) leaves White hard put to justify his sacrifice. He must attend to the protection of his attacked KP and there is no convincing way to build up pressure on Black's most vulnerable point, his backward QP. If 17 B–N4 R–K1 18 Q–R3 N–B5 and Black has quite an active game as well as being a piece ahead. Instead, Black's greed tempted him to think that he could recapture the bishop *and* get castled.

16 B×B!   **R×Q**
17 B×QP   **R×N**

17 ... Q–B3 18 B×R/8 R–B1 (or 18 ... R–B7 19 R–Q8+ K–R2 20 R–Q6 Q–B4 21 P–K7) 19 P–K7 R–K1 20 B–Q6 is hopeless for Black. The text leaves him a piece ahead but ...

18 B×Q   **R×B**
19 R–Q8+   **K–R2**
20 R–B1!

... none of his pieces has a good move.

20 ...   **R–K2**

The threat was 21 R–B7 followed by P–K7.

21 R/1–B8   **P–KR4**

Since on 21 ... R×P White forces mate by 22 B–R5 etc.

22 R–R8+   **K–N3**
23 R/Q–B8   **B×P**

Or 23 ... R×P 24 B×KRP+ K–N4 25 R–B5+ K–R5 26 P–KN3+ K–R6 27 B–B3+ R–R3 28 R–R5+ R×R 29 R×R mate.

24 R×R   **B–N5**
25 B×P   **1–0**

I. Zaitsev–Dementiev
USSR Ch 1970

1 P–K4	P–QB4
2 N–KB3	P–Q3
3 P–Q4	P×P
4 N×P	N–KB3
5 N–QB3	P–QR3
6 B–QB4	P–K3
7 B–K3	P–QN4

Black may, of course, transpose into the Sozin Variation by 7 ... N–B3.

8 B–N3   Q–B2

As is usual in such positions Black gets no joy from winning White's KP: 8 ... P–N5 9 N–R4 N×P 10 N×P! and now:

a) 10 ... P×N 11 N–N6 B–N2 12 N×R B×N 13 B×P and Black's king is stuck in the centre; or

b) 10 ... B×N? 11 B–Q5 when White regains the piece and enjoys a clear advantage.

9 P–B4   P–N5

Played not with the idea of winning the KP but to deprive White's knight of the Q5 square after Black has played ... P–K4 in reply to White's P–B5.

10 N–R4   QN–Q2

10 ... N×P 11 P–B5 P–K4 12 N–KB3 leaves White with the unpleasant threat of 13 N–N6. If 12 ... N–Q2 13 B–Q5 wins a piece, while 12 ... N–B4 13 N×N P×N 14 Q–Q5 is also very good for White (14 ... B–N2 15 B–R4+!). Best is 10 ... B–K2.

11 P–B5   P–K4

This position was reached in a five-minute game Fischer–Stein, played in Havana during the 1966 Olympiad. 'I win positions like this

in my dreams' exclaimed Fischer who then played 12 N–K2 and eventually lost.

12 N–K6!!   P×N
13 P×P   N–B4

If 13 ... N–QN1 14 N–N6 B–N2 15 B–R4+! keeps Black's king in the centre since 15 ... N–B3 16 N–Q5 is hardly appetizing for Black and 15 ... B–B3 is simply refuted by 16 N×R.

14 N×N   P×N
15 0–0

The critical position. White threatens 16 R×N P×R 17 Q–R5+ K–K2 18 Q–B7+ K–Q3 19 QR–Q1+ K–B3 20 B–Q5+ K–N3 21 B×R±±

15 ...   P–B5?

The soundness of Zaitsev's sacrifice may be demonstrated by an exhaustive analysis of Black's alternatives:
a) 15 ... Q–Q3 16 R×N! Q×Q+ (or 16 ... P×R 17 Q–R5+ K–K2 18 Q–B7+ K–Q1 19 Q×BP+±±) 17 R×Q P×R 18 B–R4+ K–K2 19 B×P+ K×P 20 B–N3 mate.
b) 15 ... B–K2 16 B–R4+ K–B1 17 R×N+ B×R (17 ... P×R 18 B–R6+ K–N1 19 Q–N4 mate) 18 Q–Q5 B–N2 (or 18 ... R–QN1

19 P–K7 +! B × P 20 R–KB1 + B–B3
21 B × P + etc.) 19 Q–B4! (threat
20 B × P + B–K2 21 Q–B1 +) and
now:

b1) 19 ... P–N3 20 B × P + K–N1
21 P–K7 + K–N2 22 P–K8 = Q +
KR × Q 23 B–B8 + winning the
queen;

b2) 19 ... B–K2 20 R–Q1 R–Q1
21 Q–B1 + B–KB3 22 R × R + Q × R
23 B × P + K–N1 24 P–K7 and
25 B–N3 + ± ±;

b3) 19 ... R–B1 20 R–Q1 B–B3
21 R–Q7 Q–R4 (if 21 ... B × B
22 R × Q R × R 23 Q × RP B–K1
24 Q–Q6 + R–K2 25 B × P and
Black is completely tied up, or
21 ... B × R 22 P × B R–Q1 23
B–N3 R × P 24 B × P + etc.) 22 B × B
R × B 23 Q–Q5 P–N6! 24 P–B3
P × P 25 R–KB7 + K–N1 26 P–K7
P–R8 = Q +   27 K–B2 B–R5 +
28 P–KN3 Q × NP + 29 K–B3 P–R4
30 P–K8 = Q + K–R2 31 R × P +
and mate next move.

c) During the post mortem Tal
pointed out 15 ... B–Q3! as being
the best defence: 16 R × N (Possibly
16 B–N5 is a stronger continuation,
e.g. 16 ... R–B1 17 B × N P × B
18 Q–R5 + K–Q1 19 QR–Q1 with
a winning attack.) 16 ... P × R
17 Q–R5 + K–Q1 18 R–Q1 Q–N3
19 Q–B7 R–K1 20 P–K7 + R × P
21 Q–Q5 B–N2 22 B × P B × Q
23 B × Q + B–QB2 24 B–B5. Now
24 ... R–Q2 is forced since other

rook moves lose to 25 B × B. After
24 ... R–Q2   25 P × B B–Q3
26 B–N6 + B–B2 comes 27 B–B2
with the idea of 28 B–QR4. White
would certainly have more than
adequate compensation for the
exchange because of his strong
passed pawn but the game would
still be a fight.

After the text Black loses by force.

16 R × N!

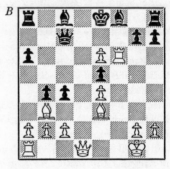

16 ...   P × R

If 16 ... P × B 17 Q–R5 + P–N3
18 R × P P × R 19 Q × NP + K–K2
20 R–Q1 with mate to follow.

17 Q–R5 +   K–K2

Since 17 ... K–Q1 18 R–Q1 +
B–Q3 loses to 19 B × P R–QN1
20 P–K7 +

18 Q–B7 +   K–Q3
19 P–K7!   Q × P

Or 19 ... B × P 20 Q–Q5 mate.

20 Q × QBP   1–0

Zaitsev was awarded a special
brilliancy prize for this game.

Malevinsky–Petkevich
USSR Spartakiade 1975

1 P–K4 P–QB4 2 N–KB3 P–Q3 3
P–Q4 P×P 4 N×P N–KB3 5 N–QB3
P–QR3 6 B–KN5 QN–Q2 7 Q–K2
P–K3 8 P–B4 Q–B2 9 0–0–0 P–QN4
10 P–QR3 B–N2 11 P–KN4 R–B1 12
B×N P×B 13 P–B5 P–K4 14 N–Q5
Q–Q1

15 N–K6!   **P×N**
If 15 ... Q–R4 16 P–N5 P×P 17
N×P, threatening (amongst other
things) 18 N×BP and 19 Q–R5+ with
a mating attack.

16 P×P   **B×N**
Black cannot keep the extra piece,
since 16 ... N–B4 is met by 17 P–N5!
N×P/3 18 Q–R5+ K–Q2 19 B–R3,
with decisive threats. ·

17 P×N+	**Q×P**
18 R×B	

The material balance has been
restored but Black's king is wide open to
an attack on the light squares.

18 ...	**R–B4**
19 P–KR4	**P–KR4**
20 R×R	**P×R**
21 B–R3	

21 P–N5 would open up the position
still further while retaining the threat of
B–R3.

21 ...	**P×P**
22 R–Q1	**Q–K3**
23 B×P	**Q–R7**
24 B–R5+	**K–K2**
25 P–B3	**B–R3+**
26 K–B2	**P–N5?**

Black should probably try passive
defence, with 26 ... Q–B5 27 Q–N4
Q–K3, though after 28 Q–N1 Q–B3 29
R–Q5 his chances of survival would be
minimal.

27 BP×P	**P–B5**

27 ... P×P 28 Q×P is an easy win.

28 Q–N4	**Q–N6+**
29 K–N1	**R–Q1**
30 R×R	**K×R**
31 Q–N8+	**K–B2**
32 Q–R7+	**K–B3**
33 Q×B	**Q–Q6+**
34 K–R1!	**1–0**

9 BxKP

The sacrifice B×KP almost always arises in variations of the Sicilian in which White has played B–QB4 though occasionally the bishop reaches the K6 square via KR3. The skeleton position is one in which White has a knight at Q4 and his KB attacking the K6 square. Black has pawns at Q3 and K3. Black's KP is defended only by the KBP, the QB has been developed at QN2 or it has had its view of K3 obstructed by a knight on Q2.

For the sacrifice to be played in its best form the skeleton position must contain two other features. Black's queen must be on Q1 or QB2 so that after the moves B×KP P×B; N×KP, White's knight is attacking the queen. Secondly, Black's KB must be at K2 so that White's knight at K6 does not only attack the black queen but forks the queen and the KNP.

Here are two examples of the sacrifice being played under these optimal conditions. In each case White gets three pawns for the bishop, but more important than any mere material consideration is the fact that Black's king is exposed to the wrath of White's attack and without anywhere for his king to hide the second player never reaches the endgame in which his piece would be superior to White's three pawns.

The game concluded **10 B×KP P×B 11 N×P Q–B5 12 N×P+ K–B2 13 N–B5 P–KR4 14 0–0–0 Q–B3 15 N×B K×N 16 N–Q5+ K–B2 17 N×N N×N 18 B×N K×B 19 R×P+ Q×R 20 P–K5+ 1–0** Mann–Gollnick, Corres 1963.

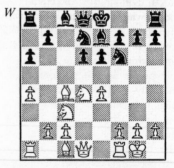

Play continued **9 B×KP P×B 10 N×P Q–N3 11 N–Q5! N×N 12 N×P+ K–B2 13 Q–R5+ K–N1 13 ... K×N 14 B–R6+ K–N1 15 Q–N4+! 14 N–B5! N–K4**

15 N × B+ N × N 16 Q–K8+ K–N2 17 Q × N+ N–B2 18 R–R3 and White won quickly, Gruzman–Galster, Moscow 1960.

When played under these optimal conditions the sacrifice is inevitably successful. The destruction of the pawn mass protecting Black's king is a blow from which, if White plays forcefully, the second player is never allowed to recover. Indeed, the sacrifice is so devastating that nowadays it is rare for a strong player to permit it. Nevertheless, there are three further examples (*64, 65* and *66*), two of which are from comparatively recent games.

One important fundamental difference between this sacrifice and those on the QN5 square which also give White three pawns for the piece, is that after the sacrifice on QN5 Black's QRP, QNP and QP have been eliminated with the result that White has three connected passed pawns (QRP, QNP, and QBP). The sacrifice on K6 however, eliminates Black's KP, KBP and KNP, a process which presents White with only one passed pawn (his KBP). This means that White cannot afford to play an ending with his three pawns against a piece—Black can easily hold off the passed KBP while his extra piece is working elsewhere. In (*67*), for example, White's sacrifice fails because in order to eliminate Black's KNP he must exchange off too many minor pieces and he is left with insufficient attacking forces.

Even if White fails to eliminate Black's KNP the black king can still suffer from exposure after the KP and KBP have disappeared. It is sometimes possible therefore, to make the sacrifice on K6 when Black's bishop is still on KB1 protecting the KNP (*69, 70* and *71*). In the first two of these examples Black's king seeks a haven on KB2. White plays N–Q5 so as to exchange the knight at KB6 which gives some protection to the black king, and if Black exchanges on his Q4 square (*71*) the K-file is opened by White's recapture with the KP.

The sacrifice on K6 might seem plausible when Black has castled but it is much less likely to meet with success. After B × KP P × B; N × KP, White's knight forks the black queen (on Q1 or QB2) and KR (on KB1). White thus 'wins' a rook and two pawns for two minor pieces but we can class this transaction as a sacrifice because in the middle-game the two minor pieces are usually of more value.

In (*74*) White only picks up two pawns for the bishop because Black's KNP has already advanced to the protected square KN4. As additional compensation however, there is the open KB-file which offers White tactical chances of a kind that do not normally go hand-in-hand with this sacrifice.

(*75*) is unusual in that Black need not (and should not) accept the sacrifice after B × KP. Instead, Black maintains the material balance by capturing White's pawn which has advanced to K5.

Bazan–Szabo
Buenos Aires 1960

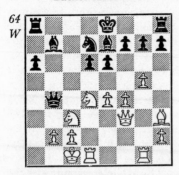

Poutainen–Dieks
Groningen 1971/72

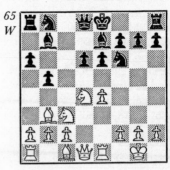

17 B × P! P × B 18 N × P N–B4 If
18 . . . K–B2 19 P–B5! threatening
20 P–N6 + **19 N × P +**

Thematic. As is usual after the
sacrifice on K6, grabbing the
exchange only serves to help Black's
game because White exchanges off a
minor piece which is needed for his
attack: 19 N–B7 + K–Q1 20 N × R
B × N 21 KR–K1 K–B2 and Black
will continue with . . . R–QN1 when
White is suddenly facing a strong
attack.

19 . . . K–Q1 20 Q–K3 K–B2 Not
20 . . . N × P 21 KR–K1! **21 R–Q4**

Perhaps 21 P–K5! would have been
the most effective continuation, e.g.
21 . . . QR–Q1 22 R–Q4 Q–N3
23 P–N4 N–Q2 24 N–K6 + K–N1
25 P × P B–KB1 26 N × R Q × N
27 P–B5 with an overwhelming game.
21 . . . Q–N3 22 P–N4? After
22 N–B5! QR–K1 23 P–N6 P × P
24 R × NP B–KB1 25 N × P Black's
plight would be desperate. But now
Black whipped up a counterattack
against White's exposed king: **22 . . .
N–Q2 23 P–K5 P–QR4! 24 N–R4
Q–N4 25 KP × P + B × QP 26
N–K6 + K–N1 and Black won.**

**10 B × P!? P × B
11 N × KP Q–B1?**

Better is 11 . . . Q–Q2 when
Poutainen had intended 12 N–Q5
B × N 13 P × B K–B2 14 P–KN4
with a complicated position (compare
the Klundt–Petrosian example, page
127). If instead White tries 12
N × KNP + K–B2 13 N–B5 P–N5
14 N–Q5 B × N 15 N × B Q × N
16 P × B Black can play 16 . . . Q–B2
when he has reached a position
almost identical to that in the game—
The important difference being that
Black's queen is defending the QP so
that 17 R–K6 can be met by 17 . . .
QN–Q2 when White has nothing to
show for the sacrificed material.

**12 N × KNP + K–B2 13 N–B5
P–N5 14 N–Q5 B × N 15 N × B
K × N 16 P × B + K–B2 17 R–K6
R–K1 18 B–N5** If 18 R × P Q × P!
18 . . . R × R? After 18 . . . QN–Q2
19 R × P Q–B4 20 B–B4 White has
only a small advantage. The text is a
gross blunder. **19 P × R + Q × KP
20 B × N N–Q2** Since either recapture
loses the rook to a queen fork. **21
B–Q4 and White won easily.**

Vadasz–Kluger
Hungarian Ch 1969

66
W

13 B×P!	**P×B**
14 N×KP	**Q–R4**
15 N×KNP+	**K–B2**
16 P–K5!	

White must play with direct threats otherwise Black's counterplay may gain too much momentum.

16 ...   **N×P**

If 16 ... P×P 17 N–B5 with all sorts of nasty threats (18 R×N, 18 N×B K×N 19 R×N+ etc.).

17 P–B4	**R×N**
18 P×N	**R/1–QB1?**

Too slow. Black had to try 18 ... R×P+! and if 19 K×R? B–K5+ 20 R–Q3 Q–R5+! 21 K–Q2 (or 21 K–N1 B×R+ 22 Q×B Q×B!∓∓) 21 ... B×R 22 Q×B P×P! 23 B×N R–Q1!. Therefore, after 18 ... R×P+, White must play 19 Q×R R–QB1 20 Q×R B×Q 21 P×N and after 21 ... B–B1 22 R–K4! leaves White in command of the board.

19 P×R	**Q×RP**
20 R–Q3!	

A very powerful move, finishing

Black's counterplay and bringing the rook into the attack by introducing the possibility of a check at KN3 in some variations.

20 ...   **N–K5**

20 ... P×P 21 Q×P would be no fun for Black.

21 Q–R5+	**K×N**
22 B–B6+	**N×B**
23 P×N+	**B×BP**

W

24 R–N3+	**B–N4+**
25 R×B+	**P×R**
26 Q×P+	**K–R1**
27 Q–B6+	**K–N1**
28 R–K7	

Forcing Black to exchange queens into a lost ending.

28 ...	**Q–R8+**
29 K–Q2	**Q×P+**
30 Q×Q	**R×Q**
31 K×R	**B×P**
32 K–N4	**K–B1**
33 R–QR7	**B–K5**
34 P–B3	**B–Q6**
35 R×P	**K–K2**
36 R–N6	**K–Q2**
37 R×NP!	

The simplest.

37 ...	**B×R**
38 K×B	**1–0**

Walther–Matanovic
Munich 1958

Klundt–Petrosian
Bamberg 1968

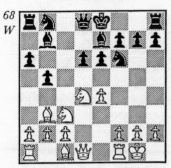

9 B×KP P×B 10 N×KP Q–N3 11 N–Q5 Q–B3 12 0–0 More propitious would have been 12 N/6–B7+ K–B2 13 N×R Q×N/1 14 0–0 with chances for both sides. **12 ... B–N2 13 Q–B4 K–B2 14 B×N N×B 15 N–N5+ K–N1 16 N×N+ P×N 17 Q×BP Q–Q2!** Now Black holds everything. White has exchanged most of his attacking pieces in order to win the third pawn and expose Black's king further. Now, with his attack dying, White meanders towards the endgame. **18 QR–Q1 R–K1 19 P–K5 Q–N2 20 Q×Q+ K×Q 21 P×P** Although White has accumulated four pawns for the piece he is totally lost. His QP is artificially isolated and will soon fall, he has only one other passed pawn and that on the second rank, Black's bishops are very powerful on the open board and lastly Black's king is aggressively placed. **21...K–B3 22 P–Q7 R–Q1 23 KR–K1??** Made under a hallucination. **23 ... K×N 24 R–K8 B–N2** So simple. It was this move that the Swiss master had overlooked. **White resigned five moves later.**

9 B×KP?! Premature. The difference between this example and the next three is that here Black has not yet played ... QN–Q2 and as a result his queen can be employed as a defensive piece along the second rank. **9 ... P×B 10 N×KP Q–Q2 11 N–Q5 B×N 12 P×B K–B2** Ivkov suggested 12 ... P–KR4 so as to prevent White's next move. True this would have created new weaknesses in Black's K-side but it is by no means clear that White can take advantage of them in any way, e.g. 13 N–N5? B–K2 followed by ... 0–0, or 13 B–N5 K–B2 14 B×N P×B. **13 P–KN4! P–R3 14 P–KB4 Q–R2+ 15 K–R1 QN–Q2 16 P–N5 Q–N2** If Black tries to hold on to the piece by 16 ... N–K1 (or 16 ... N–R2 or 16 ... N–KN1) 17 Q–N4! (threatening 18 N–Q8+ and 19 Q–K6 mate) is strong. **17 P×N N×P 18 Q–B3** 18 P–B5 is also strong. Now that White is no longer behind in material his position has suddenly become almost overwhelming because of his strong knight, but in the game Klundt failed to make the most of his advantage and only drew.

Velimirovic–Parma
Yugoslavia 1963

69
W

Nei–Tolush
USSR Ch 1959

70
W

13 B×P!? White obtains only two pawns for the piece and Black's well centralised knight is a stalwart in defence. **13 ... P×B 14 N×KP Q–Q2 15 N–Q5 K–B2! 16 N–B5?** Flashy but incorrect. White should have tried 16 P–KB4 **16 ... P×N 17 B×N B×N 18 Q–B3 B–KN2 19 QR–Q1 Q–N5! 20 Q×Q N×Q 21 B×B KR–Q1 22 B×P N×B 23 P×B R–K1 24 P–KB3 N–B4 25 K–B2 R×R 26 R×R R–K1 27 R×R K×R 28 P–KN4!** The best chance. **28 ... N–K2 29 K–K3 N×P+ 30 K–K4 N–N5 31 K–B5 N×BP 32 K×P N–N5??** 32 ... N–K8! wins one of the K-side pawns or the QNP. In the latter case the advance of Black's QBP will decide the game. **33 K–B6! K–B1 34 P–KR4 P–B5 35 P–R5 N–Q6 36 P–R6 K–N1 37 P–N5 P–N5??** And here Black misses a draw by 37 ... K–R2 38 P–N6+ K×P 39 P–N7 K–R2 40 K–B7 N–K4+ 41 K–B8 N–N3+ when White must submit to a perpetual check in order to hold on to his KNP. **38 P–N6 P–B6 39 P×P P×P 40 P–R7+ K–R1 41 P–B4!** **1–0**

11 B×P?! Much better is 11 Q–K2 (threatening 12 N–Q5!) or possibly even 11 P–QR4 P–N5 12 N–Q5!? P×N 13 P×P+ K–Q1 14 Q–K2. **11 ... P×B 12 N×KP Q–B5** Also possible is 12 ... Q–N1 (to defend the QP) 13 N–Q5 B×N 14 P×B K–B2. **13 N×B R×N 14 Q×P 0–0–0?** 14 ... Q–B3 15 Q–N3 K–B2 gives Black good chances of consolidating his position with ... K–N1 in the near future. **15 N–Q5?** Not forceful enough. 15 R–K3! is more active, preparing to transfer the rook to the Q-side, e.g.

a) 15 ... N–N5 16 N×P! P×N 17 R–QB3 Q×R 18 P×Q QR–K1 19 P–QR4 and Black is busted;

b) 15 ... P–N5 16 N–Q5 P–QR4 17 P–QR3; or

c) 15 ... Q–B3 (or B4) 16 Q–N3 threatening 17 N–Q5. **15 ... QR–K1 16 B×N** Not 16 N–K7+ K–Q1 when White has lost his initiative. **16 ... R×B?** Mistakes galore! After 16 ... P×B! 17 R–K3 B×N 18 R–QB3 Q×R 19 P×Q B–N2, the position is clearly unclear. **17 N×R N×N 18 QR–Q1! Q–QB2 19 P–KB3 Q×Q 20 R×Q** and White won.

Jansa–Adamski
'Fraternal' Armies Ch 1970

Bivshev–Furman
USSR Ch 1954

9 B ×P!	**P ×B**
10 N ×KP	**Q–N3**
11 N–Q5	**B ×N**
12 P ×B	**N/1–B3**

Better would have been 12 ...
N/2–B3 with the idea of hiding the
king on Q2. Even so, Black's K-side
would be congested and undeveloped
and White could start to smash open
the Q-side by 13 P–QR4 P–N5
14 P–QB4 followed by B–K3, R–B1
and P–B5.

13 Q–K2	**N–K4**
14 B–K3	**Q–N2**
15 B–Q4	**K–B2**
16 P–KB4	**Q ×P**
17 P ×N!	**Q ×N**

If 17 ... P ×P 18 N–N5+ K–N3
(18 ... K–N1 19 Q ×KP± ±)
19 Q–Q3+ P–K5 20 R ×N+± ±

| **18 P ×N!!** | **1–0** |

Because 18 ... Q ×Q (forced)
loses to 19 P ×P+ Q ×R+ 20
R ×Q+ etc.

| **12 B ×KP?!** | |

Correct is 12 B–N3! maintaining
the pressure on Black's centre.

12 ...	**P ×B**
13 N ×P	**Q–B5**
14 N ×R	**B ×N?**

It would be correct to recapture
with the knight so as to leave this
bishop on the more active square K2
and to free the QB, e.g. 14 ... N ×N
15 N–Q5 N ×N 16 P ×N B ×B
17 Q ×B P–R3∓ and if 18 Q–Q8?
then 18 ... Q ×BP+!

| **15 P–B4!** | **N–N3** |
| **16 B ×N?!** | |

It is tempting to expose Black's
king in this way but the correct
continuation of the attack would be
16 P–K5! and now:

a) 16 ... N–K1 17 P–K6 B ×P
18 Q–K3 B–N5 19 Q ×N/6 etc.; or
b) 16 ... P ×P 17 P ×P N–K1
18 P–K6 B–N5 (18 ... B ×P come
to the same thing as **a**) 19 Q–Q8 B ×P
20 Q ×N/6 B ×N 21 Q ×B+ etc.

| **16 ...** | **P ×B** |
| **17 Q–B2** | **Q–QB2** |

17 ... Q–B4 18 Q–R4 B–N2
allows 19 P–K5! when Black's
defences fall apart.

18 Q–Q4   **B–K3!**

If 18 ... B–K2 (or 18 ... Q–Q1) 19 P–K5!

19 Q×BP

Possibly 19 P–B5 at once would be even stronger.

19 ...	R–K1
20 P–B5	**B–B1**
21 R–K3	**B–N2**
22 R–N3	**K–R1**
23 Q×P	**Q×Q**
24 R×Q	**N–B5**
25 R–Q1	**P–N4**
26 R/3–Q3	

Threatening 27 R–Q8

26 ...	B–B3
27 N–Q5	**B×NP**
28 N–B7	**R×P?**

A time-trouble error. 28 ... R–N1 29 R–Q8 B–B3 30 R×R+ K×R would have offered Black better defensive chances.

29 R–Q8+	**K–N2**
30 R×B	**B–R6**
31 R–K8	

After 31 N×RP Black can force a draw by 31 ... N–Q7+! 32 K–R1 R–QN5 33 R×N B–N7+ 34 K–N1 B–R6+ etc.

31 ...	**R–KN5**
32 R–Q7+	**K–R3**

Or 32 ... K–B3 33 N–Q5+ K×P 34 N–K3+ N×N 35 R×N+ +

33 R–K6+	**K–N4**
34 R–N7+	**K×P**
35 R×R	**K×R/5**
36 R×P	**P–N5**
37 N–N5	**N–Q7+**
38 K–R1	**B–B8**
39 R–R4	**K–B5**
40 R×P+	**K–K6**
41 P–QR4	**N–K5**
42 P–R5	**B–Q7**

1–0 The time scramble is over.

Sodeborg–Kraidman
Budapest 1959

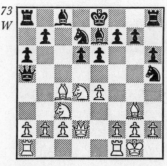

73
W

12 B×KP! It is somewhat unusual for this sacrifice to be successful when Black's queen is not attacked by the second white capture N×P. Another unusual feature of this position is that Black's KNP is defended even though his KB has been developed. But each of these two apparently adverse factors react in White's favour—With Black's KN on KR4, White has more control over his Q5 square and in some variations White wins because the knight is undefended and can be picked up by a queen fork. Also, Black's queen can be driven from the defence of the QB2 square by the move P–QN4, thereby allowing White to redress the material situation. **12 ... P×B 13 N×P N–K4** There is no better defence. 13 ... K–B2 fails to 14 P–QN4! Q×NP 15 N–B7 R–QN1 16 Q–Q5+ K–B1 17 N–K6+ etc. **14 P–QN4!** The key to White's combination. **14 ... Q×NP 15 N–B7+ K–Q1 16 B×N Q–B4 17 N×R Q×B** The rest is a massacre. **18 N–Q5 B–Q2 19 P–KB4 Q–N7 20 Q–R5+ P–N3 21 N/8×P Q–Q5+ 22 K–R1 B–R6 23 N–R8+ K–K1 24 N/5–B7+ 1–0**

Tal–Petrosian
Belgrade 1959

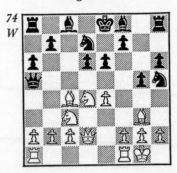

74
W

Bebchuk–Korzin
Moscow Ch ½-final 1964

75
W

12 B×KP! P×B 13 N×P N×B
Not 13 ... N–K4 14 N×B and
15 Q×QP. **14 BP×N N–K4 15
R×B+! R×R 16 Q×QP
R–B3** Not 16 ... B×N? 17 Q×B+
K–Q1 18 R–Q1+ K–B2 19 Q–Q6+
K–B1 20 Q×R+. **17 N–B7+?** 17
N–Q5 could have been answered by
17 ... R×N 18 N–B7+ Q×N 19
Q×Q R–K2, but much stronger than
the text would have been 17 Q–B7!
when White has excellent winning
chances. **17 ... K–B2 18 R–KB1
R×R+ 19 K×R N–B5!** If 19 ...
R–N1 20 N/7–Q5. **20 Q×KRP
Q–QB4!** 20 ... R–N1 is bad on
account of 21 N/3–Q5! N–Q7+ 22
K–K2 B–N5+ 23 K–Q3! After the
text Black is threatening 21 ...
N–K6+. **21 N×R** If 21 Q–R5+
K–N2 22 N×R B–N5! **21 ...
N–Q7+ 22 K–K2** Naturally not 22
K–K1?? Q–K6+ 23 K–Q1 B–N5+
with mate to follow. **22 ... B–N5+
23 K–Q3** 23 K×N Q–Q5+ **23 ...
Q–B5+ 24 K–K3 Q–B4+ ½–½** If
Black plays for a win by 24 ...
N–B8+ White's king can escape:
25 K–B2 Q–Q5+ 26 K×N and the
king hunt is over.

11 B×P   N×P
11 ... P×B loses to 12 N×KP
Q–R4 (12 ... Q–N3 13 N–Q5)
13 N×KNP+ K–B1 14 0–0+, and
11 ... P–N5 to 12 B×P+
12 B–KB4   P×B??
Black still cannot afford to accept
the sacrifice. Correct is 12 ... B×B
13 N×B Q×Q+ 14 R×Q P×N
15 B×N, when White has slightly the
better ending because of Black's
isolated KP.
13 B×N 0–0 14 Q–K2 B–Q3
After 14 ... B–B3 15 0–0–0 White
has much the better development and
pawn-structure but this was Black's
best chance.
15 B×B
Not 15 0–0–0?? Q–N4+ winning a
piece.
15 ... Q×B 16 0–0–0 N–B3 17 Q–K4
A necessary preliminary since 17
N/4×NP?? loses to 17 ... Q–B5+
17 ... B–Q2 18 N/4×NP Q–K2
The rest is easy.
**19 N–Q6 QR–N1 20 P–QR3 R–B7
21 P–KR4 K–R1 22 N–B4 P–K4
23 N–K3 B–K1 24 KR–B1 R×R
25 R×R Q–N2 26 R–B8 mate**

Matanovic–Gufeld
Yugoslavia–USSR match 1969

1 P–K4	P–QB4
2 N–KB3	P–Q3
3 P–Q4	P×P
4 N×P	N–KB3
5 N–QB3	P–QR3
6 B–KN5	P–K3
7 P–B4	QN–Q2!?

Polugayevsky's move.

8 B–B4

For 8 Q–B3 see the game Vitolinsh–
Yuferov p. 149.

8 ...   **P–QN4?!**

Boleslavsky suggests 8 ... Q–N3
9 B–N3 B–K2 10 Q–Q2 N–B4 with
good counter-play for Black.

9 B×KP!?

Westerinen has pointed out another
sacrificial possibility in this position—
9 B–Q5 P×B   10 P×P   B–N2
11 N–B6 B×N   12 P×B   N–B4
13 N–Q5 'with very good chances for
White'.

9 ...	P×B
10 N×KP	

10 ...   **Q–N3**

10 ... Q–R4 has been universally
recommended as an improvement but
experience has so far failed to provide

conclusive evidence either way:
a) 11 0–0?! (threatening 12 P–K5)
11 ... P–N5   12 N–Q5 K–B2
(Lundin's 12 ... N×N is met by
13 P×N K–B2 14 B–Q8!) 13 N/5–B7
R–R2   14 P–K5 P×P   15 P×P
Q×KP 16 Q–B3 R×N   17 QR–K1
B–B4+   18 K–R1 B–N2? (After
18 ... Q×N! 19 R×Q K×R
Black has a substantial material
advantage and it is doubtful whether
White's attack has any more bite.)
19 Q–KR3! Q×R   20 R×Q R–K1
21 B×N N×B   22 Q–KN3 N–K5
23 Q×R+ R–K2 24 N–Q8+ K–K1
25 Q×R+ B×Q   26 N×B N–Q7
27 N–Q6+ K–B1   28 R–K2 1–0
Westerinen–Hamann, Lidköping
1969;
b) 11 Q–Q4 P–N5 (On 11 ... K–B2
12 P–K5 is rather strong. But a
better possibility is 11 ... B–N2 when
White cannot afford to win the
exchange because he is left with a
very bad ending: 12 P–QN4? Q–N3
13 Q×Q N×Q   14 N–B7+ K–B2
15 N×R B×N∓) 12 N–Q5 N×N
13 P×N N–B3 (So far we have been
following Olsson–Jakobsen, Lidköping 1969) 14 N×P+ B×N   15
B×N±;
c) 11 N×B R×N   12 Q×P Q–N3
(Not 12 ... P–N5? 13 N–Q5 N×N??
14 Q–K6+ N–K2   15 Q×N/K7
mate) 13 0–0–0 Q×Q   14 R×Q
P–N5   15 N–R4 P–R3   16 B–R4
P–QR4 17 R/1–Q1, with an obscure
position in which White's chances are
probably slightly better, Tseitlin–
Polugayevsky, USSR Ch 1971.

11 N–Q5   **N×N**

O'Kelly asks 'Is 11 ... Q–B3
better?' but makes no attempt to
answer this question. Who are we to

differ with such a profound judgement?

12 Q×N!

Threatening mate in three by 13 N–B7+ Q×N 14 Q–K6+ etc.

12 ...	Q–K6+
13 K–B1	N–N3
14 N–B7+	K–Q2
15 Q–B7+	K–B3
16 N–Q5!	

16 N×R N×N 17 Q–Q5+ K–B2 18 P–K5! left White with a very big plus in Parma–Szabo, Solingen 1968. But the text wins with ease.

16 ...	Q×KP
17 Q–B7+	K×N
18 R–Q1+	K–K3
19 R–K1	Q×R+
20 K×Q	P–R3

If 20 ... N–Q4 21 Q–B6 R–QN1 22 K–B2 followed by 23 R–K1+±±, or 20 ... N–Q2 21 K–B2 and 22 R–K1+±±.

21 P–B5+!   **K–Q4**

Or 21 ... K×P 22 Q–B7+ K–K4 (22 ... K–K5 23 B–Q8) 23 B–B4+ and mate soon follows after 24 K–B2.

22 Q×N	P×B
23 K–B2	R–R5
24 R–Q1+	K–K4
25 Q–B6	R–N1
26 Q–K8+	1–0

Tal–Polugayevsky
USSR Ch 1959

1 P–K4	P–QB4
2 N–KB3	P–Q3
3 P–Q4	P×P
4 N×P	N–KB3
5 N–QB3	P–QR3
6 B–KN5	QN–Q2
7 B–QB4	Q–R4

| 8 Q–Q2 | P–K3 |
| 9 0–0 | B–K2 |

9 ... P–R3 10 B–R4 P–KN4 11 B–N3 N–R4 leads to the position of example 74.

10 QR–Q1   **N–B4**

On 10 ... 0–0 11 N–Q5! is strong.

| 11 KR–K1 | B–Q2 |
| 12 P–QR3! | Q–B2 |

Black cannot afford to capture the KP because after 12 ... N/4×P 13 N×N Q×Q 14 B×Q N×N 15 R×N P–Q4 16 B×QP P×B 17 R–K2 K–B1 comes 18 B–N4! B×B 19 P×B when White has an immense advantage in the ending (good knight *v* bad bishop, active rooks, better pawn-structure).

13 P–QN4!   **N–R5**

The KP is still taboo: 13 ... N/4×P! 14 N×N Q×B 15 B×N P×B 16 N–KB5! Q–B2 17 N/4× QP+ B×N 18 N×B+ K–K2 19 N×BP and White wins.

13 ... P–N4? is refuted by 14 N/4×NP P×N 15 N×NP B×N 16 B×B+ N/4–Q2 17 P–K5! N–Q4 18 B×B K×B 19 P×P+ Q×QP 20 B×N and 21 P–QB4.

Lastly, the indirect attempt 13 ... R–QB1 14 P×N Q×P gives White the tempo that he needs to open up the centre: 15 P–K5! Q×B (or 15 ... P×P 16 B×NP P×B 17 N×P B×N 18 B×B P×B 19 Q–Q7+ K–B2 20 N–K4!) 16 P×N P×P 17 N–K4 P×B 18 N–KB5 etc.

14 N×N   **B×N**

See diagram next page

| 15 B×KP! | P×B |
| 16 N×P | Q×P |

Black has achieved a certain measure of counterplay but his most active pieces are both offside.

17 Q–Q4

Naturally not 17 N×P+?? K–B2 when suddenly White is lost.

17 ...	**K–B2**
18 R–QB1	**Q–R7**
19 P–K5!	

Exposing Black's king even more. The combination 19 N×P K×N 20 R–B7 Q–K3 21 B×N+ Q×B 22 R×B+ K–N3 23 Q×Q+ K×Q 24 R×NP would leave Black with much the better of the ending because White has only one passed pawn.

19 ...   **P×P**

If 19 ... Q×N 20 P×N B×P 21 B×B Q×B 22 Q–Q5+ K–B1 23 Q×NP (23 R–K6 is also strong) 23 ... R–K1 24 Q×RP, Black's king is still in danger, his KR is out of play and White's Q-side pawns will meet little opposition on their road to promotion.

20 Q×P   **Q×BP+**

Polygayevsky returns his extra material in order to reduce Tal's attacking forces. This is Black's best chance since 20 ... KR–K1 21 B×N B×B 22 R–B7+ K–N1 fails to 23 R×KNP+! while on 20 ... Q–Q4 comes 21 Q–N3 when Black is under pressure from all sides (the immediate threat is 22 N–B7).

21 K×Q	**N–N5+**
22 K–N1	

22 K–N3 may appear more logical but after 22 ... N×Q 23 R–B7 N–Q2! Black threatens 24 ... B–Q3+.

22 ...	**N×Q**
23 R×N	**B×B!**

Best. If 23 ... QR–QB1 24 R–B1+ B–B3 25 N×P! will be decisive.

24 N×B+   **K–N3**

24 ... K–B3 25 R/1–B5 KR–K1 26 N–K4+ would be even less pleasant for Black.

25 N–K6

25 R–K6+? K×N 26 R–B5+ K–B5 27 K–B2 would be too esoteric even for Tal. After 27 ... B–B3 28 P–R3 (28 P–N3+ K–N5 29 R/6×B P×R 30 K–N2 loses to 30 ... P–N4) 28 ... B×P 29 K×B the game would be drawn.

25 ...	**KR–K1**
26 R–K3!	**QR–B1**

Or 26 ... R–K2 27 R–KN3+ K–R3 28 R–B4±±

27 R–B1	**B–N4**
28 R–KN3+	**K–R3**
29 N×P	**R–B1**

29 ... B×R 30 N×R R×N leads to a lost rook ending—The 2:1 K-side majority is not, in itself,

sufficient for a win but the presence of two pawns each on the Q-side makes Black's defensive task impossible. Also, Black's king is badly placed.

30 R–K1

Threatening mate in two.

30 ...   **R–KB3**

If 30 ... B–Q2 31 P–R3 (not 31 R–K4?? R–QB8+) 31 ... R–KB2 32 R–K4.

31 P–R3	**R–QB7**
32 R–K4	**R–QB5**
33 R–K5	**R–QB8+**
34 K–R2	**1–0**

Keres–Sajtar

Amsterdam 1954

1 P–K4	**P–QB4**
2 N–KB3	**P–Q3**
3 P–Q4	**P×P**
4 N×P	**N–KB3**
5 N–QB3	**P–QR3**
6 B–KN5	**QN–Q2**
7 B–QB4	**P–K3**

If Black is determined to employ the difficult 6 ... QN–Q2 defence he should play more actively with 7 ... Q–R4 which is examined in many other examples in this volume.

8 0–0   **Q–B2?!**

8 ... N–N3 is preferable.

9 B×KP!   **P×B**

10 N×KP   **Q–B5**

If 10 ... Q–N1 11 N–Q5 K–B2 (or 11 ... N×N 12 P×N when Black gets annihilated on the K-file) 12 B×N N×B 13 N–N5+ etc.

See diagram next column

11 N–Q5   **K–B2**

Again 11 ... N×N 12 P×N leaves Black's king too exposed, e.g.

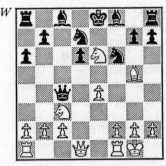

12 ... N–B3 (or 12 ... N–K4) 13 P–QN3! Q–B6 14 B–Q2 and Black cannot keep his guard on QB2, or 12 ... K–B2 13 P–QN3! Q–B6 14 B–Q2 Q–KB3 15 B–N5 Q–N3 16 P–KB4 N–B3 17 P–B5 Q–R4 18 Q–Q4 B–K2 19 QR–K1 (threatening 20 N×P) 19 ... R–KN1 20 P–KR4 B–Q2 21 P–KN4 Q×NP+ 22 Q×Q N×Q 23 B×N K×B 24 N–B7+ K–B3 25 R–K6+ K–B2 26 N×R R×N 27 R×P±± Brander–Wells, Marienbad 1962.

12 B×N   **K×N?**

Black should give up his queen for rook and knight by 12 ... N×B 13 P–QN3! Q×R+ (other queen moves allow a knight fork) 14 Q×Q B×N 15 N–B7 R–B1 16 N×B K×N when a heterogenous material balance has been restored and it is not clear how White can best take advantage of the exposed position of Black's king.

13 B–B3   **N–B3**

Black hopes to escape with his king to the Q-side. Running the other way is hopeless: 13 ... K–B2 14 Q–R5+ P–KN3 15 Q–B3+ K–N1 16 N–B6+ N×N 17 Q×N±±

14 B×N	**P×B**
15 N–N6	**Q–B3**
16 N×R	

16 Q–Q5 + is also strong; the rook will not run away while queens are being exchanged.

16 ...   **B–K2**
17 P–QR4!

But now on 17 Q–Q5 + Black can play 17 ... K–Q2 so that after 18 Q × Q + K × Q White's knight cannot escape from R8. The text threatens to exchange queens and then bring the knight out by P–R5 and N–N6.

17 ...   **P–QN3**
18 Q–Q5 +   **K–Q2**
19 R–R3

Threatening to exchange queens followed by R–QB3 + and N–B7.

19 ...   **B–Q1**
20 N × P +!   **1–0**

Because of 20 ... Q × N   21 Q–KB5 + K–B2   22 R–QB3 + or 20 ... B × N   21 Q–B7 + K–Q1 22 Q × BP +

Henkin–Furman
USSR Team Ch 1954

1 P–K4	P–QB4
2 N–KB3	P–Q3
3 P–Q4	P × P
4 N × P	N–KB3
5 N–QB3	P–QR3
6 B–QB4	P–K3
7 0–0	B–K2
8 B–N3	0–0
9 B–K3	

Vasyukov–Averbakh, played in the same event, went instead 9 P–B4 QN–Q2 10 Q–B3 N–B4 11 B–K3 Q–B2 12 P–N4 P–QN4 13 P–N5 N/3 × P! 14 N × N B–N2. Now White tried 15 N × KP?! P × N 16 B × N P × B 17 B × P + K–R1 and found himself unable to deal with the simultaneous threats 18 ... B × P and 18 ... Q–B3. A better chance would have been 15 N × N B × Q   16 N/5 × KP Q–N2   17 R × B P × N 18 N × KP, e.g. 18 ... K–R1   19 R–R3.

9 ...   **P–QN4**
10 P–QR3   **B–N2**
11 B × P!?   **P × B**
12 N × KP

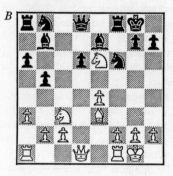

12 ...   **Q–K1**

After the game, Tal and Kliavin analysed the alternative 12 ... Q–B1 13 N × R N × P. Their analysis ran 14 N × RP N × N   15 Q–R5 Q–B3 16 P–B3 N–Q4   17 B–N5! when Black's position is rather precarious, e.g. 17 ... Q × P   18 B × B N × B 19 N–B6 + P × N 20 Q–K8 + K–N2 21 Q × N/K7 + and 22 Q × B; or 17 ... Q–B4 +   18 K–R1 N–Q2 19 B × B N × B· 20 N–N5 Q–B4 21 QR–Q1 N–Q4 (or 21 ... B–Q4 22 P–KN4 N–KB3 23 P × Q N × Q 24 KR–K1 when White wins material) 22 R–Q4 when White has a dangerous attack along the KR-file.

13 P–B3!

And not 13 N × R B × N 14 P–B3 P–Q4! when White must lose a pawn.

13 ...   **QN–Q2**

Now 13 ... P–Q4 fails to 14 P × P
(not 14 P–K5 B × P!) 14 ... B–Q3
15 B–Q4 R–B2 16 N–K4 when
White has restored the material
equilibrium and maintained his
initiative.

13 ... R–B2 would clearly be
pointless because of 14 N–B7.

14 N × R   B × N

White has 'sacrificed' two minor
pieces for rook and two pawns but
there are various aspects of the position that are to his advantage:
a) Black's forces are rather cramped.
b) Black's QP is isolated and it
restricts the scope of his dark-squared
bishop.
c) White has a firm grip on the centre.
d) There is the possibility of P–QR4
at some time in the future, opening
up the Q-wing so as to make good use
of White's QR.

Henkin now bolsters his centre and
then proceeds to cash in on his other
advantages.

15 R–K1	**Q–B2**
16 Q–K2	**R–K1**
17 K–R1	**N–K4**
18 Q–B2	**N–B5**
19 B–Q4	**N–KR4**

It would be dangerous for Black to
grab the QNP because of 19 ...
N × NP 20 KR–QN1! N–B5 21
P–QR4 P × P 22 R × P when White
has taken the initiative on the
Q-wing.

In contrast, after 19 ... N × NP
20 N × P would be a mistake on
account of 20 ... N × P! 21 P × N
(not 21 Q–B1 N–Q7 22 Q–N1
N × P!) 21 ... Q × Q 22 B × Q P × N
23 QR–N1 N–B5 24 R × P B × P
when Black's minor pieces are
co-operating rather well.

20 N–Q1	**N–K4**
21 B–B3	**R–K3**
22 P–QR4	**P × P**
23 R × P	**N–N3**
24 R–R5!	**N–K4**
25 R–B1!	

Overprotecting the queen so that
White will be able to play N–K3
without fear of the reply ... B × P.

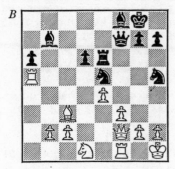

25 ...	**B–K2**
26 N–K3	**B–Q1**
27 R–R4	**N–KB5**

After 27 ... B–N3 28 B–Q4 B × B
29 R × B White will continue with
R/1–Q1 and N–B5, piling the pressure
onto Black's weak QP.

28 R–Q1

Threatening 29 B × N winning a
pawn.

28 ...	**B–K2**
29 R–N4	**B–KB1**
30 R/4–Q4	**P–N3**
31 R/4–Q2	**Q–B2**

So as to free the KB from its
defence of the QP.

32 Q–R4!	**Q–B2**

32 ... N–R4 would be answered
by 33 N–B5! and if 33 ... P × N
34 P × P! R–R3 35 B × N P × B
36 R–Q7 with a very strong attack.

33 B × N	**R × B**

Black must keep the Q-file closed:

33 ... P×B 34 R–Q7 R–K2
35 N–N4! and the game is over.

34 N–N4	R–K3
35 R×P!	R×R
36 R×R	N–R4

36 ... B×R?? 37 N–R6+
would be the quickest way to end the
game.

37 Q–Q8	Q–KB5
38 R–Q1	B×P
39 P×B	Q×N
40 R–KB1	N–B5
41 P–KN3	N–K3
42 Q–Q5	

Threatening 43 R–B6.

42 ... K–N2

If 42 ... B–K2 43 R–B4! Q–R6
44 P–KN4! or 42 ... K–R1 43 R–B6
B–B4 (43 ... B–N2 44 Q–R8+)
44 Q–K5! and in each case Black can
resign.

43 Q–Q7+	K–N1
44 R–B4!	Q–R6
45 Q–KB7+	K–R1
46 R–R4	1–0

Matsukevich–Vooremaa
Corres 1966–7

1 P–K4	P–QB4
2 N–KB3	P–Q3
3 P–Q4	P×P
4 N×P	N–KB3
5 N–QB3	P–QR3
6 B–KN5	QN–Q2
7 B–QB4	Q–R4
8 Q–Q2	P–K3
9 0–0–0	P–N4

9 ... B–K2 10 KR–K1 0–0
11 K–N1! leaves White threatening
12 N–Q5! If then 11 ... Q–B2 we
have reached the position of example
72.

10 B–N3

10 B×KP P×B 11 N×KP seems
difficult to justify after 11 ... K–B2!
Shianovsky–Aronin, USSR Ch
½-final 1959, continued: 12 B×N
N×B 13 N–N5+ K–N1 14 P–B4
P–N5 15 N–Q5 P–R3 and Black was
well on top. In Tal–Kolarov, Reykjavik 1957, White tried 12 N×B
R×N 13 Q×P and after 13 ...
P–N5! 14 N–Q5 Q×P 15 KR–K1,
Kolarov could have drawn by 15 ...
Q–R8+ 16 K–Q2 Q×P 17 P–K5
Q–Q5+ 18 K–B1 Q–R8+ etc.
Instead he chose a more difficult
course: 15 ... K–N1 16 B×N P×B?
(the losing move. 16 ... N×B
17 N–K7+ K–B2 18 N–B6 K–N1
should lead to a draw, but not 18
P–K5 because of 18 ... B–N5!
19 Q–B7 N–K1 20 Q–N7 Q–R8+
21 K–Q2 Q×P 22 N–Q5+ K–N1
23 Q×R B×R 24 R×B Q×KP
when White has no satisfactory move.)
17 R–Q3! Q–R8+ 18 K–Q2 Q×P
19 P–KB4 P–N6 20 N–K7+ K–R1
21 R×P and White soon won.

10 B–Q5? is also a mistake, not
because of 10 ... P×B? (11 N–B6
Q–N3 12 P×P when Black runs into
grave difficulties on the K-file as in
many examples of chapters 6 and 7),
but because of 10 ... P–N5! 11 B×R
P×N 12 P×P N–N3 13 B–B6+
B–Q2 14 B×B+ N/B3×B when
White's Q-side is in shreds.

10 ... B–N2

Now 10 ... P–N5 would be to no
avail because White has the traditional sacrifice 11 N–Q5! at his
disposal, e.g. 11 ... P×N 12 P×P
B–N2 (12 ... B–K2? 13 N–B6)
13 KR–K1+ with a strong attack, or
11 ... N×P 12 Q×P! when Black

is completely lost (12 ... Q × Q
13 N–B7 mate).

11 KR–K1

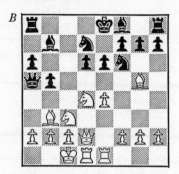

11 ...   N–B4

There are four alternatives worthy
of examination:

a) 11 ... P–N5? 12 N–Q5! P × N
(or 12 ... N × P 13 N × KP! N × Q
14 N/5–B7+ Q × N 15 N × Q mate)
13 P × P+ K–Q1 14 N–B6+ B × N
15 P × B N–K4 16 Q–B4 and Black
has no good move.

b) 11 ... R–B1 12 P–K5! and now:

b1) 12 ... P–N5 13 P × N P × N
14 Q–B4 N–B4 15 B × P! P × B
16 N × P N–K5 (if 16 ... N × N
17 BP × P B × P 18 R × N+ K–Q2
19 Q × P mate) 17 P–B7+ K–Q2
18 N × B+ QR × N 19 R × N K–B1
(or 19 ... B × R 20 Q × P+ K–B1
21 Q–K6+ etc.) 20 R–B4+ 1–0
(after 20 ... K–N1 21 K–N1!
Black has no swindling chances)
Berta–Kallinger, Corres 1965/6;

b2) 12 ... P × P 13 B × N N × B
(13 ... P × B 14 N × KP!) 14 R × P
led to a quick win for White in
Gligoric–Sofrevski, Yugoslav Ch
1959: 14 ... B–N5 15 N × KP! P × N
16 R × KP+ B–K2 17 R × B+ 1–0;

b3) 12 ... N × P 13 N × KP! P × N
14 R × N P × R 15 B × N Q–B2 (if

15 ... B–Q4 16 B × KP!) 16
B × P/K5 Q–B2 (after 16 ... Q–B3
17 N–K4 White has ample compensation for his slight material deficit)
17 P–B4 B–B3 18 Q–K2 B–K2 (so far
we have followed Shamkovich–Titen-
ko, Trud TU Ch 1963) 19 P–N4 ±

c) 11 ... B–K2 12 P–B4 N–B4
13 B × N P × B! (The game Korchnoi–
Polugayevsky, USSR Ch 1958,
showed that if Black recaptures with
the bishop his centre is very weak and
prone to sudden collapse: 13 ...
B × B 14 P–K5 B–R5 15 P–N3 B–Q1
16 P × P 0–0 17 P–QR3! B–KB3
18 B–R2 Q–N3 19 P–QN4 N–Q2
20 N × KP! P × N 21 B × P+ K–R1
22 B × N P–QR4 and now 23 Q–K3!
would have been strong ±) 14 Q–K3
0–0–0 (not 14 ... P–N5? 15 N–Q5!
B–Q1 16 Q–N3! N × B+   17
N × N ±) 15 P–QR3 N × B+ 16
N × N Q–B2   17 P–B5 K–N1
18 N–Q4 B–QB1 19 R–Q3 B–Q2
20 K–N1 R–QB1 21 Q–R3 Q–B4
22 Q–R5 QR–B1 23 N/3–K2 B–Q1
24 R/1–Q1 B–K2 25 R–QN3 K–R1
26 R–QB3 Q–R2 27 N–B4! P–K4
28 N–Q5 B–Q1 29 N–B6 and Black
can hardly move, Estrin–Titjen,
5th World Corres Ch ½-final 1962–5.

These three variations and the
game itself all show how precariously
placed is Black's king in the centre
and how easily it can be laid bare
by a sacrificial attack. There is one
remaining alternative at move eleven
and this may actually make the whole
system playable for Black:

d) 11 ... 0–0–0! (Black's king moves
away from the centre at once and
... P–N5! now becomes a genuine
possibility) and now:

d1) 12 P–QR3 B–K2 13 K–N1 K–N1

14 P–B3 P–KR3   15 B–K3 N–K4
16 N–R2 Q × Q   17 B × Q N/3–Q2
18 B–N4 N–B4   19 N–B1 P–N4
20 B–R2 P–KN5 21 N/1–N3 P × P
22 P × P N–B5 and White's position
is becoming somewhat constricted;
Sherwin–Reshevsky, USA Ch 1959–
60;

d2) 12 P–B3 P–R3 (12 ... B–K2 may
also be playable and if 13 K–N1?
P–N5 14 N–R4 N × P winning a
pawn, Kahyai–Saidy, Tel Aviv 1964)
13 B–K3 P–N5 14 N/3–K2 P–Q4
15 P × P N × P 16 B–N1 N–B4
17 P–QB4 P × Pep 18 N × BP N × N
19 Q × N Q × Q+ 20 P × Q P–N4
21 B–QB2 B–Q3 with roughly even
chances, Langeweg–Saidy, Tel Aviv
1964;

d3) 12 P–B4 P–N5 13 N–R4 P–R3
14 B × N N × B with an unclear
position.

12 P–K5!   **P × P**

12 ... P–N5 is met by 13 N–R4!,
e.g. 13 ... N × N 14 P × N N–B4
15 B × P! or 13 ... N × B+ 14
RP × N N–Q4   15 P × P B × P
16 N–KB5!

13 B × P!!   **P × B**
14 N × KP   **N/4–Q2**
Or 14 ... N × N 15 B × N!
15 B × N   **N × B**

In Ivkov–Petrosian, Bled 1961, the
players now agreed to a draw because
of mutual fright. But White has much
more.

16 R × P   **K–B2**
17 Q–K3

17 Q–B4 K–N1   18 R–KB5
(followed by R × N) also wins as
Ivkov discovered during the post-
mortem of his game with Petrosian.

17 ...   **P–R3**

O'Kelly shows that there is nothing
better than returning the piece:

a) 17 ... K–N1 18 N × B R × N
(18 ... N–N5 19 Q–N5 N × R loses
to 20 N–K6 N–N3 21 R–Q7)
19 R–K7 B–B1 20 Q–R7! with
killing pressure, e.g. 20 ... N–K1
(or 20 ... N–R4) 21 Q–B5 N–B3
22 N–K4 Q × P 23 N × N+ P × N
24 Q–B7!++

b) 17 ... B–B1 18 N–N5+ K–N1
19 R–K8!! (threatening 20 R × QB)
19 ... N × R 20 Q × N Q–B2
21 R–Q8 Q–KB5+ 22 K–N1 and
Black has no answer to the threat of
23 N–Q5, e.g. 22 ... Q × BP 23
N–B3! or 22 ... P–R3 23 N–Q5!

18 N × B   **KR × N**

If 18 ... K × N 19 R–K7 (threatening 20 Q–K6), and now 19 ...
R–K1 20 R/1–Q7± or 19 ... B–B1
20 Q–B5 K–N1 21 N–K4!±

19 R–K7+   **K–N1**
20 R × B

White has two extra pawns and a
strong attack.

20 ...   **P–N5**
21 N–Q5!   **N × N**
22 Q–K5!   **R–B3**

Or 22 ... R–B2 23 R × N and
24 Q–K6.

23 R × N   **1–0**

If 23 ... Q × P 24 R × KNP+!

There are two distinct themes associated with the sacrifice of White's Q4 knight on K6. If Black has already castled K-side the purpose of the sacrifice is to answer the recapture ...P×N with B×KP+ (or Q×KP+), driving Black's king into the corner, and then to launch an attack which will hopefully lead to mate or substantial material gain:

16 N×KP! P×N If 16 ... Q–B1 17 Q–R3 **17 Q×KP+ K–R1 18 Q–R3 P–K5** If 18 ... P–R3 19 P×P and White's attack is very strong. **19 B×KP N–B3 20 N–Q5 Q–B1 21 B–B5 Q–Q1 22 N×N P–R3 23 QR–Q1 B×N 24 R×Q and White won,** Vasiliev–Karasev, USSR Armed Forces Team Ch 1967.

Bannik–Suetin (76) is another typical example.

But the sacrifice is normally made when Black's king is still in the centre—the point then is to keep it there. White's task is easiest when Black has played ... P–KR3 for then it is possible to start the attack with a disrupting check on the KR5–K8 diagonal. The three examples that follow all exhibit this idea as does Lobzhanidze–Buslayev (77).

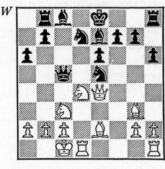

16 N×P P×N 17 B–R5+ K–B1 18 KR–B1+ B–B3 If 18 ... K–N1 19 R×N B×R 20 B×N R–KB1 21 R×R+ B×R 22 Q–N6 Q–K6+ 23 K–N1 Q–N4 24 Q–B7+ K–R2 25 N–K4 ± ± **19 B×N N×B 20 R–Q8+ K–K2 21 R×R N–B3 22 R–K8+ K–Q3 23 Q–KB4+ P–K4 24 N–K4+ and White won,** Filipowicz–Drozd, Polish Ch 1964.

See diagram next page

13 N×KP! P×N 14 P–K5 P×P 15 Q–N6+ K–B1 If 15 ... K–Q1 16 B×B Q×B 17 Q×NP R–KN1 18 Q–B7 with an irresistible attack.

16 B × N B/K2 × B Or 16 ... N × B
17 B × B Q × B 18 P × P and 19
P × N. **17 B–R5 N–B4 18 P × P
B × KP 19 KR–B1+ B–KB3 20
P–QN4! B–K5** If 20 ... N–R5
21 R × B+ P × R 22 Q × BP+
K–N1 23 Q × KP+ ± ± **21 R × B+
P × R 22 Q × BP+ K–N1 23 N × B
1–0** Because of 23 ... N × N 24
Q × KP+ followed by a fatal rook
check, Mukhin–Platonov, TU Spar-
takiad 1969.

16 N × KP P × N 17 Q–N6+ If
17 Q × P immediately, Black may
eventually be able to consolidate his
K-side and castle long. **17 ... K–Q1
18 Q × NP R–KB1 19 B–N4 Q–B5
20 R × N+! K × R 21 R–Q1+
K–B3 22 Q × B** Threat 23 Q–Q6
mate **22 ... Q–B5+ 23 K–N1
Q × KP 24 B–B3+ R × B 25 P × R**
and White had a sound extra pawn
and the better position, Cherskikh–
Gaspariants, Lokomotiv TU Ch 1961.

Bannik–Suetin
Minsk 1962

Lobzhanidze–Buslayev
Georgian Ch 1962

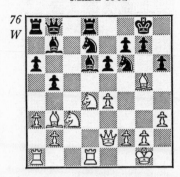

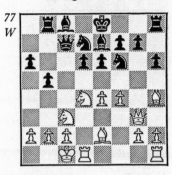

**16 N×KP! P×N 17 B×KP+ K–R1
18 B/5×N N×B?** Not 18 ... P×B
19 Q–R5. But better was 18 ...
B–R7+ 19 K–R1 N×B 20 R×R+
Q×R 21 K×B Q–Q3+ 22 P–K5
Q×B 23 P×N Q×P when Black's
pieces are more active than in the
game. **19 P–K5 B×KP 20 R×R+
Q×R 21 Q×B Q–N3** If 21 ...
Q–Q7 22 Q–K2 Q×Q 23 N×Q
R–Q1 Black's active rook is insufficient compensation for the pawn.
21 ... Q–K2 is answered by 22 N–K2
and 23 N–B4. **22 B–B7 R–Q1
23 B–N6 N–Q2 24 Q–N3 N–K4
25 B–B5 N–B5 26 P–N3!** Giving back
the pawn so that Black's knight will
be out of play when White com-
mences the next wave of his attack.
**26 ... N×P 27 R–Q1! R×R+
28 N×R B–Q4 29 N–K3 B–N1**
On 29 ... B×QNP 30 N–N4 comes
with gain of tempo. **30 N–N4 B–R2
31 Q–K5 B×B 32 Q×B P–N5
33 N–K5 Q–B2?** The losing move.
Better is 33 ... Q–N1, keeping
White's queen out of the eighth rank.
**34 N–N6+ K–N1 35 Q–KB8+
K–R2 36 N–K7 Q–B8+ 37 K–R2
P–KR4 38 P–B4 Q–B7 39 Q–B7 1–0**

**13 N×KP   P×N
14 Q×P   R–R2**
If 14 ... R–N1 15 B–R5+ K–Q1
16 Q×P threatening 17 P–K5.
15 Q–N6+   R–B2
Forced. 15 ... K–Q1 loses to
16 B×N N×B 17 P–K5.
**16 P–K5   P×P
17 R×N   Q×R**
If 17 ... N×R 18 B–R5 ± ±
18 B×N?
Surely 18 R–Q1 is the correct
winning idea, e.g. 18 ... N–Q4
19 B–R5 B×B 20 Q–N8+ K–K2
21 N×N+ P×N 22 Q×R+ K–Q1
23 R×P ± ±
**18 ...   B×B
19 R–Q1   Q–K2**
The point. In the previous note
this move was not available to Black.
**20 B–R5   B–QN2
21 Q–N8+   Q–B1
22 B×R+   K–K2
23 Q–N6   Q–N2**
23 ... Q×B?? 24 R–Q7+
**24 P×P Q×Q 25 B×Q B×KP
26 P–KN3 ½–½**
After 26 ... B×N 27 P×B,
Black's passed KP is adequate compensation for White's extra QBP.

Christiansen–Reshevsky
USA Ch 1977

W

15 N×P!

If 15 P×P at once, 15 . . . N–KN6 16
Q–N4 N×R 17 R×N N×B 18 P×N,
and White has nothing to show for his
material deficit.

15 . . .	**P×N**
16 P×P	**N–KN6**
17 B–N6+	

The difference. Now Black's QB4
knight has nothing to capture on . . .
Q6.

17 . . .	**K–Q2**
18 Q–N4	**N×N+**

18 . . . N×R is met by 19 B×N, and if
19 . . . P×B 20 R–Q1+ B–Q4 21
R×B+

19 Q×N	**N–K5**

Black cannot keep his extra piece and
his king is horribly placed in the centre.

20 B–Q4	**N–B3**
21 KR–K1	**P–K4**
22 P×P	**P×P**
23 B×P	**Q–N3+**
24 K–R1	**B–Q3**
25 QR–Q1	**N–Q4**
26 B–K4	**KR–K1**
27 B/K4×B	**K–B2**
28 Q–B4+	**1–0**

Panchenko–Psakhis
Vilnius 1978

W

12 N×KP

The point here is simply to expose
Black's king in the centre so that it will
have to run to the Q-side, where it will
be quite unsafe.

12 . . .	**P×N**
13 B×P	

It is clear that Black will never be
able to castle short so he now seeks the
only route to (temporary) safety.

13 . . .	**Q–B4**
14 N–Q5	**B×N**

On 14 . . . 0–0–0 White has, at the
very least, 15 N×N P×N 16 B×P,
forcing the win of material.

15 P×B	**0–0–0**
16 R–Q3	**K–N2**
17 R–QB3	**Q–Q5**
18 P–QR4	**Q–K4**
19 B–K3	**N–B4**
20 P×P	**P–QR4**
21 P–N6!	

The pawn cannot be taken: 21 . . .
K×P 22 R–N3+ and 23 Q–N5,
winning at once.

21 . . .	**B–K2**
22 R–R1	**R–R1**
23 Q–N5	**R–R3**
24 Q–B6+	**K–N1**
25 Q–B7+	**K–R1**
26 P–N7+	**N×P**
27 Q–B8+	**1–0**

Robatsch–Tal
Leipzig 1960

1 P–K4 P–QB4   2 N–KB3 P–Q3
3 P–Q4 P×P   4 N×P N–KB3
5 N–QB3 P–QR3   6 B–QB4 P–K3
7 P–QR3 B–K2   8 B–R2 0–0
9 0–0 P–QN4   10 P–B4 QN–Q2

Fischer prefers 10 ... B–N2
11 P–B5 P–K4 12 N/4–K2 QN–Q2
13 N–N3 R–B1!, e.g. 14 B–K3 N–N3
15 B×N Q×B+ 16 K–R1 Q–K6!
with a good game for Black,
Robatsch–Fischer, Havana 1965.
After Robatsch lost that game he
telephoned Fischer (who was playing
by telegraph from New York) to find
out where he had gone wrong and
was informed that '... the whole
variation is worthless'!

11 R–B3!

A strong manoeuvre, preparing for
a direct attack against the black king.

11 ...   **B–N2**
12 R–R3!   **R–B1**

It would be a great mistake to take
the pawn: 12 ... N×P? 13 N×KP!
P×N 14 B×P+ K–R1 (or 14 ...
R–B2 15 Q–R5) 15 R×P+! K×R
16 Q–R5 mate.

13 B–K3   **Q–B2?!**

The KP is still poisoned, but a more
active possibility was 13 ... R×N!
14 P×R B×P with good counterplay.

See diagram next column

14 N×KP!   **P×N**
15 B×P+   **K–R1**
16 B–Q4   **B–Q1!**

If 16 ... N–B4 17 B–B5 with
dangerous pressure against KR7.

17 Q–K2?

If 17 B–KB5 as suggested by
Ragozin, not 17 ... P–R3? 18 K–R1!
Q–B5 (or 18 ... Q–B3 19 R×P+!

P×R 20 Q–R5 N–K4 21 Q×P+
K–N1 22 B–K6+ N–B2 23 R–KB1
and Black can resign) 19 B×N/7
N×B 20 R×P+ K–N1 21 Q–R5!
P×R 22 Q–N6 mate. Instead 17 ...
Q–B5! at once is very strong (the
threat is 18 ... Q×B+), e.g.
18 P–K5 P×P 19 P×P B–N3
20 B×B Q–B3 21 Q–K2 Q×B+
22 K–R1 KR–K1 and Black should
win.

Correct is 17 P–KN4 N–B4 18
B–B5 N/4×P 19 P–N5 when Black's
chances are rather dismal.

17 ...   **Q–B3**
18 K–R1

Otherwise 18 ... B–N3 will be
even stronger.

18 ...   **B–N3!**

The start of Black's counterattack.

19 B×N/7   **Q×B**

Not 19 ... N×B 20 Q–R5±±

20 B×B   **R–B5!**
21 P–QN3   **Q×R!!**
22 P×Q   **R×N**
23 K–N1   **B×P**
24 R–QB1   **R×RP**

Black has quite good value for his
queen sacrifice. White's bishop is
rather impotent, his rook passive and
his king indecently exposed.

25 B–B2   **P–Q4**

26 B–N3   **N–R4**
27 Q–K3

If 27 Q–N4 N×B!   28 Q×R
N–K7+   29 K–B2 N×P∓ ∓

27 ...   **P–N4?**

Why? Simply 27 ... N×B   28
P×N P–KR4 and 29 ... P–R5 is
devastating. 29 Q–B2 allows mate in
one and if 29 Q–Q2 R×NP+
30 K–B2 R–KB6+ and 31 ...
R/1×P. Black will win either by
direct force of arms or by eventually
promoting his KRP.

28 Q–Q4+   **K–N1**
29 R–K1!   **N×B**
30 R×B!

30 P×N R×NP+ is still very
dangerous for White.

30 ...	**P×R**
31 Q–Q5+	**R–B2**
32 Q–Q8+	**K–N2**
33 Q×P+	**K–R1**
34 Q–Q8+	**K–N2**
35 K–N2	**R–R3**
36 P×N	**R–K3**
37 Q–N5+	**K–B1**
38 P–B5	**R–K1**
39 P–B6	**P–K6**
40 Q–QB5+	**K–N1**
41 Q–B6	

White plays for a win!

41 ...   **R/1–KB1**

Naturally not 41 ... R/2–B1
42 Q–Q7± ±

42 Q–K6 K–R1	**43 Q×KP R×P**
44 Q–Q4 P–R3	**45 P–R4 P×P**
46 Q×P R–KN3	**47 Q–Q4+**
R/1–B3 ½–½	

Kostov–Minev
Bulgarian Ch 1960

1 P–K4 P–QB4   2 N–KB3 P–Q3
3 P–Q4 P×P   4 N×P N–KB3
5 N–QB3 P–QR3   6 B–KN5 P–K3
7 P–B4 P–KR3   8 B–R4 B–K2
9 Q–B3 Q–B2   10 0–0–0 QN–Q2
11 B–K2

11 B–Q3! P–QN4! 12 P–K5! B–N2
13 N×KP! is the theoretical continuation, taking advantage of Black's
weakness at KN3: 13 ... P×N
14 B–N6+ K–B1 (if 14 ... K–Q1
15 Q–R3 P×P   16 Q×P with an
unavoidable attack) 15 P×N! B×Q
16 P×B+ K–N1   17 P×B N–B3!
18 B×N P×B 19 P–K8=Q+ R×Q
20 B×R K–B1! with a very double-
edged position which Black can
probably hold. Unger–Bengtsson,
Corres 1967.

The text became well known in the
line without ... P–KR3, B–R4
through the famous game Keres–
Fischer, Bled 1959, in which Keres
sacrificed his queen in the same
manner as White does here.

11 ...   **P–QN4!**

Not 11 ... P–KN4 12 P×P N–K4
(12 ... N–R2? 13 P–N6!) 13 Q–B1
P×P   14 B×NP when Black has
nothing to show for the pawn.

12 P–K5	**B–N2**
13 P×N	**B×Q**
14 B×B	**P–Q4**

Probably best is 14 ... B×P 15 B×B N×B 16 B×R P–Q4, reaching a position identical to the Keres–Fischer game with the unimportant exception that in that game Black's KRP was on KR2. This variation is roughly equal with Black having whatever chances are going. But after the text the game becomes very unclear.

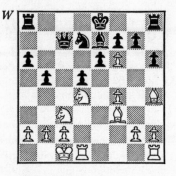

15 N×KP

Not 15 P×B?? Q×P+ winning back the piece.

15 ...   P×N
16 B–R5+   K–Q1?

Pachman recommends 16 ... P–N3 (creating a safe square for the king at KN2) 17 B×P+ K–B1 18 P×B+ K–N2 when 19 P–B5 loses to 19 ... Q–B5+. But White can improve with 19 B–N3! and if 19 ... N–B3 then 20 P–K8=Q N×Q 21 B×N KR×B 22 P–B5 with an unclear position.

Now Black is lost.

17 P×B+   K–B1
18 KR–B1!

Preventing the fork ... Q×P+ and preparing to smash Black's pawn centre.

18 ...   K–N2
19 P–B5!

Smash.

19 ...   Q–QB5

If Black moves, or captures with, the KP his king becomes exposed to a raging attack from White's rooks and bishops.

20 B–N3 N–B3   21 B–K2 Q–B4 22 P×P QR–QB1 23 R–Q2 N–K5 24 N×N P×N   25 B–Q6 Q–N4 26 B–KB4 Q–N3 27 R–Q7+ K–R1 28 R/1–Q1   Q×KP   29 B–K3 Q–QB3 30 P–B3 Q–B3 31 R–R7+ K–N1 32 R/1–Q7 1–0

Boleslavsky–Aronin
USSR 1960

1 P–K4 P–QB4 2 N–KB3 N–QB3 3 P–Q4 P×P   4 N×P N–B3 5 N–QB3 P–Q3 6 B–QB4 P–K3 7 0–0 B–K2 8 B–K3 0–0 9 B–N3 P–QR3 10 P–B4 N–QR4
11 Q–B3   Q–B2?

After this move Black has little Q-side counterplay. Stronger was 11 ... P–QN4, e.g. 12 P–N4 P–N5 13 N/3–K2 N×B 14 RP×N B–N2 with much pressure against White's KP, or 12 P–K5 B–N2 13 Q–R3 (13 P×N B×Q 14 BP×B Q×P 15 R×B is unsound—Black has too much control of the centre) 13 ... N–K1 14 P–B5 QP×P 15 P×P P×N 16 P×P+ K–R1 17 P×N=Q R×Q 18 QR–Q1 B–KB3 with a very good game for Black.

12 P–N4!   P–QN4

But here this move is not so forceful. Nevertheless, it is probably best. 12 ... N×B 13 RP×N B–Q2 14 P–N5 N–K1 15 P–B5 leaves Black with a very passive position and the only other way to continue his Q-side counterplay, 12 ... N–B5, also fails to distract White from the persuance of his attack: 13 P–N5 N–K1 (if 13 ... N–Q2 14 N–B5! P×N 15 N–Q5 Q–Q1 16 B×N with a decisive positional advantage) 14 P–B5 N×B 15 Q×N, and Black's position is most unpleasant, e.g.

a) 15 ... P–K4? 16 N–Q5! P×N 17 Q–N3 Q–Q2 18 R–B4 and Black, with all his pieces badly placed, is faced with unsurmountable defensive problems; or

b) 15 ... Q–B4 16 K–R1 N–B2 (16 ... P–K4 17 N–Q5 B–Q1 18 N–KB3 Q×Q 19 N×Q is relatively best but Black's badly placed pieces, his lack of space, and the gaping hole at his Q4 would be sufficient to cause his demise) 17 P–B6 B–Q1 18 N–R4 Q–R2 19 N–N6! P–K4 (if 19 ... R–N1? 20 N×B R×N 21 P×P K×P 22 N–B5+ winning the queen; or 19 ... Q×N 20 P×P R–K1 21 Q–B4 R–K2 22 P–N6! RP×N 23 Q–R6±±) 20 N×B Q×N (or 20 ... P×N 21 Q–R3±±) 21 Q×Q P×Q 22 N×P with a decisive advantage.

13 P–N5   N–Q2?

Better was 13 ... N–K1 14 P–B5 N×B 15 RP×N when Black has a difficult game but there is nothing immediately killing for White.

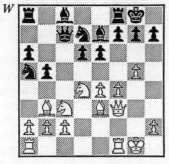

14 N×KP!	P×N
15 B×P+	K–R1
16 N–Q5	Q–Q1
17 Q–R5	

Having seized the key squares in the centre, White goes over to attacking mode. The dual threats are 18 B–KB5 and 18 P–B5 followed by 19 P–N6.

17 ...   N–B4

Boleslavsky suggested 17 ... Q–K1 18 P–N6 N–KB3! (not 18 ... Q×P+ 19 Q×Q P×Q 20 N×B) 19 N×N Q×P+ 20 Q×Q P×Q as the best defence, but Shamkovich points out that after 21 N–Q5 (not 21 B–Q5 B×N 22 B×R N–B5! 23 B–B1 B–R6 24 R–B3 B–Q5+ 25 K–R1 B–N5 26 R–KN3 N–K4! 27 K–N2 P–N4! with counterchances) White is a pawn to the good with the better position.

18 B×B	R×B
19 P–B5	B×P

The only move. If 19 ... K–N1 20 P–N6 P–R3 21 B×P P×B 22 Q×P R–KB2 23 P×R+ K×P 24 Q–N6+ K–B1 25 P–B6 with mate to follow.

20 B×B	Q–K1
21 Q×Q	KR×Q
22 P–B6!	

Now 22 ... P×P 23 B×P+ K–N1 24 P–N4 costs Black a piece.

22 ...   N–Q2

After 22 ... N×P 23 P–B7 N×B 24 P×R=Q+ R×Q 25 N–B7 White's material advantage will be ample.

23 P–B7 R×KP   24 N–N6 N–B1 25 N×R R–KN5+   26 K–R1 R×B 27 N×P P–N3   28 QR–K1 R–Q4 29 R–K8 K–N2   30 R–Q8 R–K4 31 N–K8+ K–R3   32 N–B6 1–0

Rossetto–Larsen
Portoroz 1958

1 P–K4	P–QB4
2 N–KB3	P–Q3
3 P–Q4	P×P
4 N×P	N–KB3
5 N–QB3	P–QR3
6 B–KN5	QN–Q2
7 Q–Q2	

7 B–QB4 is well known to be the strongest move.

7 ...	P–R3
8 B–R4	P–K3
9 B–K2	P–QN4?

9 ... N–B4 10 P–B3 B–K2 gives Black a comfortable game.

10 N×KP!

For the piece White obtains only one pawn but the important issue is the strength of his attack and not the material situation.

10 ...	P×N
11 B–R5+	K–K2
12 0–0–0	Q–B2
13 KR–K1!	K–Q1

If 13 ... P–N5? 14 N–Q5+! P×N 15 P×P+ N–K4 16 R×N+, or 13 ... P–N4? 14 B–N3 N–K4 15 N×P! P×N 16 B×N and 16 ... P×B? loses at once to 17 Q–N4+

14 P–K5!	P×P
15 P–B4	

Opening files for the attack. 15 ... P×P can be answered by 16 N–Q5! P×N? 17 R–K8 mate.

15 ...	B–K2
16 R×P	P–N5

If 16 ... N×B 17 B×B+ K×B (or 17 ... K–K1 18 B–Q6 followed by 19 R×N and the attack still rages) 18 N–Q5+ ±±

17 N–K4	N×N
18 B×B+	K×B

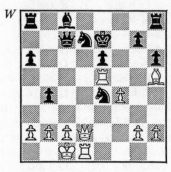

19 R×P+?

After 19 R×N! White's attack would be very dangerous, e.g. 19 ... Q–B4 20 P–B5 P–K4 (or 20 ... N–B3 21 R–QB4! Q–N3 22 R–B6!) 21 R–N4 R–KN1 22 R–N6; 19 ... N–B4 20 R–B4; or 19 ... P–R4 20 R×KP+! K×R 21 R–K1+ K–B3 22 Q–Q4+.

19 ...	K×R
20 Q–Q5+	K–K2
21 Q×N/4+	K–Q1
22 Q×R	Q–N2

Forcing a very favourable endgame.

23 Q×Q	B×Q
24 B–N4	B–B3
25 R–Q6	K–B2
26 R–N6	R–KN1
27 B–K2	P–QR4

28 K–Q2 If 28 B–B4 B–K5 29 R–R6 R–QR1.

28 ...	N–B3
29 B–Q3	B–K1

30 R–N3 B–B2   31 P–QR3 P×P
32 P×P N–R4   33 R–K3 R–K1
34 P–N3 N–B3   35 P–R3   35 R×R
and 36 K–K3 might have offered
slightly more hope. **35 ... N–R4
36 R–B3 B–Q4   37 R–B1 B–N7
38 R–KN1 B×P   39 K–B3 R–K6
0–1**

Vitolinsh–Yuferov
USSR 1972

1 P–K4	P–QB4
2 N–KB3	P–Q3
3 P–Q4	P×P
4 N×P	N–KB3
5 N–QB3	P–QR3
6 B–KN5	P–K3
7 P–B4	QN–Q2

This double-edged alternative to
7 ... B–K2 was introduced into
master praxis by Polugayevsky in
1967.

8 Q–B3	Q–B2
9 0–0–0	P–N4

The point of Polugayevsky's idea—
Black intends to start his Q-side
counterattack even before he has
completed his development and seen
to the safety of his king.

10 P–K5!
The most direct attempt at refutation. White smashes open the centre
to denude the black king.

10 ...	B–N2
11 Q–R3	P×P

See diagram next column

12 N×KP	P×N
13 Q×KP+	B–K2
14 B×P!?	

This second sacrifice is possibly not
the best way for White to continue
his attack. Zhelyandinov–Polugay-

evsky, USSR Ch 1967 went 14 N×P
P×N 15 B×P 0–0–0 16 Q×B P×P
17 Q–N4 N–K4   18 Q×P R–Q4
19 R×R N×R   20 Q–B5+ K–N1
21 R–K1 N–KN3, and now 22
P–KN3 would have left White on
top. Since that game 14 N×P has
not been played in master chess but
unless Espig's 18 K–N1 (see the note
to 18 Q×B) turns out to be completely convincing 14 N×P may soon
replace 14 B×P as the main line.

14 B×N is not so good: 14 ...
P×B (not 14 ... N×B 15 B×P+!
K–B1 16 P×P B–B1 17 Q–B6—
*17 N–Q5 B×Q   18 N×Q is also
strong*—17 ... Q–R2 18 P×N P×P
19 B–B4 K–N2 20 KR–K1 R–QN1
21 R–Q3 B–KB4 22 R–N3+ B–N3
23 N–Q5 1–0. Richardson–Mostowfi,
6th Corres Olympiad) 15 B–K2
P–KR4   16 N–Q5 (not 16 N×P
P×N   17 B×NP 0–0–0!   18 Q×B
N–B4   19 Q×BP B–K5   20 B–B4
B×NP 21 KR–N1 B–B6 22 R×R+
R×R 23 P×P B–N5∓ Westerinen–
Jacobsen, Raach 1969) 16 ... B×N
17 R×B N–N3   18 B×RP+ R×B
19 Q–N8+ B–B1 20 Q–K6+ with a
draw by perpetual check.

14 ...   **P×B**
If 14 ... 0–0–0   15 B×N/7+
R×B 16 P×P±±

15 N×P   **Q–B3**
16 N–Q6+   **K–Q1**
17 P×P

Not 17 N×B+ K–B2 18 Q×B R×P with counterplay, nor 17 N–B7+? K–B2 18 Q×B because of 18 ... N–Q4! 19 R×N Q×R 20 N×R R×P 21 K–N1 R–R1∓ ∓ Haag–Kluger, Hungary 1968.

This position is crucial for the assessment of the variation beginning with 14 B×P. Although two pieces down White has all the winning chances because of his numerous immediate threats based on the exposed position of Black's king.

17 ...   **K–B2**

Two other moves have been tried:
a) 17 ... N–Q4 18 B×B+ N×B 19 Q–B7! B–R3 20 P–K6 N–QB4 21 R–Q4 N–Q6+ 22 K–N1 N–K4 23 N–B5+ N–Q4 24 R×N+! 1–0 (because of 24 ... Q×R 25 P–K7+) Astashin–Freider, USSR 1968;
b) 17 ... R–K1 18 P×N P×P 19 N×B+ K–B2 20 R×N+! Q×R 21 B–B4+ K–B1 (so far we have been following the game Bronstein–Ciocaltea, Kislovodsk 1968) 22 Q–N3! Q–R5! 23 Q–KB3 R–R3 24 R–Q1 with a slight advantage to White. Analysis by Estrin.

18 Q×B

18 K–N1 may be better, the idea being to protect the QRP before continuing with the attack and thereby to deprive Black of any counterplay based on ... R×P followed by ... R–R8+. Espig–Bromeyer, East Germany 1970 continued 18 ... N–Q4 19 B×B R×P 20 P–B4! (20 K×R?? N–N5+) with a persevering attack.

Another possibility is Bondarevsky's suggestion of 18 B×N which deprives Black of the defensive resource ... N–Q4.

18 ...   **R×P**

Also possible is 18 ... N–Q4! 19 R×N Q×R 20 R–Q1 Q×KP with a very unclear position.

19 P×N   **R–R8+**
20 K–Q2   **Q–Q4+**

Not 20 ... Q×NP+? 21 K–B3 Q–B3+ 22 N–B4± ±

21 K–B3   **Q–R4+**

If 21 ... R×R 22 R×R Q×R 23 P×P R–KN1 24 N–K8+± ±

22 K–Q3   **Q–Q4+**

Not 22 ... R×R+ 23 R×R Q×B 24 N×B± ±

23 K–B3   ½–½

Neither player can avoid the repetition.

Stean–Browne
Nice Olympiad 1974
(Notes by Stean)

1 P–K4	P–QB4
2 N–KB3	P–Q3
3 P–Q4	P×P
4 N×P	N–KB3
5 N–QB3	P–QR3
6 B–KN5	QN–Q2

7 B–QB4	P–K3
8 O–O	P–R3
9 B×N	

If 9 B–R4, then 9 . . . N–K4 followed by 10 . . . P–KN4 gives Black a very comfortable position.

9 . . .	N×B
10 B–N3	P–QN3

A crucial stage in the game for Black, since natural development by 10 . . . B–K2 allows 11 P–KB4 O–O 12 P–B5 P–K4 13 N4–K2 followed by N–N3–R5 with clear advantage to White through control of his Q5 square. The other natural move for Black is 10 . . . P–QN4, when 11 P–QR4! is very embarrassing e.g. 11 . . . P–N5 12 N–B6 Q–N3 13 P–R5! Q–B4 14 N–Q5; also 11 R–K1 B–N2 12 P–QR4 P–N5 13 N–Q5 gives a strong attack. Hence the unusual-looking text move.

11 P–B4	B–N2
12 Q–Q3	B–K2

After 12 . . . R–QB1 13 B–R4+ is strong – 13 . . . P–QN4 14 N3×P P×N 15 Q×P+ Q–Q2 16 Q–R5 or `13 . . . N–Q2 14 P–K5 and 15 N×P

13 N×P

Probably the best of the many sacrificial possibilities. Firstly, observe that the positional continuation 13 P–B5 P–K4 14 N4–K2 R–B1 is not as

good as in the previous note, as White no longer has the manoeuvre N–N3–R5; so White tries tactically to exploit the white square weaknesses created by . . . P–KR3.

The other possibilities I considered were:
a) 13 B×P P×B 14 N×P Q–Q2 15 N×P+ K–B2 16 N–B5 QR–KN1! (threat Q×N) and Black has the attack.
b) 13 B×P P×B 14 P–K5 P×P 15 Q–N6+ K–Q2 16 P×P B–B4 17 QR–Q1 K–B2! and Black stands better.
c) 13 P–K5 P×P 14 N×P Q×Q 15 N×P+ K–Q2! (*15 . . . K–B1 16 P×Q K×N 17 P×P* regains the piece with advantage) 16 P×Q R–KN1! with advantage to Black again.

13 . . .	P×N
14 B×P	

The forcing 14 P–K5 N–Q4 15 Q–N6+ K–Q2 is unconvincing, as the black king will be quite safe on QB2.

14 . . . **P–QN4**

Trying to force the issue by threatening . . . Q–N3+ and . . . K–Q1–B2. Against purely passive defence to the threat (i.e. 15 P–K5), I was intending simply to improve my position with moves like QR–Q1 and K–R1 before breaking with P–K5, since it is difficult for Black to find any constructive moves, e.g. 14 . . . B–QB1 15 B–N3 does not relieve Black's position. If 14 . . . N–Q2 (to meet *15 P–K5* with *15 . . . N–B1*) 15 QR–Q1 N–B4 16 Q–R3 N×B 17 Q×N, then 18 P–K5 will be very strong.

15 P–K5	Q–N3+
16 K–R1	P×P
17 Q–N6+	K–Q1
18 Q–B7	

It is important not to play 18 QR–Q1+ K–B2 first, as Black can then defend with QR–K1.

18 . . .   Q–B4

There is no other defence to 19 QR–Q1+ e.g. 18 . . . B–B4 19 QR–Q1+ B–Q5 20 P×P.

19 P×P

Now Black is lost, as 19 . . . Q×P 20 QR–Q1+ wins a piece with check and 19 . . . N–Q2 20 KR–Q1 B–QB3 allows 21 B×N and P–K6. Hence the following counter-sacrifice.

19 . . .   B×P+
20 K×B   R–KB1

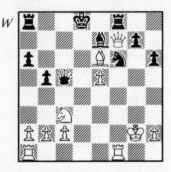

21 QR–Q1+

The clearest win. After 21 Q×P Q–B3+ 22 B–Q5 N×B 23 R×R+ K–Q2 there are still complications to be resolved. Also 21 Q–N6 Q×P is not clear at all.

21 . . .   K–B2
22 Q×P   R–KN1
23 P×N

Clearer than 23 B×R.

23 . . .   R×Q+
24 P×R   B–Q3

The point of White's play is that after 24 . . . Q–N4+ 25 K–R1 Q×P, 26 R–B7 wins a piece by 27 R×B+ and 28 N–Q5+

25 R–B7+   K–B3

25 . . . K–N3 26 N–Q5+ K–B3 27 B–Q7+ K–N2 28 B×P+ wins everything.

26 B–Q5+   K–N3
27 B×R   Q–N4+
28 K–R1   B–K4
29 P–N4

Threat N–Q5 mate. If 29 . . . B×N 30 R–Q6 mate.

29 . . .   P–QR4
30 R–N7+   K–B3

If 30 . . . K–R3 either 31 P–QR4 or 31 R×P Q×P 32 R×P+ K–N3 33 N–Q5 mate.

31 P–N8=Q   Q×Q
32 R–N8+   Resigns

This game won the Turover $1,000 brilliancy prize.

11 ... P–Q4

In one sense Black's pawn sacrifice ... P–Q4 does not belong in this volume: Its aims are far less clearly defined than those of the other, more substantial offers considered in the earlier chapters, and it is therefore impossible to single out a common theme which links our examples of this sacrifice. But for the sake of completeness and because the move ... P–Q4 is so fundamental to Sicilian theory I have decided to include this appendix.

As every Russian schoolboy knows, Black's strategy in the Sicilian revolves largely around his control of his Q4 square and his preparations for the pawn push ... P–Q4. If he can play this thrust without incurring the loss of a pawn Black will normally be able to achieve full equality (or better). Many examples of this theme can be found in the classical form of the Dragon Variation: **1 P–K4 P–QB4 2 N–KB3 P–Q3 3 P–Q4 P×P 4 N×P N–KB3 5 N–QB3 P–KN3 6 B–K2 B–N2 7 B–K3 N–B3**

See diagram next column

a) 8 P–KN4? P–Q4 9 P×P N×QP 10 N/B3×N Q×N 11 B–B3 Q–B5 12 N×N P×N 13 P–N3 B–B6+!∓
b) 8 P–KR3 0–0 9 Q–Q2 (If 9 P–KN4? P–Q4! 10 P×P N×QP 11 N/3×N N×N 12 B–QB4 B–K3 13 B×N B×N 14 B×B/N7 B×R∓

Shores–Sämisch, Berlin 1920) 9 ... P–Q4 10 P×P N×P 11 N/3×N N×N 12 N×P+ (12 B×N Q×N 13 B×B Q×NP loses a pawn) 12 ... Q×N 13 B×N B×B 14 Q×B R–K1 15 Q–K3 Q×Q 16 P×Q R×P=
c) 8 0–0 0–0 9 P–KR3 P–Q4! 10 P×P N×P 11 N/3×N Q×N 12 B–B3 Q–QR4! 13 N×N P×N 14 B×BP R–N1 15 Q–Q5 Q–B2 16 B–R4 B×NP 17 QR–Q1 B–R3∓ Ravinsky–Lisitsin, USSR Ch 1944
d) 8 0–0 0–0 9 P–B3 P–Q4! 10 P×P N×P 11 N/3×N Q×N=
e) 8 0–0 0–0 9 N–N3 B–K3 10 P–KR3 (or 10 P–B3) 10 ... P–Q4 11 P×P N×P 12 N×N Q×N 13 Q×Q B×Q=

In each case Black's ... P–Q4 leads to a liquidation that neutralises White's centre control and destroy's White's initiative.

The effectiveness of ... P–Q4 in the Dragon led to the development of the Accelerated Dragon, sometimes called the Simagin Variation. Black's philosophy in the Accelerated Dragon is to omit the move ... P–Q3 on the grounds that (a) he can play it later if he so wishes; and (b) he may be able to force ... P–Q4 at one stroke, without wasting a tempo by first playing ... P-Q3 and then ... P–Q4. Strategy (b) only works after insipid play by White: **1 P–K4 P–QB4 2 N–KB3 N–QB3 3 P–Q4 P×P 4 N×P P–KN3 5 N–QB3 B–N2 6 B–K3 N–B3 7 B–K2 0–0 8 0–0** or 8 Q–Q2? P–Q4! 9 P×P N×P 10 N/3×N N×N 11 B×N Q×N 12 B×B Q×NP 13 Q–Q4 P–K4!∓∓ Pogrebisky–Simagin, USSR 1950 **8...P–Q4!** 9 P×P or 9 N×N P×N 10 P×P P×P 11 B–Q4 P–K3 12 P–QR4 P–QR4 13 N–N5 B–QR3 14 P–QB3 N–K5! with an excellent game for Black, Pilnik–Petrosian, Budapest 1952 **9 ... N–QN5 10 N–N3** 10 P–Q6 Q×P 11 N/4–N5 Q–N1 12 B–QB4 N–B3 is good for Black **10 ... N/3×P 11 N×N N×N 12 B–Q4 N–B5** with equal chances. But in this variation White can play 5 P–QB4, setting up a Maroczy bind which prevents ... P–Q4 forever.

It was not only in the Dragon systems that ... P–Q4 proved to be such an effective blow. Nowadays almost the whole of Sicilian theory is founded on White's attempts to control his Q5 square and Black's aims of frustrating this control and breaking open the centre with ... P–Q4. If White is able to keep his grip on the centre and to prevent Black from freeing himself, the first player will usually triumph through the traditional motif of the K-side attack.

Because modern technique and theory normally suffice to prevent Black from playing ... P–Q4 with impunity, the question arises 'Under what circumstances can Black afford to sacrifice his QP?' It has long been known that the best answer to an attack on the wing is counterplay in the centre and with this in mind it is hardly surprising that Black's ... P–Q4 sacrifice has often been employed to counter a K-side attack. Perhaps the earliest well-known example is the famous Alekhine–Botvinnik game from Nottingham 1936: **1 P–K4 P–QB4 2 N–KB3 P–Q3 3 P–Q4 P×P 4 N×P N–KB3 5 N–QB3 P–KN3 6 B–K2 B–N2 7 B–K3 N–B3 8 N–N3 B–K3 9 P–B4 0–0** 9 ... P–QR4 10 P–QR4 0–0 is now known to be more accurate; e.g. 11 P–N4? P–Q4 12 P–B5 B–B1 13 KP×P N–QN5 14 P×P RP×P 15 P–Q6 Q×P 16 Q×Q (Alekhine's idea, 16 B–B5, accomplishes nothing in this case because the interpolation of P–QR4 on both sides has left Black's QN protected, cf the Alekhine–Botvinnik game.) 16 ... P×Q 17 0–0–0 N×NP 18 B–N6 B–R3+ 19 K–N1 N–K6∓ **10 P–N4 P–Q4?!** 10 ... N–QR4 is correct. **11 P–B5 B–B1 12 KP×P N–QN5 13 P–Q6?!** Stronger is 13 B–B3! P×P 14 P–QR3! P×P 15 B–N2 N–R3 16 Q–Q3! with a very good game for White. **13 ... Q×P** The only move. If 13 ... KP×P 14 P–QR3 N–B3 15 P–N5 and 16 P–B6. **14 B–B5 Q–B5!** After 14 ... Q×Q+?

15 R×Q N–B3 16 P–N5 N–Q2
17 P–B6 B–R1 18 N–Q5 Black's
position is gravely ill. **15 R–KB1
Q×RP 16 B×N N×P** 16 . . .
Q–N6+ 17 R–B2 N×P is inadequate
after 18 N–K4! and 16 . . . B×P
17 P×B Q–R5+ fails to 18 R–B2
Q×B 19 B–Q3. **17 B×N Q–N6+
18 R–B2 Q–N8+ 19 R–KB1** ½–½.
This game illustrates two important
features of the . . . P–Q4 sacrifice:
Black can often regain the pawn
immediately by meeting KP×P with
. . . N–QN5 and in such cases White
may be able to return the pawn under
favourable circumstances by advancing it to Q6 instead of allowing Black
to recapture it on a central square.

In many Sicilian variations Black
is saddled with pawns at K4 and Q3
(or K4 and Q2). In such cases it often
makes very good sense for Black to
sacrifice his QP in order to increase
the activity of his pieces, since
otherwise White will usually be able
to increase his grip on the vulnerable
Q5 square and to intensify his
pressure on the backward QP.

Fischer–Najdorf, Santa Monica 1966.
In this position Najdorf missed an
excellent opportunity in **12 . . .
P–Q4!**, e.g.

a) **13 N×P R–B1** Or 13 . . . B/1×N

14 P×B Q–R4+ **15 P–QB3** (on
15 K–B1 0–0–0 Black has a strong
initiative) 15 . . . B×N 16 B×B
Q×BP+ 17 K–B1 R–QB1! with
an excellent game. **14 B–N3** Or
14 Q–Q3 P–B4 **14 . . . B/1×N
15 P×B P–B4;**

b) **13 P×P B×N 14 NP×B** Or
14 QP×B B×P 15 P×P+ K–B1
14 . . . Q–R4 15 Q–Q2 R–QB1; or
c) **13 B×QP B×N 14 P×B Q–R4
15 Q–Q2 R–QB1.**

'In every case the prospects are
excellent'—Najdorf. Instead he
played 12 . . . P–N4? 13 B×B P×B
14 N–K2 N–B3 (14 . . . N×N
15 Q×N P–Q4 was better—Fischer)
and he failed to get sufficient play to
counteract White's mounting
pressure.

The Rauser–Botvinnik example
(77) is particularly favourable to
Black because of the presence on the
Q-file of White's queen and Black's
rook.

With . . . P–Q4 leading to so much
activity in the centre, it is obviously to
Black's great advantage for the white
king still to be on its original square.
In Tuomainen–Lee, Cracow 1964,
White paid a stiff penalty for launch-
ing a premature K-side attack while
his king was left exposed:

See diagram next page
**10 . . . P–Q4! 11 KP×P P–K5
12 B–K2 N–N3** Threatening 13 . . .
N×NP 14 B×N Q–R5+ **13 P–N5
N/B3×P 14 N×KP Q–K2 15 N–B2
R–K1** and Black had a terrific attack
for the pawn. After **16 K–B1** Black
could have won quickly by 16 . . .
B×P 17 R–QN1 B×B but Lee chose
another course which ultimately was
just as decisive.

In the first game of his 1971 match with Fischer, Petrosian played a very powerful theoretical innovation which should have netted him the full point: **1 P–K4 P–QB4 2 N–KB3 P–K3 3 P–Q4 P×P 4 N×P N–QB3 5 N–N5 P–Q3 6 B–KB4** Because of Black's eleventh move, this system may well go out of fashion. **6 ... P–K4 7 B–K3 N–B3 8 B–N5 B–K3 9 N/1–B3 P–QR3 10 B×N P×B 11 N–R3**

11 ... N–Q5 has been played in this position: Estrin–Borisenko, USSR Corres Ch 1960 continued 12 N–B4 P–B4 13 P×P N×KBP 14 B–Q3 R–B1 15 B×N R×N 16 B×B P×B 17 Q–B3 ±. Black also has unsatisfactory possibilities in 11 ... P–QN4 12 N–Q5!, 11 ... B–K2 12 B–B4! and 11 ... P–B4? 12 B–B4! B×B

13 N×B P×P 14 N/3×P P–Q4 15 Q×P! 'and in all cases White's advantage cannot be contested'— Gipslis. Petrosian now introduced a move that had been discovered by Suetin in 1962: **11 ... P–Q4! 12 P×P** On 12 N×P Black can simplify with 12 ... B/1×N 13 P×B Q–R4+ 14 Q–Q2 Q×Q+ 15 K×Q 0–0–0 followed by 16 ... P–B4, or maintain the tension by 12 ... B/1×N 13 P×B P–B4! **12 ... B×N 13 P×B Q–R4 14 Q–Q2 0–0–0! 15 B–B4 KR–N1 16 R–Q1** and now Petrosian could have maintained his (probably decisive) initiative by 16 ... R×NP.

There are some Sicilian variations in which the sacrifice ... P–Q4 forms an integral part. Let us first consider one of White's strongest systems against the Löwenthal Variation: **1 P–K4 P–QB4 2 N–KB3 N–QB3 3 P–Q4 P×P   4 N×P P–K4 5 N–N5 P–QR3   6 N–Q6+ B×N 7 Q×B Q–B3   8 Q–Q1! Q–N3 9 N–B3 KN–K2 10 P–KR4 P–KR4 11 B–KN5 P–Q4 12 P×P**

Does Black have enough compensation for the pawn? From the variations which follow the answer would appear to be 'No' and I feel that

White's whole system is the refutation of the Löwenthal.

a) 12 . . . N–Q5   13 B–Q3 B–B4 14 B×B Also strong is the simple 14 0–0 P–B3 15 B–K3 B×B 16 P×B 0–0 17 B×N P×B 18 P–Q6 N–B4 19 N–Q5 QR–K1   20 N–B4± Winiwarter–N. Littlewood, Tel Aviv 1964. **14 . . . N/2×B 15 Q–Q3 P–B3 16 B–K3 Q–N5** Or 16 . . . Q×NP 17 0–0–0 Q–B6   18 N–K4 0–0 19 P–B3 N–K7+   20 K–N1 N–B5 21 B×N Q×Q?   22 R×Q P×B 23 N–B5± Sakharov–Shianovsky, Ukraine Ch 1962. **17 B×N P×B 18 N–K2 Q×NP 19 0–0–0 Q×BP 20 K–N1** with an overwhelming position, Vasyukov–Malich, East Germany 1962.

b) 12 . . . N–N5   13 B×N K×B 14 B–Q3 N×B+   15 Q×N Q×Q 16 P×Q P–QN4 17 0–0–0! R–Q1 Weaker is 17 . . . P–N5? 18 N–K4 P–B4 19 N–N5 R–Q1 20 P–Q4 R×P 21 P×P! when White's extra pawn was decisive. Zuckerman–Bleiman, Netanya 1971. **18 KR–K1** White has a significant advantage because he retains his initiative while Black struggles to win back the pawn.

The next case is a line in the Dragon in which Black sacrifices his QP in order to shift the action from the K-side, where he is most vulnerable, to the Q-side and the centre: **1 P–K4 P–QB4 2 N–KB3 P–Q3 3 P–Q4 P×P 4 N×P N–KB3 5 N–QB3 P–KN3 6 B–K3 B–N2 7 P–B3 N–B3 8 Q–Q2 0–0 9 0–0–0 P–Q4**

See diagram next column

10 P×P N×P 11 N/4×N P×N 12 N×N White can decline the pawn by 12 B–Q4. **12 . . . P×N 13 Q×P Q–B2** The immediate consequence of

Black's pawn sacrifice has been the exchange of both pairs of knights. Since White's knights were helping to form a protective barrier in the region of his king the exchanges have increased Black's Q-side attacking chances. **14 Q–QB5** 14 Q×R B–B4 15 Q×R+ K×Q 16 R–Q2 P–KR4 is slightly better for Black because his queen is so active. **14 . . . Q–N1 15 P–QN3** Not 15 P–B3 P–QR4 16 Q×KP B–K3 17 Q–R3 R–K1! nor 15 Q–R3 B–B4 16 B–Q3 Q–K4 17 B×B Q×B/4 with good chances for Black in each case. **15 . . . P–QR4! 16 Q–N6 Q–K4 17 B–Q4 Q–B5+ 18 B–K3 Q–K4** with a draw by repetition since 18 K–N1 loses to 18 . . . R–N1   19 B–K3 Q–K4 20 Q–Q4 Q×Q   21 B×Q R–Q1. The current opinion on this whole variation is that if White accepts the pawn sacrifice he should never be able to achieve more than a draw.

In the illustrative game at the end of this chapter we examine one more variation which depends for its viability on the sacrifice . . . P–Q4 though in that case the word 'sacrifice' may be considered a misnomer since White is virtually compelled to return the pawn.

Rauser–Botvinnik
Leningrad 1939

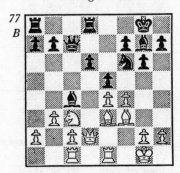

Grottke–Vogt
East German Ch 1977

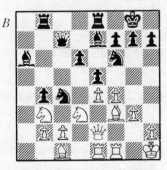

| 16 ... | P–Q4! |
| 17 KP×P | |

If 17 BP×P N×P 18 B×N P×B
19 Q–B2 B×KP 20 N×P P–B4! or
17 N×B B×N 18 P×B P–K5!
19 B–K2 N×P, and in each case
Black has the more active game.

17 ...	P–K5!
18 P×B	P×B
19 P–QB5	Q–R4

Threatening 20 ... N×P as well
as 20 ... N–N5.

20 KR–Q1?

Better was 20 Q–Q3. Now White is
annihilated.

20 ...	N–N5!
21 B–Q4	P–B7+!
22 K–B1	

If 22 K–R1 R×P! 23 N×R
P–B8=Q+

22 ...	Q–R3+
23 Q–K2	B×B
24 R×B	Q–KB3
25 R/1–Q1	Q–R5
26 Q–Q3	R–K1
27 R–K4	P–B4
28 R–K6	N×P+
29 K–K2	Q×P
0–1	

If 30 R–KB1 QR–Q1!

| 21 ... | P–Q4! |

Smashing open the centre to take
advantage of the fact that White's king
will soon be vulnerable along the
diagonals.

22 KP×P

If 22 BP×P P×P 23 P×N P×B 24
Q×B (or 24 Q–K4 P–B7!) 24 ... R×Q
25 P×R R–K1, winning easily.

22 ...	P–K5
23 B×P	B–Q3
24 Q–N2	

The only way out of the pin. If 24
N–B2 N×B 25 N×N P–B4, winning a
piece.

24 ...	N×B
25 R×N	R×R
26 Q×R	N–N3!

Suddenly Black's pressure along the
diagonals has become overwhelming.
There is no defence to the threat of ...
N×P and ... B–N2.

27 R–K1	N×P
28 N–Q4	B–N2
29 N–N5	N–B3!
30 N×Q	N×Q
0–1	

Gaprindashvili–Timoshchenko
USSR 1977

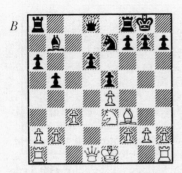

18 ...   P–Q4!
19 P×P

It is easy to see that 19 N×P N×N 20 P×N can be met by 20 ... P–K5 21 B–K2 (21 B×P?? R–K1) 21 ... Q–N4, and on 22 0–0 comes 22 ... QR–Q1, winning back the pawn with the more active game.

19 ...   Q–Q3

If 19 ... P–B4 20 P–Q6!, but now ... P–B4 can be stopped for good.

20 P–KN4!   QR–Q1
21 Q–Q3   R–Q2

Black cannot afford to capture on Q4 at the moment: 21 ... N×P 22 B×N B×B 23 R–Q1 (not 23 0–0–0? Q–R3+) 23 ... B×R 24 Q×Q R×Q 25 R×R, when White will probably win the endgame.

22 0–0–0   KR–Q1
23 N–B5

If 23 R–Q2 Q–KB3, and White does not have time to triple on the Q-file.

23 ...   Q–KB3
24 N×N+   Q×N
25 KR–K1?

White should have simplified into a drawn ending with 25 Q–K3 B×P 26 B×B R×R 27 R×R R×R 28 R–Q1. Now she discovers that two rooks can sometimes be worse than a queen.

25 ...   B×P
26 B×B   R×B
27 Q×R   R×Q
28 R×R   Q–N4+!
29 R–K3

Better was 29 R–Q2.

29 ...   P–KR4!
30 R×KP   Q×P
31 K–B2   Q–KB5

Picking up another pawn, whereupon Black's K-side pawns become the decisive factor.

32 P–KR3   Q×BP+
33 K–N3   P–R5
34 R–Q3   Q–B5
35 R–K8+   K–R2
36 R–Q4   Q–N6

There goes another one.

37 R/8–K4   P–N4
38 R–K7   K–N3
39 R–R7   Q×RP
40 R×RP+   P–B3
0–1

White has no defence against ... Q–B4 (or B6) followed by the advance of the passed pawns.

Oesch–Moran
Correspondence 1958

1 P–K4	P–QB4
2 N–KB3	P–Q3
3 P–Q4	P×P
4 N×P	N–KB3
5 P–KB3	

The idea of this move is to leave the QBP free to set up a Maroczy bind and only then to develop the QN. In order to combat this plan Black must strike quickly.

5 ...	P–K4!
6 B–QN5+	

On 6 N–N3 P–Q4 Black has no problems, while 6 N–N5? P–QR3 7 N/5–B3 B–K3 8 B–KN5 QN–Q2 also makes life easy for Black.

6 ...	QN–Q2
7 N–B5	P–Q4!
8 P×P	P–QR3
9 B×N+	

9 B–K2 is passive: 9 ... N–N3 10 N–K3 N/N3×P 11 N×N N×N 12 P–QB4 B–QN5+! (13 B–Q2 N–K6!∓∓). 9 B–R4 P–QN4 10 B–N3 N–B4 is also satisfactory for Black, e.g. 11 N–K3 N×B 12 RP×N B–N2 13 P–QB4 B–B4 14 0–0 0–0 15 N–B3 Q–N3.

9 ...	Q×B
10 N–K3	P–QN4

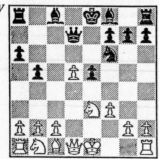

11 P–QB4

Various other moves have been tried:
a) 11 N–B3 B–N2 12 Q–K2 P–N5!
b) 11 P–QR4 (probably best) 11 ... B–N2 12 P×P P×P 13 R×R+ B×R 14 Q–K2 B–B4 15 N–B3 0–0 16 N–K4 (after 16 Q×P Q×Q 17 N×Q N×P 18 N×N B×N 19 N–B3 B–N2, Black has ample play for the pawn because White's king is stuck in the centre—the main threat is ... R–R1–R8) 16 ... B×N and Black wins back his pawn with a good game.
c) 11 P–QN3? B–B4! 12 P–QR4 R–QN1 13 P×P P×P 14 Q–Q3 0–0! with a great lead in development to compensate for the pawn, Tartakower–Najdorf, Amsterdam 1950.

The idea of the text is that 11 ... P×P? can be met by 12 N–B3! and White will eventually recapture on QB4 while keeping his Q5 pawn.

11 ...	B–B4
12 N–B3	0–0
13 N–K4?	

White should look to the safety of his king: 13 P×P P×P 14 0–0 B–Q5 15 K–R1 B–R3 16 N–K4 N×P 17 N×N Q×N 18 B–K3 P–N5! when Black is certainly better but White may be able to defend.

Now Black unleashes a ferocious attack.

13 ...	N×N
14 P×N	P–B4!

Completing the undermining of White's pawn centre. Also good is 14 ... Q–R2 15 Q–B3 P–B4 16 KP×P P–K5! Bely–Gereben, Hungary 1954. The text is just a little sharper.

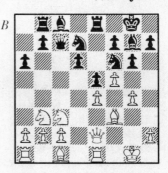

15 KP×P

If 15 N×P Q–Q1, threatening
16 ... B×N followed by 17 ...
Q–R5+

15 ...	**Q–R2**
16 Q–K2	**B×P**
17 P×P	**B–Q2**
18 P×P	

Klaeger–Kottnauer, 1954 concluded: 18 P–QR4 R–B5! 19 R–B1
R–K5   20 R–R3 (or 20 R–B3
B–KN5!) 20 ... B×R 21 P×B P×P
22 P×P Q–B4 0–1. Clearly Oesch
was unaware of that game otherwise
he wouldn't have come this far.

18 ...	**B–QN5+**
19 K–Q1	

Or 19 B–Q2 B–N4   20 Q×B
Q×N+

19 ...	**B–R5+**
0–1	

Shternberg–Zhidkov
USSR 1976

1 P–K4 P–QB4 2 N–KB3 P–Q3 3
P–Q4 P×P 4 N×P N–KB3 5 N–QB3
P–QR3 6 B–K2 P–KN3 7 0–0 B–N2 8
N–N3 QN–Q2 9 P–B4 0–0 10 B–B3
R–N1 11 Q–K2 Q–B2 12 R–K1 P–K4
13 P–B5 R–K1 14 P–N4

14 ...	**P–Q4**

As every Russian schoolboy knows
the correct response to a flank attack is a
counterattack in the centre.

15 BP×P

If 15 KP×P P–K5 and 16 ... N–K4;
or if 15 P–N5 QP×P 16 B–N2 NP×P 17
P×N N×P, with three pawns for the
piece and active counterplay against
White's K-side.

15 ...	**RP×P**
16 P–N5	

Again P×P is met by ... P–K5.

16 ...	**P×P**
17 B–N2	**N–R4**
18 N–Q5	**Q–Q1**
19 Q×KP	**N–N3**
20 N×N	**Q×N+**
21 B–K3	**Q–B2**

Despite his somewhat understated
development Black certainly does not
stand badly. His K-side is quite safe and
he has the prospect of a long range
offensive against the somewhat exposed
white king.

22 B–R7	**R–R1**
23 B–B5	**P–R4**
24 B–K3	**R–N1**

·Intending to advance the QNP and
follow with ... B–N2.

25 Q–QR4	**B–B4**

26 Q×P	Q×P
27 QR–Q1	R–R1
28 Q–N5	Q×P
29 R–Q2	Q–B6
30 B×P	QR–N1
31 Q–B5	P–K5
32 R–QB1	Q–K4!
33 R–Q5	Q–N7
34 B–B6	KR–QB1
35 R–Q2	Q–K4

Now White should probably content himself with 36 R–Q5 Q–N7.

36 Q×Q	B×Q

Black has a very slight plus because of White's straggly pawns on QR2 and KN5 and the passed pawn on ... K5.

37 R–KB2

Too passive.

37 ...	R–Q1
38 R–K1	

Too passive.

38 ...	B–B6
39 R–QB1	R–Q6

Suddenly White's game is on the verge of collapse.

40 B–R7	R/1–Q1
41 R/2–B2	B–K4
42 R–K1	N–B5
43 R/2–B1	

43 B×P fails to 43 ... R–Q8 44 R–QB1 N–K7+, winning a whole rook.

43 ...	B–B6
44 R×P	B×R
45 B×B	N–K7+
	0–1

INDEX OF COMPLETE GAMES

Bold indicates that the first player had White

INDEX OF POSITIONS

Bold indicates that the first named player had White

INDEX OF OPENING VARIATIONS

1: 1 P–K4 P–QB4 2 N–KB3 P–K3 3 P–Q4 P×P 4 N×P P–QR3 5 N–QB3:
5 ... Q–B2 6 B–Q3 P–QN4   74
5 ... P–QN4 6 B–Q3 B–N2 7 0–0 Q–B2 8 R–K1 P–Q3 9 B–N5   60
5 ... P–QN4 6 B–K2 B–N2 7 B–B3 Q–B3 8 0–0 N–QB3 9 R–K1   75

2: 1 P–K4 P–QB4 2 N–KB3 N–QB3 3 P–Q4 P×P 4 N×P P–K4
Löwenthal:
5 N–N5 P–QR3 6 N–Q6+ B×N 7 Q×B Q–B3 8 Q–Q1   174

3: 1 P–K4 P–QB4 2 N–KB3 N–QB3 3 P–Q4 P×P 4 N×P P–K3:
5 N–N5 P–Q3 6 B–KB4 P–K4 7 B–K3 N–B3 8 B–N5   174
5 N–QB3 P–Q3 6 B–K3 N–B3 7 P–B4 B–K2 8 Q–B3 0–0 9 0–0–0   109
5 N–QB3 Q–B2 6 B–K3 P–QR3 7 B–Q3 N–B3 8 0–0 N–K4   42

4: 1 P–K4 P–QB4 2 N–KB3 N–QB3 3 P–Q4 P×P 4 N×P N–B3 5 N–QB3 P–Q3 6 B–QB4 Sozin:
6 ... Q–N3   120
6 ... P–K3:
   7 0–0 B–K2 8 B–K3 0–0 9 B–N3 P–QR3   164
   7 B–K3 B–K2 8 Q–K2
     8 ... 0–0   121
     8 ... P–QR3   28

5: 1 P–K4 P–QB4 2 N–KB3 N–QB3 3 P–Q4 P×P 4 N×P N–B3 5 N–QB3 P–Q3 6 B–KN5 Richter–Rauser:
6 ... P–QR3 7 Q–Q2 B–Q2 8 0–0 P–N4   61

6: 1 P–K4 P–QB4 2 N–KB3 P–Q3 3 P–Q4 P×P 4 N×P N–KB3 5 N–QB3 P–KN3
Dragon:
6 B–K2 B–N2 7 B–K3 N–B3   171, 172
6 B–K3 B–N2 7 P–B3 N–B3 8 Q–Q2 0–0:
  9 0–0–0 P–Q4   175
  9 B–QB4 N–Q2   30
  9 B–QB4 B–Q2   16

7: 1 P–K4 P–QB4 2 N–KB3 P–Q3 3 P–Q4 P×P 4 N×P N–KB3 5 N–QB3 P–K3
Scheveningen:
6 P–KN4 P–QR3 7 P–N5   117
6 P–KN4 B–K2 7 P–N5 KN–Q2 8 P–KR4   125
6 B–K2 P–QR3 7 0–0 Q–B2 8 P–B4 N–B3 9 B–K3 B–Q2   43
6 B–KN5 B–K2 7 Q–B3 QN–Q2 8 0–0–0 P–QR3   72
6 P–B4 P–QR3 7 B–K2 Q–B2 8 0–0 B–K2 9 K–R1   32
6 P–B4 B–K2 7 B–K3 P–QR3 8 Q–B3 Q–B2 9 0–0–0   62

8: 1 P–K4 P–QB4 2 N–KB3 P–Q3 3 P–Q4 P×P 4 N×P N–KB3
5 P–B3 P–K4   178
5 N–QB3 P–QR3 Najdorf:
6 B–K2   45, 47, 179
6 B–QB4 P–K3:
  7 P–QR3   162
  7 B–K3 P–QN4 8 B–N3   137
  7 B–N3 P–QN4 8 0–0:
  8 . . . P–N5 9 N–R4 N×P   27
  8 . . . QN–Q2   106, 136
  8 . . . B–N2 9 R–K1 QN–Q2 10 N–Q5   123
  7 0–0 B–K2 8 B–N3:
  8 . . . N–B3 9 P–B4   15
  8 . . . 0–0   153
6 B–KN5:
6 . . . QN–Q2:
  7 Q–Q2   166
  7 Q–K2   139
  7 B–QB4 P–K3 8 0–0   152, 169
  7 B–QB4 Q–R4 8 Q–Q2 P–K3:
  9 0–0 B–K2   150
  9 0–0–0 P–N4   119, 155
6 . . . P–K3 7 Q–B3   56, 58, 59
6 . . . P–K3 7 P–B4:
  7 . . . P–KR3   163
  7 . . . QN–Q2 8 B–B4   149
  7 . . . QN–Q2 8 Q–B3   167
7 . . . B–K2 8 Q–B3 Q–B2 9 0–0–0 QN–Q2:
  10 B–Q3 P–QN4 11 KR–K1 B–N2 12 N–Q5   114
  10 P–KN4 P–N4 11 B×N N×B 12 P–N5 N–Q2:
    13 P–QR3 R–QN1   26
    13 P–B5   101, 104, 105

9: 1 P–K4 P–QB4 2 N–KB3 N–QB3 3 P–Q4 P×P 4 N×P N–B3 5 N–QB3 P–K4
Pelikan:
6 N/4–N5 P–Q3 7 B–N5 P–QR3 8 B×N P×B 9 N–R3   63, 76

"Besides its straightforwardness, clarity, and grounding in Scripture, what I like most about this book is its practicality. By following its counsel and being led by the Holy Spirit, Christians will be well equipped to discern and commit to God's will for their lives!"

Gregg R. Allison, Professor of Christian Theology, The Southern Baptist Theological Seminary; Pastor, Sojourn Community Church; author, *Sojourners and Strangers*; *Roman Catholic Theology and Practice*; and *Historical Theology*

"In my forty-five years of pastoral ministry, there is one question that I've been asked more than any other: *How might I know God's will?* That is why I'm so happy to recommend Grudem's short treatment of this topic. His analysis is not only thoroughly biblical, but also incredibly practical and easy to grasp. So whether you are a seasoned believer or a young Christian, were you to ask me that all-too-familiar question, I would send you to this book. I highly recommend it!"

Sam Storms, Senior Pastor, Bridgeway Church, Oklahoma City, Oklahoma

"I wholeheartedly recommend Wayne Grudem's book. These principles have guided my own decisions, and I'm thrilled to know they are in a book I can give to others."

Jason Fritz, Lead and Founding Pastor, Illuminate Community Church, Scottsdale, Arizona

What the Bible Says about
How to Know God's Will

Books in This Series

What the Bible Says about Abortion, Euthanasia, and End-of-Life Medical Issues

What the Bible Says about How to Know God's Will

What the Bible Says about
How to Know God's Will

Wayne Grudem

CROSSWAY®

WHEATON, ILLINOIS

The content of this book has been adapted from "How to Know God's Will: Factors to Consider in Making Ethical Decisions" in Wayne Grudem, *Christian Ethics: An Introduction to Biblical Moral Reasoning* (Wheaton, IL: Crossway, 2018), 148–86 (chap. 6).

Cover design: Jeff Miller, Faceout Studios
Cover image: Shutterstock

First printing, 2020

Printed in the United States of America

Trade paperback ISBN: 978-1-4335-6990-6
ePub ISBN: 978-1-4335-6993-7
PDF ISBN: 978-1-4335-6991-3
Mobipocket ISBN: 978-1-4335-6992-0

Library of Congress Cataloging-in-Publication Data

Names: Grudem, Wayne A., author.
Title: What the Bible says about how to know God's will / Wayne Grudem.
Description: Wheaton: Crossway, 2020. | Includes bibliographical references and index.
Identifiers: LCCN 2019034901 (print) | LCCN 2019034902 (ebook) | ISBN 9781433569906 (trade paperback) | ISBN 9781433569913 (pdf) | ISBN 9781433569920 (mobi) | ISBN 9781433569937 (epub)
Subjects: LCSH: God (Christianity)—Will—Biblical teaching. | Christian Ethics—Biblical teaching. | Decision making—Religious Aspects—Christianity—Biblical teaching.
Classification: LCC BT135 .G78 2018 (print) | LCC BT135 (ebook) | DDC 241—dc23
LC record available at https://lccn.loc.gov/2019034901
LC ebook record available at https://lccn.loc.gov/2019034902

Crossway is a publishing ministry of Good News Publishers.

BP		28	27	26	25	24	23	22	21	20
14	13	12	11	10	9	8	7	6	5	4	3	2	1

Contents

INTRODUCTION

What factors should we consider in making decisions?

What does it mean to be "led by the Holy Spirit"?

Christians instinctively want to live in a way that pleases God. In fact, Jesus said, "If you love me, you will keep my commandments" (John 14:15). But sometimes it is unclear what "keeping God's commandments" implies when facing a specific decision. There are many times when it does not seem as if any specific teaching of Scripture can decide an issue for us.

This book is intended to provide helpful guidelines whenever people wonder, "What is God's will for me in this specific situation?"

A. DECISIONS CAN BE QUICK OR DRAWN-OUT, AND CAN INVOLVE MAJOR EVENTS OR SMALL DAILY ACTIVITIES

Some decisions must be made instantly. When Joseph was working in Potiphar's house in Egypt, one day Potiphar's wife "caught him by his garment, saying, 'Lie with me.' But he left his garment in her hand and fled and got out of the house" (Gen. 39:12; notice also his earlier pattern of wise responses in vv. 7–10). Joseph had only an instant to respond, and he made a wise decision and fled.[1]

Other decisions take more time. In this book I will explain multiple factors that can and should be considered when we have more time to make a decision and when the decision itself is important enough to consider in greater detail.

Sometimes knowing God's will involves major decisions, such as what career to aim for, what subject a student should choose as a college major, or whom to marry. Sometimes the question is whether to take a new job or stay in the present job, which church to join, or whether to volunteer for a charitable cause or church activity. Still other situations may involve difficult end-of-life decisions regarding a terminally ill family member. And yet other decisions relate to convictions about public-policy issues, such as abortion, capital punishment, euthanasia, war, marriage laws, or the legalization of marijuana.

---

1. In another case, Uzzah had an instant to decide and made the wrong decision. God had given a clear commandment that the people "must not touch the holy things, lest they die" (Num. 4:15, referring to the various furnishings for the tabernacle). But the magnitude of God's holiness behind that prohibition had not penetrated deeply enough into Uzzah's heart, because when King David and the people of Israel were bringing the ark of the covenant to Jerusalem, Uzzah actually touched the ark: "And when they came to the threshing floor of Nacon, *Uzzah put out his hand to the ark of God and took hold of it*, for the oxen stumbled. And the anger of the LORD was kindled against Uzzah, and God struck him down there because of his error, and he died there beside the ark of God" (2 Sam. 6:6–7). There was also a failure of leadership in this situation, because the ark was wrongly being carried on a cart rather than with poles placed through the rings on the corners of the ark (see Ex. 25.14–15; 2 Sam. 6:3–4).

At other times Christians desire to have God's wisdom regarding simpler, everyday decisions, such as which emails to respond to or delete, which phone calls to make or postpone, or how to schedule various tasks that have to be done on certain days.

For all such questions, whether large or small, the following process should be helpful (even if only parts of this process are used in some situations).

The next two sections will discuss *four dimensions of every action* and *nine sources of information* that should be considered in any moral decision.

B. FOUR DIMENSIONS OF EVERY ACTION

Human actions have at least four dimensions that need to be considered when decisions need to be made:

1. The action itself
2. The person's attitudes about the action
3. The person's motives for doing the action (the reason why the person does something)
4. The results of the action

While the action itself, as soon as it is done, will be visible to you and to others, your attitudes and motives will be mostly invisible, and the results of the action will also be mostly invisible because they have not happened yet.

We can consider these four dimensions to every action in more detail.

1. The Action Itself. The first question to ask is, Is this a morally good action? To decide that, we need to know the commands of Scripture regarding the action.

Some actions are clearly prohibited by Scripture. The Bible tells us not to murder (Ex. 20:13), not to commit adultery (v. 14), not to steal (v. 15), not to bear false witness (v. 16), and so on. Other actions are commanded. Scripture says to "honor your father and your mother" (v. 12). Elsewhere the Bible tells us that we are to "pay . . . taxes to whom taxes are owed" (Rom. 13:7).

But many actions that we have to consider are neither specifically commanded nor specifically prohibited by Scripture, such as whether to accept a particular job offer, which used car to purchase, which church to join, or whom to marry. For such decisions, we need to consider other dimensions of the action in question, and we need to consider all nine sources of information.

2. The Person's Attitudes about the Action. Because "the LORD looks on the heart" (1 Sam. 16:7), it is not enough for us simply to do morally right actions. God also wants the attitudes of our hearts to be right before him:

> Every way of a man is right in his own eyes,
> but *the LORD weighs the heart.* (Prov. 21:2)

In some cases, an *action* can be right and the *results* can be morally good, but a person's *attitudes* might be wrong. For instance, if Julie's mother tells her that she has to clean her room before she can go out to play with friends, she might do the right action (clean the room in a hurry) and get the right results (a clean room) but with the wrong attitude (she slams the door and cleans the room in anger and with simmering resentment against her mother).

3. The Person's Motives for Doing the Action. Jesus taught us to beware of doing good actions with wrong motives, such as the desire to be praised by other people:

> Beware of practicing your righteousness before other people *in order to be seen by them*, for then you will have no reward from your Father who is in heaven. Thus, when you give to the needy, sound no trumpet before you, as the hypocrites do in the synagogues and in the streets, that they may be praised by others. Truly, I say to you, they have received their reward. (Matt. 6:1–2; cf. 23:5–7)

For example, consider a couple who are talking together about whether they should agree to help with their church's youth ministry one night a week. If they honestly ask themselves why they want to do this, they might find that their motives are very positive ones, such as a desire to minister effectively to young people who come to their church, to be involved in a church activity in which their children participate, to do some kind of ministry together, to meet a need because of a shortage of volunteers at the time, or because of other similar motives. They might simply want to honor God in the way they conduct their lives and to advance his kingdom, as Jesus taught: "Seek first the kingdom of God and his righteousness, and all these things will be added to you" (Matt. 6:33).

On the other hand, they might find that their motives are not appropriate. They might be thinking about helping in the youth ministry because a neighbor has been putting pressure on them to do so and they are tired of telling him no, even though they do not feel it is the right thing for them to do. Or they might want to become better known and gain recognition from others in the church, which is a simple appeal to their pride. Or they might be seeking an opportunity to observe the youth pastor so they can lodge more criticisms against him with the church leaders! All of these would be wrongful motives.

4. The Results of the Action. Other passages in Scripture encourage us to take thought about the results of our actions. For example, Paul wanted the Christians at Corinth to evaluate what was happening in their worship services to see if various activities actually contributed to building up one another in the Lord:

> What then, brothers? When you come together, each one has a hymn, a lesson, a revelation, a tongue, or an interpretation. *Let all things be done for building up.* (1 Cor. 14:26)

To take another example, Paul was persuaded that the unclean foods in the Old Testament were no longer unclean for Christians to eat ("Nothing is unclean in itself,"

Rom. 14:14), and therefore the action of eating pork (for example) was not morally wrong in itself. But it could bring a wrongful result, and in those cases it should not be done:

> For *if your brother is grieved by what you eat*, you are no longer walking in love. By what you eat, do not destroy the one for whom Christ died. So do not let what you regard as good be spoken of as evil. (Rom. 14:15–16; see also 1 Cor. 8:13; 10:24)

In writing to the Corinthian church, Paul concluded a long section of advice with a general requirement for them to consider the results of their actions: "Whether you eat or drink, or whatever you do, do all to the glory of God" (1 Cor. 10:31).

We need to consider all four of these dimensions for any action: (1) the action itself, (2) attitudes, (3) motives, and (4) results. An action that is pleasing to God will follow the teachings of Scripture in all four of these areas.

5. Most Actions Contain a Mix of Different Attitudes, Motives, and Results. Even simple actions can involve a complex mixture of *attitudes*. Any parent who has been awakened in the middle of the night to care for a sick child will attest to feeling deep love for the child, but also perhaps mild irritation or even resentment at the interruption of a sound sleep, coupled with thankfulness to God for the privilege of being a parent, plus a slight tinge of anxiety about being able to do a good job at work the next day with less sleep, plus concern about whether the disturbance will wake the other children, plus a deep sense of peace at knowing God's presence, plus a renewed sense of gratitude for the sacrifices made by his or her own parents, plus perhaps a bit of weariness and discouragement because of having so many responsibilities, and so forth. Our hearts are complex, and we are capable of having multiple attitudes at once in any given situation.

Then our *motives* for an action might be mixed. While our primary motive for giving time or money to a church or charitable organization might be to further the work of the church and to earn heavenly rewards from God, there might also be a small bit of desire to gain recognition from others. It is often difficult to know our own hearts or to fully understand our motives for our actions.

As for *results*, while we can usually predict the most likely outcome of an action, it is seldom possible to predict the results with certainty or to know how extensive the results will be. Often people are surprised by the "unintended consequences" of their actions. For example, someone could make a business investment in a morally good project (a right action), with right attitudes and motives, but have bad results (the investment could fail and the principal be lost, perhaps because the investment was in a product for which there was no consumer demand).[2]

But these complexities do not mean that it is impossible to know or to evaluate the attitudes, motives, and results

---

2. A tragic biblical example of unforeseen results is Jephthah's foolish vow in Judg. 11:30–31.

of an action. Usually we can know the dominant attitudes and dominant motives for an action (at least for ourselves). It is often possible to predict the most likely results that will come from an action. Therefore, we can analyze these four factors when considering any particular action or situation.

C. NINE SOURCES OF INFORMATION AND GUIDANCE

As I mentioned earlier, sometimes there is no time to ponder a decision, and a person simply has to use his or her best judgment at the moment and make the decision quickly. But at other times there is more opportunity to ponder it, and in that case, several different sources of information should be considered, especially if the decision is quite significant.

Here are nine sources of information to consider.

1. Information from the Bible. Our first source of information about any ethical decision should be the teachings of the Bible. The Bible is our only source of inerrant and absolutely authoritative ethical guidance.

2. Information from Studying the Situation. Jesus gives examples from ordinary life that illustrate how people typically learn more about a situation before they agree to a course of action:

> For which of you, desiring to build a tower, does not first sit down and count the cost, whether he has enough to complete it? Otherwise, when he has laid

a foundation and is not able to finish, all who see it begin to mock him, saying, "This man began to build and was not able to finish." Or what king, going out to encounter another king in war, will not sit down first and deliberate whether he is able with ten thousand to meet him who comes against him with twenty thousand? And if not, while the other is yet a great way off, he sends a delegation and asks for terms of peace. (Luke 14:28–32)

Many decisions about medical care, colleges, job offers, marriage partners, ministry opportunities, political positions, and numerous other things require us to find more information about the actual facts of a situation before we are able to make a responsible choice.

Studying the situation should also include reflection on "what might be," which comes from our imagination. John Frame explains why imagination is a useful factor in ethical decisions. He defines imagination as "our ability to think of things that are not," then says that imagination is helpful in making ethical decisions because it "enables us to conceive of alternative courses of action as we ponder what to do in the future."[3]

3. Information about Oneself. It is important to understand oneself and one's specific role in the situation at hand. Paul encourages such sober self-reflection:

---

3. John M. Frame, *The Doctrine of the Christian Life: A Theology of Lordship* (Phillipsburg, NJ: P&R, 2008), 369–70.

For by the grace given to me I say to everyone among you not *to think of himself* more highly than he ought to think, but *to think with sober judgment*, each according to the measure of faith that God has assigned. (Rom. 12:3)

Therefore, a person should honestly ponder his or her own skills, interests, desires, and sense of life calling from God when deciding whether to take a specific action or not. Advice from friends and spiritual leaders can be helpful in this regard (see next section).

4. Advice from Others. Christians can get helpful advice from other people regarding an ethical decision. Personal friends as well as spiritual leaders such as pastors can give useful advice. Paul encouraged the Christians in Rome (whom he had not yet met!) that they were able, in general, to give one another wise advice:

I myself am satisfied about you, my brothers, that you yourselves are full of goodness, filled with all knowledge and *able to instruct one another.* (Rom. 15:14)

The Greek word translated as "able to instruct" is *noutheteō*, "to counsel about avoidance or cessation of an improper course of conduct, admonish, warn, instruct."[4] In a similar way, we read in the Old Testament, "In an abundance of counselors there is safety" (Prov. 11:14).

---

4. Walter Bauer et al., *A Greek-English Lexicon of the New Testament and Other Early Christian Literature*, 3rd ed. (Chicago: University of Chicago Press, 2000), 679.

Reading books and articles about the subject of the decision is another important source of "advice from others," only in this case the others are not personally present but have written their advice and published it.

Finally, the historical teachings of the church can be another source of "advice from others" that is helpful in making ethical decisions. Many of the wisest Bible teachers in the history of the church have given extensive time and thought to the common ethical questions that confront people in each generation, and a tradition of accepted church teaching on some ethical questions has accumulated over time. Sometimes that tradition finds expression (for Protestants at least) in some of the longer statements of faith, such as the Westminster Confession of Faith and the Westminster Larger Catechism, the Heidelberg Catechism, or the Philadelphia Baptist Confession.

5. Changed Circumstances. When your circumstances change, might that be an indication of God's will for you? A correct evaluation will require wisdom to discern whether the circumstances indicate something of God's purposes for us, and this requires prayer for God to give us discernment to understand the circumstances correctly. But there are several examples of circumstantial guidance in Scripture.

A famous example of seeking guidance from changed circumstances is found in the story of Gideon putting out a fleece of wool overnight and asking God to cause the fleece to be wet with dew and the ground dry, and then the next night asking God to cause the fleece to be dry and the ground wet with dew (see Judg. 6:36–40). God granted Gideon's request on both nights.

However, it is not at all clear that the biblical narrative holds this up as an example to imitate. God had already told Gideon clearly what he should do and had already promised to give him victory (see Judg. 6:14–16), and Gideon was essentially saying to God, "If you will do *what you have said you will do*, give me this sign." He was certainly not demonstrating faith in God's promise. Moreover, Gideon had understood God's promise clearly, for he said to God, "If you will save Israel by my hand, *as you have said*, behold I am laying a fleece of wool on the threshing floor" (vv. 36–37). Often in the book of Judges, the events are reported truthfully, but they are not always portrayed in the narrative as examples for us to imitate.

I am not aware of any New Testament example in which God's people similarly sought guidance by asking God to perform a specific miracle. However, there are some other examples in the New Testament of guidance by changed circumstances. When Jesus sent his twelve disciples out to preach, he instructed them that the response of the town would tell them whether to stay there or leave:

> And if anyone will not receive you or listen to your words, shake off the dust from your feet when you leave that house or town. (Matt. 10:14)

Circumstances also seem to have played a significant role in how Paul determined whether to stay in a city or depart during his missionary journeys. Whenever violent hostility arose against his preaching, he left that city and went on to the next one (see Acts 13:50–51; 14:5–6, 20; 16:40; 17:10, 14; 20:1, 3).

He did not face violent opposition in Athens, but when he received only a minimal response, he left there and went on to Corinth, where he stayed a year and six months (Acts 18:1, 11). But the positive circumstance of God's blessing on Paul's ministry did not always indicate that he should stay in a city. He found an "open door" for ministry in Ephesus and decided to stay there longer, but then he found an "open door" for ministry in Troas and decided not to stay. Here is the situation in Ephesus:

> But I will stay in Ephesus until Pentecost, *for a wide door for effective work has opened to me*, and there are many adversaries. (1 Cor. 16:8–9)

And here is the contrasting situation in Troas:

> When I came to Troas to preach the gospel of Christ, *even though a door was opened for me in the Lord*, my spirit was not at rest because I did not find my brother Titus there. *So I took leave of them and went on to Macedonia.* (2 Cor. 2:12–13)

In this second case, in spite of a door for ministry that was "opened for me in the Lord," Paul left Troas, because his spirit was deeply concerned to find Titus, whom he had sent on ahead of him. (A reading of the larger context of these events shows that it was not merely Paul's concern for Titus as an individual, but his deep concern for the well-being of the church at Corinth, and the expectation that Titus would bring him the news from Corinth that he was longing to hear.) Apparently Paul did take account of changed circumstances when seeking to know God's will for his ministry, but at Troas the circumstances included not only the open door for the gospel but also the absence of Titus. And Paul may have taken other factors into account as well.

I will not examine here in detail the numerous additional examples of decision-making in the light of changed circumstances that are found in Scripture, but from these examples we can draw this conclusion: we should take changed circumstances into consideration, but changed circumstances are only one factor in a decision-making process, and we need to pray for wisdom from God in understanding how to evaluate these circumstances.

6. Conscience. Conscience is a person's instinctive inward sense of right and wrong. Peter encourages his readers that they should take care to have "a *good conscience*" (1 Pet. 3:16), and Paul said, "I always take pains to have a *clear conscience* toward both God and man" (Acts 24:16). He told the Christians in Rome that one reason they should be obedient to government was "for the sake of conscience" (Rom. 13:5).

This does not mean that conscience is always a reliable guide, because some people can have a "weak" conscience (1 Cor. 8:10), and when Paul says that he wants his hearers to develop a "good conscience" (1 Tim. 1:5),[5] he implies that others can have a bad conscience or one that is not as reliable. Nevertheless, conscience must be taken into account when making an ethical decision. Serious consequences come to those who reject the testimony of their consciences, for Paul said that Timothy should "wage the good warfare" while "holding faith and a good conscience." Then he added, "By rejecting this [that is, by rejecting their consciences],[6] some have made shipwreck of their faith" (vv. 18–19). Therefore, people reject the testimony of their consciences at great peril.

7. Heart. While conscience is an instinctive *inward sense* of right and wrong, the "heart" in Scripture is a broader concept, for the heart is seen as the inward center of a person's deepest moral and spiritual inclinations and convictions, especially in relationship to God.[7]

Believers in the new covenant age have God's laws written on their hearts in a fuller and deeper sense than in the old covenant. As part of the superiority of the new covenant over the old, God promises, "I will *put my laws on their hearts*, and write them on their minds" (Heb. 10:16;

---

5. Andrew David Naselli and J. D. Crowley discuss how a person can train his or her conscience in *Conscience: What It Is, How to Train It, and Loving Those Who Differ* (Wheaton, IL: Crossway, 2016), 55–83.

6. The word *this* translates the Greek pronoun *hēn*, a feminine singular pronoun that refers back to "conscience" (*suneidēsis*), which is also feminine singular in Greek and the nearest antecedent.

7. Non-Christians are said to have "an evil, unbelieving heart" (Heb. 3:12; see also Rom. 1:21, 24; 2 Pet. 2:14). However, by God's common grace, they still have some inward sense of right and wrong, because Paul says that every person still has, to some extent, an innate understanding of the moral standards of God's laws: "The work of the law is *written on their hearts*" (Rom. 2:15).

cf. 8:10). In addition, Paul assumes that Christians in general have become "obedient from the *heart*" to God's will (Rom. 6:17). But we should not think that our hearts are yet perfect, because Paul also says that his goal in ministry is that Christians would come to practice "love that issues from a *pure heart* and a good conscience and a sincere faith" (1 Tim. 1:5; see also 2 Thess. 3:5). Paul also says that God "*tests our hearts*" (1 Thess. 2:4), assuming that Christians can have hearts that are more or less pure before God (see also Prov. 4:23; 1 Cor. 4:5; Eph. 1:18; 6:6; 1 Thess. 3:13; James 3:14; 4:8).

As far as ethical guidance is concerned, sometimes Scripture speaks of people following their heart desires so as to do what is pleasing to God. Paul told the Christians in the church at Corinth that, regarding the giving of money to the Lord's work, "each one must give as he has decided *in his heart*" (2 Cor. 9:7). He also said that God "*put into the heart of Titus* the same earnest care I have for you" (8:16; see also Acts 7:23).

Even in the old covenant, David could write of a heart that had been to some measure transformed by God:

> Delight yourself in the LORD,
>   and he will give you the desires of your *heart*.
>   (Ps. 37:4)

This indicates that the deep, heartfelt desires of a person who loves God and takes delight in him will often be the very desires that God wants that person to have, the desires that God will be pleased to grant. In this case, a person's desires indicate the will of God for that person.

A similar idea of deep inward desires that accord with God's will is found in other passages that do not specifically use the word *heart* (Hebrew, *lēb*; Greek, *kardia*) but carry a similar meaning:

> If anyone *aspires* [Greek, *oregeō*, "to seek to accomplish, aspire, strive for"] to the office of overseer, he *desires* [Greek, *epithumeō*, "to have a strong desire, long for"] a noble task. (1 Tim. 3:1)

With respect to the remarriage of a woman whose first husband has died, Paul writes:

> A wife is bound to her husband as long as he lives. But if her husband dies, she is free to be married *to whom she wishes*, only in the Lord. (1 Cor. 7:39)

Here the Greek term for "wishes" is *thelō*, "to have a desire for something, wish to have, desire, want." Paul is saying that a widow has considerable freedom to marry anyone she wants to marry, as long as he is a Christian believer ("only in the Lord"). I do not think there is a convincing reason to refrain from applying this guideline to marriage decisions generally, even though here it is speaking specifically of widows who wish to remarry. The principle is that people should be married to someone they *want* to be married to.

In my 42 years of teaching theology to undergraduate and graduate students, I have found this principle to be important when students have come to me asking for counsel regarding decisions they have to make between job opportunities, career directions, or sometimes whether to make a commitment to marry a certain person or not. Again and again, after learning about the specific situation, I have found it helpful to ask, "What do you most deeply *want* to do? What is in your heart?"

I find this question helpful because in many situations the Lord has already put in the person's heart a deep desire to follow a particular course of action, and it would be foolish to ignore that desire. I am not saying that such a desire is always reliable, for James warns his readers (who are for the most part Christian believers) that they might have "bitter jealousy and selfish ambition" in their hearts (James 3:14), and some of them need to "purify [their] hearts" (4:8; see also 1:26; 5:5, 8). But in general, Christian believers have become "obedient from the heart" to God's teachings (Rom. 6:17), and I have found again and again that, for Christians who are walking in obedience to the Lord, staying in fellowship with him, and maintaining regular prayer and Bible reading, their heart desires should be a large factor in discerning God's will in particular situations. (But let me be clear that a person's heart desires are not the only factor to take into account, for the other sources of information discussed in this entire section must also be considered.)[8]

---

8. At this point someone might object that Jer. 17:9 says, "The heart is deceitful above all things, and desperately sick; who can understand it?" But I do not think that this description is intended to apply to Christian believers in the new

8. A Person's Human Spirit. A person's "spirit" (Greek, *pneuma*) is the nonmaterial part of a person, the part that survives when the person's physical body dies. A person's *human spirit* is not the same as the Holy Spirit who lives within us and who is himself God, for Paul distinguishes between the Holy Spirit and our human spirits when he says, "*The Spirit* himself bears witness with *our spirit* that we are children of God" (Rom. 8:16).

Paul was guided by the uneasiness of his human spirit when he was in Troas looking for Titus to bring him news from the church at Corinth:

> When I came to Troas to preach the gospel of Christ, even though a door was opened for me in the Lord, *my spirit was not at rest* because I did not find my brother Titus there. So I took leave of them and went on to Macedonia. (2 Cor. 2:12–13)

In another situation, when Paul came to the city of Athens, we read that "*his spirit* was provoked within him as he saw that the city was full of idols" (Acts 17:16). This apparently indicates that Paul had a subjective sense that in-

---

covenant, where God has fulfilled his promise, "I will put my law within them, and I will write it on their hearts" (Jer. 31:33; see also 32:39). The author of Hebrews sees this passage as indicating one of the ways the new covenant is superior to the old, and the author sees it as fulfilled in the lives of believers under the new covenant, where God has written his laws on his people's hearts (see Heb. 8:10; 10:16). Therefore, the author of Hebrews says that Christians under the new covenant can "draw near" to God "with a *true heart* in full assurance of faith, with our *hearts* sprinkled clean from an evil conscience" (10:22). For this reason, I do not think that Jer. 17:9 should be used to describe the condition of the hearts of believers in general in the new covenant, who have become "obedient from the *heart*" (Rom. 16:7) to God's laws.

visible, evil spiritual forces were active in Athens and were behind the outward physical evidences of idolatry that he saw as he walked through the city. The presence of evil in the invisible, spiritual realm registered in Paul not so much in his intellect and reason as in his subjective perception of what his spirit was sensing within him.

In a similar way, the Gospels sometimes say that Jesus perceived something "in his *spirit*" (Mark 2:8) or that he "was troubled in his *spirit*" (John 13:21).

Sometimes a person's human spirit can give indications of positive emotions, such as when Mary declared, "My soul magnifies the Lord, and *my spirit* rejoices in God my Savior" (Luke 1:46–47).

Therefore, in addition to a subjective perception about right and wrong from our own *consciences*, and in addition to the deep inward desires and convictions that we feel in our *hearts*, it is also appropriate to consider any sense of invisible spiritual dynamics in a situation that may register in our *human spirits*.

9. Guidance from the Holy Spirit. Yet another source of guidance is personal direction from the Holy Spirit. Such guidance was explicitly identified in Paul's second missionary journey:

> And they went through the region of Phrygia and Galatia, *having been forbidden by the Holy Spirit to speak the word in Asia.* And when they had come up to Mysia, they attempted to go into Bithynia, *but the*

Spirit of Jesus did not allow them. (Acts 16:6–7; see also 8:29; 13:2; 15:28)

But is direct guidance from the Holy Spirit part of the life of all Christians or was it unique to Paul and the other apostles in the book of Acts? I am convinced that the New Testament teaches that direct guidance from the Holy Spirit is a normal component of the life of Christians generally, and it is one of the factors we should take into account in seeking to know God's will.

Paul wrote to Christians in Rome, whom he had not yet met, about an experience of being led by the Holy Spirit that he seems to have thought of as characteristic of the lives of Christians in general:

For *all who are led by the Spirit of God* are sons of God. (Rom. 8:14)

The Greek word here translated "led" is *agontai*, the present passive indicative form of *agō*, which means "to direct the movement of an object from one position to another" or (in a spiritual sense) "to lead/guide morally or spiritually."[9]

Similarly, Paul writes in Galatians:

But if you are *led by the Spirit*, you are not under the law. (Gal. 5:18)

Significantly, Paul here uses the same Greek verb (*agō*) to speak of such leading by the Holy Spirit.

---

9. Bauer et al., *A Greek-English Lexicon*, 16, meanings 1 and 3.

Some commentators argue that this leading by the Holy Spirit consists only in the Spirit giving an inward desire or inclination to obey God's moral laws as revealed in Scripture. For example, Thomas Schreiner writes that being led by the Spirit is not a matter of "specific guidance for daily decisions," but rather of "being directed by the Spirit to live a life that pleases God."[10]

Other commentators, however, see guidance by the Holy Spirit as also including situation-specific direction to make a certain decision, take a specific action, or go to a particular place. Gregg Allison and Andreas Köstenberger write,

> Statements such as "The Holy Spirit is leading me to do such and such" or "The Spirit told me to say such and such" have become so commonplace that a tendency has developed in some circles to avoid discussion of the guidance of the Spirit. However, this work of the Spirit is well supported biblically and confirmed in genuine experiences of his guidance in the lives of both individual Christians and churches.[11]

And Craig Keener's book *Gift Giver* contains 34 pages on "recognizing the Spirit's voice" and "learning to hear God's heart by the Spirit," including several personal anecdotes of being guided by the Holy Spirit to walk someplace, talk to someone, and so forth.[12]

10. Thomas R. Schreiner, *Galatians*, Zondervan Exegetical Commentary Series: New Testament (Grand Rapids, MI: Zondervan, 2010), 345.

11. Gregg R. Allison and Andreas J. Köstenberger, *The Holy Spirit,* Theology for the People of God (Nashville: B&H Academic, 2020), 398.

12. Craig Keener, *Gift Giver* (Grand Rapids: Baker, 2001), 17–50.

I think that the "situation-specific guidance" view is more convincing here, primarily because of the way the Greek verb *agō* is used elsewhere in the Bible. In the Septuagint (the Greek translation of the Old Testament that was often cited by New Testament authors), the verb *agō* is used 113 times to speak of leading by a personal agent (that is, leading by a human person or by God). Every one of those 113 examples refers to situation-specific directional guidance that leads to a particular location or decision. None of the examples speaks of imparting an inclination to obey God's moral standards apart from situation-specific direction. Here are some examples (all of these examples use *agō* in the Greek text, though the English translation uses "bring" instead of "lead" in several verses):

> Now out of the ground the LORD God had formed every beast of the field and every bird of the heavens and *brought* (*agō*, "led") them to the man to see what he would call them. (Gen. 2:19)

> And the rib that the LORD God had taken from the man he made into a woman and *brought* her to the man. (Gen. 2:22)

> [Joseph, speaking to his brothers:] *Bring* your youngest brother to me. So your words will be verified, and you shall not die. (Gen. 42:20)

> And I will *lead* the blind
>   in a way that they do not know,

in paths that they have not known
   I will guide them.
I will turn the darkness before them into light,
   the rough places into level ground. (Isa. 42:16)

The Spirit lifted me up and *brought* me to the east gate
of the house of the LORD, which faces east. (Ezek. 11:1)

And the Spirit lifted me up and *brought* me in the vision by the Spirit of God into Chaldea, to the exiles
(Ezek. 11:24)

In addition, *agō* is used several times to speak of God
guiding Israel through the wilderness:

And you shall remember the whole way that the LORD
your God has *led* you these forty years in the wilderness. (Deut. 8:2)

The LORD your God . . . who *led* you through the great
and terrifying wilderness, with its fiery serpents and
scorpions and thirsty ground where there was no water,
who brought you water out of the flinty rock. (Deut.
8:14–15)

So I led them out [a related verb, *exagō*] of the land of
Egypt and *brought* [*agō*, "led"] them into the wilderness. (Ezek. 20:10)

When we turn to the New Testament, we see a similar
pattern. The verb *agō* is used 53 times in the New Testament, and in the overwhelming majority of cases it refers

again to the situation-specific directional guidance leading to a particular location or decision. Here are some examples:

> And Jesus, full of the Holy Spirit, returned from the Jordan and was *led* by the Spirit in the wilderness for forty days, being tempted by the devil. And he ate nothing during those days. (Luke 4:1–2)

> Go into the village in front of you, where on entering you will find a colt tied, on which no one has ever yet sat. Untie it and *bring* it here. (Luke 19:30)

> Then they *led* Jesus from the house of Caiaphas to the governor's headquarters. (John 18:28)

It is fair to conclude that when *agō* is used in contexts that speak about leading by a *personal agent*, it overwhelmingly refers to a situation-specific kind of leading to a specific location or decision, not merely imparting an inclination to do good or evil.[13] And since Romans 8:14 and Galatians 5:18 speak of leading by the Holy Spirit, and the Holy Spirit is surely a personal agent, being "led by the Spirit" in these verses should also be understood to refer to situation-specific detailed leading to a specific location or decision.

---

13. One possible exception to this pattern may be argued from Rom. 2:4: "God's kindness is meant to *lead* you to repentance." But even in this example, such leading is not merely to a general attitude of contrition but to specific repentance for specific sins that people have committed—a sense not inconsistent with situation-specific detailed guidance.

We should also notice that in both Romans 8:14 and Galatians 5:18, Paul uses a present-tense verb to describe a quality that characterizes the lives of "sons of God" generally, and therefore it is appropriate to understand the present tense as indicating a continuous aspect to this leading, something like "all who are *being led regularly* by the Spirit of God are sons of God." Paul does not speak of a person being guided merely by his or her own moral convictions or desires, but by the Holy Spirit himself, who is a person. Paul is speaking of personal guidance from the Holy Spirit to individuals, and he indicates that this experience is characteristic of the lives of all Christians.

In the same context in Galatians, Paul gives similar instructions to Christians in the churches of Galatia:

> But I say, *walk by the Spirit*, and you will not gratify the desires of the flesh. (Gal. 5:16)

> If we live by the Spirit, let us also *keep in step with the Spirit*. (Gal. 5:25)

All of these passages speak about an expectation that Christians in general will experience a measure of leading or guiding by the Holy Spirit, who will influence their evaluation of various choices and courses of action in a subjectively perceived way.[14]

---

14. I have discussed elsewhere the question of guidance from the Holy Spirit that can come through other people when God brings to their minds something concerning you, and they then report that to you. This is something the New Testament would call the gift of "prophecy." On the gift of prophecy, see Wayne Grudem, *Systematic Theology: An Introduction to Biblical Doctrine* (Leicester,

10. We Can Perceive Subjective Factors in Guidance Separately or in Combination. All of the last four factors listed above (the conscience, the heart, the human spirit, and guidance from the Holy Spirit) may be called "subjective factors" because we become aware of them instinctively, as something we feel or sense, rather than by logical analysis of ideas or by observation of facts in the natural world.

People who operate from a non-Christian, materialistic worldview would lump all four of these factors into the broad category of "feelings" or "emotions" because they do not have a category for the invisible guidance of the Holy Spirit or for thinking about our human spirits as real but invisible components of who we are as persons.[15]

I have listed these four factors separately because the Bible treats them as distinct factors, and we can often recognize them as distinct components of guidance (as the passages above indicate). However, there may be other times when we are simply aware of an overall instinctive sense of what to do in a situation (sometimes people informally refer to this as a "gut feeling" about a decision) without being able to specifically evaluate each of these factors separately.

UK: Inter-Varsity, and Grand Rapids, MI: Zondervan, 1994), 1049–61; *The Gift of Prophecy in the New Testament and Today*, rev. ed. (Wheaton, IL: Crossway, 2000). My understanding of Scripture is that such guidance through a gift of prophecy will continue to be valid for the entire church age until Christ returns, but caution is needed to guard against abuse of this gift. Paul says, "Do not quench the Spirit. *Do not despise prophecies, but test everything*; hold fast what is good" (1 Thess. 5:19–21).

15. Jesus speaks of the Holy Spirit as "the Spirit of truth, whom the world cannot receive, because *it neither sees him nor knows him*" (John 14:17).

11. Objection: "Subjective Impressions Can Mislead People." It is certainly possible for people to make mistakes in the area of subjective guidance. A person's instinctive sense of what to do can at times be wrong, and I am not saying that Christians should always trust such subjective impressions. Other, more objective factors must also be taken into account, especially the first five factors I listed above: (1) information from the Bible, (2) information from studying the situation, (3) information about ourselves, (4) advice from others, and (5) observation of changed circumstances. And the teaching of the Bible must always have the highest priority. Christians can make the mistake of putting too much emphasis on guidance from subjective impressions.

But I am also concerned about another kind of mistake, the mistake of teaching people not to pay any attention to subjective impressions about what decision to make. This cannot be right, because God has made us as whole persons, including a conscience, a heart, and a human spirit, and has given us the ability to relate to him through the personal presence of the Holy Spirit.

Jesus says, "And I will ask the Father, and he will give you *another Helper*, to be with you forever" (John 14:16; see also 14:26; 15:26; 16:7; 1 John 2:1). The word translated as "Helper" is the Greek *paraklētos*, which is variously translated as "Helper," "Advocate," "Comforter," or "Counselor." Jesus was saying he would give the Holy Spirit to be "another Helper" to be present with the disciples when he was no longer physically present to talk with them and teach them. All of these translations convey the idea of someone who engages in personal communication and personal interaction with the person being helped or counseled.

In response to the objection that subjective impressions can mislead people, we must recognize that we can also be misled regarding the more objective factors in guidance. We can be misled by misunderstanding the teaching of Scripture, by wrongly evaluating ourselves and our abilities, or by depending on wrong information about a situation. We can be misled by wrongfully interpreting past experience. And certainly we can be misled by sermons (which we can also apply wrongly) and by advice from others. Books and articles can mislead us as well, and sometimes the historical tradition of the church has made mistakes. Therefore, I don't find the objection that subjective impressions might mislead us to be a convincing reason not to consider subjective factors.

My conclusion is that we should pay attention to the four subjective factors as well as the first five objective factors when making decisions. God relates to us as *whole persons*, including our ability to perceive these subjective factors, not merely as people with intellectual abilities. And I must re-emphasize that we should never follow any of these subjective impressions to disobey the clear teachings of Scripture.

D. THE DANGER OF MAKING THIS PROCESS TOO COMPLICATED

Up to this point, this book has discussed four dimensions to be considered regarding any action and nine factors to be considered when making ethical decisions. I have gone into such great detail because it is helpful for Christians to have a more extensive understanding of the individual factors that form our decision-making process as we seek to know God's will for our individual situations.

However, I do not think that God wants this decision-making process to seem impossible for Christians to follow regularly or so complicated that they are discouraged by it. God wants us to be able to have wisdom to make right decisions: "If any of you lacks wisdom, let him ask God, who gives generously to all without reproach, and it will be given him" (James 1:5).

In the actual course of a person's life, all of these factors can be taken into account quite quickly in most situations— sometimes even instantly and instinctively, without consciously considering each of these factors individually. Yet in other situations, thoughtfully and explicitly considering these different dimensions and factors will provide much greater insight and discernment. In this way, wise decision-making can become a good habit for all Christians, a skill that they exercise more and more naturally through the course of a day, as they increase in "knowledge and all discernment" so that they "approve what is excellent" (Phil. 1:9–10).

A helpful analogy is a golf professional teaching a beginner how to swing a golf club. The golf pro might first take a club in his hands, step up to the ball, and swing the club once, sending the ball straight and far, making it all look so easy. But when the golf lesson gets under way, the beginner realizes how complicated a proper golf swing really is. He must learn the proper position for his fingers and his hands when holding the club, the proper position for his feet, the direction his body needs to face, and the proper position of his knees, torso, arms, elbows, wrists, shoulders, and head. And he has to learn not just the starting position for all of these things, but the movements that they need to make from beginning the golf swing to hitting the ball and following through properly. It is a genuinely complex task!

What I have done in this book is something like breaking down the golf swing into great detail to talk about its individual parts. But these individual parts can be put together into a natural process that becomes part of the way a Christian habitually lives his or her life. I think this is what the author of Hebrews is intending when he speaks about mature Christians as "those who have their powers of discernment *trained by constant practice* to distinguish good from evil" (Heb. 5:14). The process no longer seems complicated. They just take the club in their hands, step up to the ball, and hit it well.

E. ACQUIRING WISDOM: THE PERSONAL SKILL NECESSARY FOR ETHICAL LIVING

Up to this point in this book, I have discussed the importance of considering whether an *action itself* is morally right or wrong, considering the person's *attitudes* toward that action, considering the person's *motives* for the action, and considering the *results* of the action. Then I listed nine possible sources of information to be considered when making a decision about any particular action. But how can we know that we will evaluate each of these factors correctly when we "consider" them? To "consider" these factors requires skill in making correct evaluations. How can we obtain that skill, and how can we improve it? This brings us to the topic of *wisdom*.

Presumably everyone reading this book wants to gain more insight into making right decisions about different ethical situations that arise in their lives. In biblical terms, the personal skill of making such right decisions falls under the category of wisdom.

For purposes of this book, I will use the following definition:

Wisdom is the skill of understanding and applying the Bible rightly to each situation.[16]

This definition indicates that wisdom is not a mechanical process but *a skill*, one that is exercised by real human beings in real situations.[17] As with other skills, wisdom can

---

16. Someone might object that, based on this definition, people without the Bible could not become wise. But even unbelievers have, by common grace, some understanding of God's moral standards, because Paul says that "the work of the law is written on their hearts" (Rom. 2:15). Therefore, unbelievers can have an approximation of God's wisdom in some areas of life even though they do not have the Bible or access to the teachings of the Bible (see the discussion of the necessity of Scripture in Wayne Grudem, *Christian Ethics: An Introduction to Biblical Moral Reasoning* [Wheaton, IL: Crossway, 2018], 95–97). Yet their understanding, not based on the Bible itself, will also include many errors, and will not equal the true biblical wisdom that is practiced in relationship to God himself.

17. The idea of wisdom as a *skill* is found in some evangelical ethics books. Scott B. Rae says, "This concept of a craft or skill is at the heart of the Hebrew concept of wisdom." *Moral Choices: An Introduction to Ethics*, 2nd ed. (Grand

increase with time and with practice at making good decisions in different situations. Gaining mature wisdom is a process that increases over many years of godly living, and mature Christians are "those who have their powers of discernment *trained* by constant practice to distinguish good from evil" (Heb. 5:14). Children do not yet have much life experience, and as a result they are not as wise as we hope they will be later. Even Jesus grew in wisdom during his childhood:

> And Jesus *increased in wisdom* and in stature and in favor with God and man. (Luke 2:52)

John Frame speaks of the need for such a skill:

> To apply the Word of God to circumstances requires a kind of moral vision. Such applications require the ability to *see* the circumstances *in the light of* biblical principles. In moral quandaries, we often ask questions such as "Is this act murder?" Or "Is this act stealing?" For Christians, the challenge is to give biblical names to human actions. Sometimes it is obvious: taking money out of a friend's wallet without authorization is what the Bible calls stealing. Sometimes it

Rapids, MI: Zondervan, 2000), 74n6. (The chapter that contains this footnote was not included in the 3rd edition of this book in 2009, however.) Robertson McQuilkin and Paul Copan say, "Wisdom is the skill for living rightly, which means that true wisdom is anchored in a correct view of reality. Skillful living begins with being properly aligned with the intrinsically relational, triune God." *An Introduction to Biblical Ethics: Walking in the Way of Wisdom*, 3rd ed. (Downers Grove, IL: InterVarsity Press, 2014), 17. See also the quotation from Frame in the following footnote.

is less obvious: is it murder to remove this terminal patient from life support?[18]

My definition of wisdom is very similar to what he calls "a kind of moral vision" and "the ability to see the circumstances in the light of biblical principles."

The Bible places an exceptionally high emphasis on the value of wisdom. The book of Proverbs in particular extols wisdom over and over again:

> Blessed is the one who finds *wisdom*,
>   and the one who gets understanding,
> for the gain from her is better than gain from silver
>   and her profit better than gold.
> She is more precious than jewels,
>   and nothing you desire can compare with her. . . .
> Her ways are ways of pleasantness,
>   and all her paths are peace. (Prov. 3:13–17)

But how can a person become wise? The Bible speaks frequently about that subject. It is not a simple matter of following certain steps, so that if you merely complete steps A, B, and C you will automatically get the right answer. Rather, Scripture speaks often about *the character of the*

---

18. Frame, *The Doctrine of the Christian Life*, 356, emphasis in original. Frame says that Scripture often represents wisdom "as a skill, a knowing *how* rather than knowing *that*. . . . In James 3:13–17, wisdom is clearly ethical, the skill of godly living." *The Doctrine of the Christian Life*, 351, emphasis in original. If my memory is correct, I also first learned to think of wisdom as the skill of applying Scripture rightly to specific situations from Frame's ethics class in 1973 at Westminster Seminary, but I could not find it defined in exactly that way in his book *The Doctrine of the Christian Life*.

person who is making ethical decisions—what kind of person he or she must be in order to have wisdom. I have discussed the development of Christian character in some detail elsewhere.[19]

For the rest of this section, we will look at the source of wisdom and the personal character traits that accompany wisdom.

1. Wisdom Comes from God. God is infinitely wise. His wisdom is so far superior to all human wisdom that Paul can call him "the only wise God" (Rom. 16:27; see also Rom. 11:33). While human beings may obtain some knowledge, the Bible says that in Christ "are hidden *all* the treasures of *wisdom* and knowledge" (Col. 2:3).

Therefore, if we are to obtain true wisdom, we must obtain it from God himself as we walk in a personal relationship with him. "The Lord gives wisdom" (Prov. 2:6; see also 1 Kings 3:12; 4:29; 10:24; Ps. 51:6; Eccles. 2:26; Dan. 2:21–23). James tells his readers that the way to get wisdom is to ask God for it:

> If any of you lacks wisdom, *let him ask God*, who gives generously to all without reproach, and it will be given him. (James 1:5)

Other passages in the New Testament speak of Christ as the source of wisdom for us (see Luke 21:15; 1 Cor. 1:24, 30; Col. 2:3), and still others speak of the role of the

---

19. See Grudem, *Christian Ethics*, especially chap. 4, and, more broadly, the entire book.

Holy Spirit in imparting wisdom to believers (see 1 Cor. 12:8; Eph. 1:17).

If wisdom is the skill of applying the Bible rightly to each situation, then wisdom requires *discernment into situations*, an ability not only to learn the facts of a situation but also to see into the heart of it, to understand what is really going on. In addition, wisdom requires *discernment into Scripture*, the ability to evaluate various passages and understand accurately how they apply. That is why Paul prays that the Philippian Christians might grow in their discernment:

> And it is my prayer that your love may abound more and more, with knowledge and all discernment [Greek, *aesthēsis*, "discernment, insight, capacity to understand"], so that you may approve what is excellent, and so be pure and blameless for the day of Christ. (Phil. 1:9–10)

Since Paul prays for God to give discernment to these Christians, it is right for us also to ask God for the same kind of discernment for ourselves and others.

In a similar way, Paul prays for the Christians in Colossae to be filled with the knowledge of God's will "in all *spiritual wisdom* and understanding" (Col. 1:9). And the author of Ecclesiastes tells us, "To the one who pleases him God has given wisdom and knowledge and joy" (Eccles. 2:26). These passages are a further indication that wisdom comes from God, that it is right to pray to God for wisdom, and that he is especially pleased to give it to those who walk in a personal relationship with him.

2. Wisdom Comes from Scripture. If God is the source of all true wisdom, then it is not surprising that God often uses the words of the Bible as the means by which he gives wisdom to us. When Moses was giving the people of Israel the written commands of God in Deuteronomy, he told them that they should "keep them and do them," for, he said, "*that will be your wisdom* and your understanding in the sight of the peoples" (Deut. 4:6).

It is not only a small group of highly trained scholars who can be made wise by Scripture, but all of God's people, even "the simple"—those who might not be highly trained or wise in the world's eyes—can be made wise by God's words:

> The law of the LORD is perfect,
>   reviving the soul;
> the testimony of the LORD is sure,
>   *making wise the simple.* (Ps. 19:7; see also Ps.
>   119:98–100, 130; Col. 3:16; 1 Tim. 3:15)

The wisdom that comes from God through Scripture is far different from the wisdom of the world. Paul makes this contrast between worldly wisdom and the wisdom of God very clear:

> Yet among the mature we do impart wisdom, although
> *it is not a wisdom of this age* or of the rulers of this age,

who are doomed to pass away. But we impart a secret and hidden wisdom of God, which God decreed before the ages for our glory. (1 Cor. 2:6–7; see also Gen. 3:6; 1 Cor. 1:18–31; 2:1–16; 2 Cor. 1:12)

3. Wisdom Comes with a Fear of God. Scripture makes clear in several places that if we are to gain wisdom, we must begin with a fear of God:

> *The fear of the* LORD *is the beginning of wisdom*;
>> all those who practice it have a good
>>> understanding. (Ps. 111:10)

> *The fear of the* LORD *is the beginning of wisdom*,
>> and the knowledge of the Holy One is insight.
>>> (Prov. 9:10)

> *The fear of the* LORD *is instruction in wisdom*,
>> and humility comes before honor. (Prov. 15:33; see
>>> also Job 28:28)

The idea of the fear of the Lord is not an obscure topic in Scripture, for the expressions "fear of God," "fear God," "fear of the Lord," and "fear the Lord" occur 84 times in the Old and New Testaments (in the ESV).[20]

Sometimes Christians explain this "fear of the Lord" as "reverence for God," a somewhat weaker concept than fear. But I am aware of no modern Bible version that translates Psalm 111:10 as "Reverence for the LORD is the beginning

---

20. In addition, there are other verses saying "fear him," referring to God.

of wisdom," no doubt because the most common sense of the Hebrew word *yir'āh* in the Old Testament and the Greek word *phobos* in the New Testament (in verses such as Deut. 2:25; Jonah 1:10; Acts 9:31; 2 Cor. 5:11) is simply "fear."[21] While it is true that the sense "reverence" is appropriate in some contexts,[22] it does not seem to me to fit the passages about wisdom nearly as well.

It is important to affirm clearly that Christians should no longer fear eternal condemnation from God (see 1 John 4:18), for Christ has eternally saved us from final condemnation: "There is therefore now no condemnation for those who are in Christ Jesus" (Rom. 8:1). Still, there are other senses of "the fear of the Lord" that seem appropriate to the Christian life. For example, it is very appropriate for Christians to *fear displeasing God* or grieving the Holy Spirit (see Eph. 4:30). And it is very appropriate for Christians to *fear God's fatherly discipline* if they walk in willful disobedience to him (see Heb. 12:5–11).[23] But fear of God's fatherly displeasure and fear of his fatherly discipline are far different from the terror of final judgment, from which we have been freed by Christ's sacrifice for our sin.

---

21. Ludwig Koehler and Walter Baumgartner, *The Hebrew and Aramaic Lexicon of the Old Testament*, study ed., 2 vols. (Leiden: Brill, 2001), 433–34; Francis Brown, S. R. Driver, and Charles Briggs, *A Hebrew and English Lexicon of the Old Testament* (Oxford: Clarendon, 1968), 432; Bauer et al., *A Greek-English Lexicon*, 1062.

22. See Brown, Driver, and Briggs, *A Hebrew and English Lexicon*, 432, meaning 3, "fear of God, reverence, piety," and Bauer et al., *A Greek-English Lexicon*, 1062, meaning 2b, "reverence, respect." However, the meaning "reverence" does not occur in the more recent Koehler and Baumgartner, *The Hebrew and Aramaic Lexicon* (2001), 433–34.

23. See also Grudem, *Christian Ethics*, 142.

A healthy fear of God's displeasure and fear of his fatherly discipline are appropriate to acquiring wisdom. If we establish in our minds, at the beginning of a quest for wisdom, that we deeply want to avoid disobeying God or displeasing him, then we will be much more eager to learn his directions for our lives and to walk in obedience to those good commands.

The opposite is certainly not true. If we have *no fear* of displeasing God and *no fear* of his discipline, then we will not be as careful to seek to understand his ways, and we will likely not grow much in wisdom. This is because "the fear of the LORD is the beginning of wisdom" (Ps. 111:10).

Those who have *no* fear of God can engage in all sorts of horrible sin. At the culmination of nine verses in which Paul talks about the sins of Jews and Gentiles apart from God, he summarizes the problem in the last sentence by saying they have *no fear of God*:

> "None is righteous, no, not one;
>> no one understands;
>> no one seeks for God.
> All have turned aside; together they have become
>>> worthless;
>> no one does good,
>> not even one."
> "Their throat is an open grave;
>> they use their tongues to deceive."
> "The venom of asps is under their lips."
>> "Their mouth is full of curses and bitterness."

"Their feet are swift to shed blood;
    in their paths are ruin and misery,
and the way of peace they have not known."
    "There is no fear of God before their eyes."
        (Rom. 3:10b–18, quoting several passages
        from the Old Testament)

The Bible's emphasis on a spiritually beneficial fear of God suggests to us that it is important for churches to teach Christians about the value of fearing God. Such teaching would undoubtedly lead to more wisdom in our churches, and that would result in more holiness and purity, and more of God's blessing on our daily lives.

4. Wisdom Comes with Faith. Immediately after telling his readers that someone who lacks wisdom should "ask God" for it, James adds three verses (vv. 6–8) about the importance of asking in faith:

If any of you lacks wisdom, let him ask God, who gives generously to all without reproach, and it will be given him. *But let him ask in faith, with no doubting*, for the one who doubts is like a wave of the sea that is driven and tossed by the wind. For that person must not suppose that he will receive anything from the Lord; he is a double-minded man, unstable in all his ways. (James 1:5–8)

To "ask in faith" means to ask with a settled trust or confidence in one's mind that God will grant the wisdom that we have asked for. This is a specific example of the general principle about trusting in God that is found in Hebrews 11:

> And without faith it is impossible to please him, for whoever would draw near to God *must believe* that he exists and *that he rewards those who seek him.* (Heb. 11:6)

Verses like this should be a great encouragement. When we ask for something that God has approved or promised in his Word (such as wisdom), we don't have to keep wondering whether it is pleasing to him to give us what we ask, for his Word tells us that it is.[24]

5. Wisdom Comes with Knowledge. If wisdom is understood as the skill of applying the Bible rightly to each situation, wisdom often comes after we have gained *more information* about the teaching of the Bible on a topic or more information about the actual situation.

The Bible speaks of *knowledge* as an important factor that must accompany wisdom. "An intelligent heart acquires *knowledge*, and the ear of the wise seeks *knowledge*" (Prov. 18:15; see also Prov. 10:14). In Proverbs 8, when "Wisdom" calls and invites people to learn, she says, "Take my instruction instead of silver, and *knowledge* rather than choice gold, for wisdom is better than jewels" (Prov. 8:10–11). Several other passages in the Psalms and

---

24. For more discussion of prayer, including how to think about unanswered prayers in the Christian life, see Grudem, *Systematic Theology*, 355–75.

Proverbs connect wisdom and knowledge (see Ps. 119:66; Prov. 1:7; 2:6, 10; 15:2, 7; 18:15; 21:11; 22:17; 24:3–5). These passages indicate that a wise person will not only have the *skill* of applying the Bible rightly to each situation, but will also have *knowledge* about the Bible and about the situation (including himself or other people who are in the situation).

For example, a young couple seeking wisdom about how to raise their children might need to spend time searching out numerous Bible passages that teach us about parenting (there is a lot of material in Proverbs and elsewhere). That would give them more information (knowledge) about the Bible.

More information about a situation is often needed before we can make a wise decision. A person seeking wisdom about whether to take another job will need to find out a considerable amount of information about the potential job before he is able to make a wise decision. People who are buying a house will often hire a professional home inspector to give them more detailed information about the house before they buy it.

In addition, knowledge of the situation also must include knowledge about *ourselves*, for we are part of the situation. A woman who is thinking about starting a new business will need to honestly evaluate herself to determine whether she has skills and interests necessary to succeed in that particular kind of business (wise counsel from honest friends can be a great help here).

6. Wisdom Comes with Obedience to God. In the Bible, the "wicked" person is not wise, for "the words of his mouth are trouble and deceit; he has ceased to act wisely and do good" (Ps. 36:3). By contrast, people who are obedient to God are those who gain wisdom and exercise it in their actions:

> The mouth of *the righteous* utters *wisdom*,
>> and his tongue speaks justice. (Ps. 37:30)

In Proverbs 8, "Wisdom" calls out and says, "I walk in the way of *righteousness*, in the paths of justice" (Prov. 8:20). In the New Testament, James says that anyone who is a "hearer of the Word and not a doer" will quickly forget what he has heard, implying that he will not learn wisdom from reading the Bible unless he follows through and obeys it, for then he will not be a "hearer who forgets" but a "doer who acts" (James 1:23–25). James elsewhere connects wisdom with good conduct:

> *Who is wise* and understanding among you? *By his good conduct* let him show his works in the meekness of wisdom. (James 3:13)[25]

One passage in Hebrews indicates that we can become better at making wise decisions by years of "practice" in distinguishing good from evil, with the implication that

---

25. Other verses also connect wisdom with obedience to God or with personal integrity of character (see Prov. 11:3; 12:5; Eccles. 2:26).

those who constantly make morally wise choices will gain skill in such discernment:

> But solid food is for the mature, for those who have their powers of discernment *trained by constant practice* to distinguish good from evil. (Heb. 5:14)

In this verse, "powers of discernment" translates a plural form of the Greek term *aisthētērion*, which means "capacity for discernment" with regard to "the ability to make moral decisions."[26]

7. Wisdom Comes with Accepting Counsel from Others. A common theme in Proverbs is that people who are wise listen to counsel from other people. This is probably because other people can help us understand Scripture or understand a situation more accurately:

> The way of a fool is right in his own eyes,
>   but *a wise man listens to advice*. (Prov. 12:15)

> With those who take advice is wisdom. (Prov. 13:10)

> Listen to advice and accept instruction,
>   that you may gain wisdom in the future. (Prov.
>   19:20; see also 15:31; 20:18; 24:6)

But it is important to choose carefully the people from whom we take advice. It is possible to choose wise or

---

26. See Bauer et al., *A Greek-English Lexicon*, 29.

foolish companions for our source of wisdom, and the kind of companions we choose will affect whether we gain wisdom or not:

> Whoever walks with the wise becomes wise,
>> but the companion of fools will suffer harm.
>>> (Prov. 13:20)

There are repeated warnings in Proverbs to beware of counsel from people who do evil:

> My son, if sinners entice you,
>> do not consent. (Prov. 1:10; see also Prov. 16:29;
>>> 25:5)

8. Wisdom Comes with Humility. Another characteristic of people who gain wisdom is humility. "When pride comes, then comes disgrace, but *with the humble is wisdom*" (Prov. 11:2). Proud people have a wrong kind of "wisdom," a false wisdom whereby they consider themselves to be wise. Scripture warns against this repeatedly:

> *Be not wise in your own eyes*;
>> fear the LORD, and turn away from evil.
>>> (Prov. 3:7; see also Prov. 26:12; Jer. 9:23;
>>> Rom. 12:16)

In the New Testament, James says that a person who is "wise in understanding" should "show his works *in the meekness of wisdom*" (James 3:13). Then, after talking about the false kind of wisdom that comes from "selfish ambition," James goes on to describe the gentle persuasiveness of the humble wisdom that comes from God:

> But the wisdom from above is first pure, then peaceable, *gentle, open to reason*, full of mercy and good fruits, impartial and sincere. And a harvest of righteousness is sown in peace by those who make peace. (James 3:17–18)

9. Wisdom Brings Joy. For the person who finds wisdom from God, a valuable reward is the joy that comes with wisdom. "*Wisdom is pleasure* to a man of understanding" (Prov. 10:23; also note the joy that wisdom brings to God in Prov. 8:30).[27]

Elsewhere the author of Proverbs compares the joy of wisdom to the sweetness of honey:

> My son, *eat honey*, for it is good,
> > and the drippings of the honeycomb are sweet to
> > > your taste.
> Know that *wisdom is such to your soul*;
> > if you find it, there will be a future,
> > and your hope will not be cut off.
> > > (Prov. 24:13–14)

This means that when a person finds a wise solution to a puzzling situation, God will often give with that wisdom an

---

27. Other passages connecting wisdom with things that are joyful or pleasant include Prov. 2:10; 3:13; 8:11, 18–19; 16:16; Eccles. 8:1.

inward sense of joy and delight, and even a sense of being "led by the Spirit of God" (Rom. 8:14).

F. APPENDIX: A RESPONSE TO GARRY FRIESEN'S BOOK *DECISION MAKING AND THE WILL OF GOD*

First published in 1980, with a revised edition in 2004, *Decision Making and the Will of God*[28] has had a significant influence on evangelical thinking about how to know God's will. Author Garry Friesen[29] denies that God directly guides individual Christian to an "individual will" for each person that is more specific than the "moral will of God" revealed in the Bible. Because Friesen denies that God ordinarily gives additional guidance to Christians through the subjective means that I just discussed, it is appropriate to provide some comments on his book at this point.[30]

There is much that I like about this book. Friesen's sections on the moral law of God, on God's sovereignty in our lives, and on the use of wisdom in decision-making contain much valuable material on theology as it impacts practical Christian living. The entire book is a model of clarity in writing and in developing an extended argument.

---

28. Garry Friesen with J. Robin Maxson, *Decision Making and the Will of God*, rev. ed. (Colorado Springs: Multnomah, 2004). The cover of the 2004 edition says, "Over 250,000 copies sold."

29. For simplicity I have decided to refer to the book as "Friesen's even though it was written "with J. Robin Maxson," who evidently played a significant role in its composition and revision. But throughout most of the book Friesen speaks as the primary author.

30. This appendix is a brief summary of a longer interaction with Friesen's argument that is found in my *Christian Ethics*, 171–84.

Throughout every section of the book there is an evident desire to understand and submit to the authoritative teaching of Scripture. In addition, some of Friesen's criticisms of what he calls the "traditional view" provide good warnings against excessive dependence on subjective factors when seeking to know God's will.

I also think Friesen is correct in arguing that Scripture does not show any expectation that we must seek additional guidance from God in most of the ordinary, routine decisions of life. It would be hopelessly paralyzing.[31] He rightly criticizes the view that, if we miss God's special guidance at some particular point in life, we are consigned to living a life of God's "second-best."[32] And he rightly emphasizes that most of the choices we make throughout each day can and should be decided according to the teachings of Scripture and the use of our God-given wisdom (in fact, my entire *Christian Ethics* book is devoted to helping people make wise decisions in that way).

Therefore, his emphasis on the importance of making decisions based on the Bible and wisdom is helpful. However, I think it is only part of the picture.

Here is where I would disagree with Friesen: It seems to me that Friesen's exclusion of personal guidance from God to individual believers is contrary to the entire pattern of Scripture from Genesis to Revelation. I do not think there is any passage of Scripture, or any combination of passages,

---

31. See Friesen, *Decision Making*, 246–47.
32. Friesen, *Decision Making*, 29, 200, 517.

that should lead us to think that God does not communicate directly with his people throughout all of history in individual, personal ways *in addition to* his communication in and through the written words of Scripture.

If we look at the whole scope of biblical history, we see that from beginning to end God has a personal relationship with his people, a relationship in which he communicates directly and personally with them, and this communication is never limited to the words that he gave to all his people in "the book of the covenant" or the writings of the canon of Scripture. God had a personal relationship and direct interpersonal communication with Adam and Eve, Cain and Abel, Enoch (who walked with God, Gen. 5:24), Noah, Abraham, Isaac, Jacob, Moses, David, Solomon, and many other Old Testament prophets and kings.[33]

In the person of Jesus, God the Son communicated individually and personally with many people while he was on earth. After the resurrection, the Lord Jesus or the Holy Spirit interacted personally with Paul not only on the Damascus road (Acts 9:4–6), but also by directing his second missionary journey (16:6–7), encouraging him in Corinth (18:9–10), confirming his decision to go to Jerusalem (19:21), showing him what would happen in Jerusalem (20:23), encouraging

---

33. Friesen writes, "In the Bible, no believer asks, 'What is God's individual will for me in this matter?'" Friesen, *Decision Making*, 48. But this is surely incorrect. For example, David often sought specific guidance from God: "Therefore David inquired of the LORD, 'Shall I go and attack these Philistines?' And the LORD said to David, 'Go and attack the Philistines and save Keilah'" (1 Sam. 23:2; see also 1 Sam. 23:4, 9–12; 30:8; 2 Sam. 2:1; 5:19, 23–24. There are many other examples, such as the people seeking guidance from God in Judg. 1:1; 20:18, 23, 27–28; 1 Sam. 10:22.

him in prison in Jerusalem (23:11), assuring him that he would arrive safely in Rome (this time by an angel, 27:23–24), telling him he would not heal his thorn in the flesh (2 Cor. 12:9), directing him to go to Jerusalem (Gal. 2:2), and standing by him at his trial in Rome (2 Tim. 4:17).

But this was true not only with Paul, for God gave direct guidance for Philip (Acts 8:26, 29), Ananias (9:10–16), Cornelius (10:3–6), Peter (10:13–20; 12:7–8), the church at Antioch (13:2), and the church in Jerusalem (15:28).

In addition, the New Testament promises that each individual believer will have a personal relationship that the Father, Son, and Holy Spirit:

> If anyone loves me, he will keep my word, and my Father will love him, and we will come to him and *make our home with him*. (John 14:23)

> For all who are *led by the Spirit of God* are sons of God. (Rom. 8:14)

> But I say, *walk by the Spirit*, and you will not gratify the desires of the flesh. . . . But if you are *led by the Spirit*, you are not under the law. (Gal. 5:16, 18)

> [I pray] that the God of our Lord Jesus Christ, the Father of glory, may give you the Spirit of wisdom and of revelation *in the knowledge of him*. (Eph. 1:17)

> [I desire] that I may *know him* and the power of his resurrection, and may share his sufferings, becoming like him in his death. (Phil. 3:10)

Let those of us who are mature think this way, and if in anything you think otherwise, *God will reveal that also to you.* (Phil. 3:15)

Behold, I stand at the door and knock. If anyone hears my voice and opens the door, I will come into him *and eat with him*, and he with me. (Rev. 3:20)

Friesen attempts to explain many of these examples as special cases that do not establish a pattern for ordinary Christians today.[34] But my counterargument is this: look at the overall pattern of Scripture.

From beginning to end the Bible tells us of a God who relates *individually and personally* to his people. And now Friesen tells us, contrary to the experience of God's people throughout all of the Bible, that God no longer communicates personally and individually with any of his people except through the written words in the canon of Scripture.[35]

So Friesen's "Bible and wisdom only" view is asking us to believe (1) that throughout the Bible God communicated

---

34. See Friesen, *Decision Making*, 45–111: the prophets are different, Jesus is different, Paul is different, their experiences are different, and so forth. Friesen also says that instances of special guidance in the Bible are uncommon: "Even in the biblical record, special guidance is rare . . . bona fide instances of special guidance have been rare—even for the apostles." Friesen, *Decision Making*, 233–36. I disagree, because a phenomenon that occurs many dozens of times throughout all parts of the Bible can hardly be called "rare" in Scripture. The large number of examples of personal interactions with God that are recorded in Scripture should lead us to expect that this kind of interpersonal relationship between God and individual believers also occurred multiple other times that were not recorded.

35. See the previous footnote for Friesen's qualification that there are rare exceptions.

to his people both through written Scripture (as much as they had at any point) and through direct personal fellowship and interaction with people, and (2) that God now communicates *only* through the written words of the canon, and no longer through direct personal fellowship and interaction with people.

This is quite strange in light of the fact that the new covenant in which we now live is seen to be better in every way (see 2 Corinthians 3; Hebrews 8–9). But how can it be better if we have lost the elements of personal relationship with God and personal communication from him that characterized all periods of history that the Bible talks about? Where is *anything* in the Bible that would lead us to believe that?

I realize, of course, that the canon of Scripture is closed[36] and no more writings are to be added to the Bible. But that is not the question. The question is, What about communication from God to specific individuals that is not part of the canon? If the Bible is the "book of the covenant" that stipulates the terms of the relationship between God as King and us as his covenant people, then are we to say that *the King can never communicate with his people in any additional ways besides the covenant document*? Can a God who loves his people never communicate with them directly and personally?

Evangelical theologian Carl F. H. Henry rightly commented as follows:

---

36. See Grudem, *Systematic Theology,* 54–72.

Any statement of evangelical experience that does not include the possibility both of communion with God and the communication of the particularized divine will to the surrendered life seems to me artificially restrictive.[37]

Surely the vast majority of Christians throughout all history have known and experienced the guidance of the Holy Spirit in making decisions, especially while they were praying and reading the words of Scripture, and they have known that this guidance included not only the directions, commands, and principles of Scripture, but also subjective impressions of God's will, as well as thoughts or specific memories that the Lord brings to mind. And this certainly implies the validity of thinking that there is a particularized or "individual will" of God for specific people in some specific situations.

Therefore, my primary observation on Friesen's argument is to note how a position that *rules out all direct personal guidance from the Holy Spirit today* is so completely different from the whole course of biblical history and from the New Testament teaching on personal fellowship that we have with the Father, Son, and Holy Spirit.

In addition, there is no passage that teaches this position. Where is there a passage that says something like, "You should never think that God is leading you through a

---

37. Carl F. H. Henry, *Confessions of a Theologian* (Waco, TX: Word, 1986), 53.

subjective sense of his guidance. Make your decisions based only on the Bible and your own wisdom"? No passage even comes close to that kind of teaching.

Perhaps I have missed something, but I do not think the passages that imply the expectation of a closed canon provide such support for Friesen's position, nor do the passages that speak of the sufficiency of Scripture for the purposes for which it was intended. In fact, I don't think there are any strong passages of Scripture at all that support the "Bible and wisdom only" view of guidance.

Finally, I am happy to report that Friesen read an early draft of the chapter in my book *Christian Ethics* where I interacted extensively with his view, and he wrote to me as follows:

> After reading your chapter several times, I am convinced that we are closer in viewpoint than you think and than I thought. You do not hold the traditional view. You hold something like the wisdom view with exceptions. Even those exceptions are very close to my own view. But, of course, there are differences.[38]

QUESTIONS FOR PERSONAL APPLICATION

1. Have you ever had to make an instant decision, and you decided rightly? Wrongly? Can you tell what factors in your heart led to the instant decision that you made?

---

38. Email to me from Garry Friesen, Sept. 20, 2016, quoted by permission.

2. Can you think of a time when it seemed to you that a sudden change in circumstances indicated God's guidance about how you should make a decision? How did you know this?

3. Would you say today that you have "a clear conscience toward both God and man" (Acts 24:16)? Or is there something troubling your conscience? If so, what could you do to make it right?

4. Have the deep desires of your heart ever affected any decisions regarding your job or career direction, or a ministry commitment?

5. Are you ever aware of sensing something in your spirit? Can you give a specific example?

6. How do you know when the Holy Spirit is guiding you, if at all?

7. Who are some wise people you have known? How do you think they became wise?

8. Do you feel a fear of God right now? If so, can you explain how it affects your relationship with him? How does it give you wisdom?

9. Read James 1:5–6. How much faith would you say that you have right now that God will give you wisdom regarding a specific difficult decision?

SPECIAL TERMS

conscience
fear of God
heart
moral will of God

sovereign will of God
spirit
subjective impressions

BIBLIOGRAPHY

Sections in Christian Ethics Texts

Clark, David K., and Robert V. Rakestraw, eds. *Readings in Christian Ethics*. 2 vols. Grand Rapids, MI: Baker, 1994, 1:279–310.

Feinberg, John S., and Paul D. Feinberg. *Ethics for a Brave New World*. 2nd ed. Wheaton, IL: Crossway, 2010, 52–61.

Frame, John M. *The Doctrine of the Christian Life: A Theology of Lordship*. Phillipsburg, NJ: P&R, 2008, 24–36.

Geisler, Norman L. *Christian Ethics: Contemporary Issues and Options*. 2nd ed. Grand Rapids, MI: Baker, 2010, 116–27.

Grudem, Wayne. *Christian Ethics: An Introduction to Biblical Moral Reasoning*. Wheaton, IL: Crossway, 2018, 148–86.

Gushee, David P., and Glen H. Stassen. *Kingdom Ethics: Following Jesus in Contemporary Context*. 2nd ed. Grand Rapids, MI: Eerdmans, 2016, 442–48.

Jones, David Clyde. *Biblical Christian Ethics*. Grand Rapids, MI: Baker, 1994, 59–76.

McQuilkin, Robertson, and Paul Copan. *An Introduction to Biblical Ethics: Walking in the Way of Wisdom*. 3rd ed. Downers Grove, IL: InterVarsity Press, 2014, 13–23.

Rae, Scott B. *Moral Choices: An Introduction to Ethics*. 3rd ed. Grand Rapids, MI: Zondervan, 2009, 11–23.

Other Works

DeYoung, Kevin. *Just Do Something: A Liberating Approach to Finding God's Will*. Chicago: Moody, 2009.

Friesen, Garry, and J. Robin Maxson. *Decision Making and the Will of God*. Sisters, OR: Multnomah, 2004.

Howard, J. Grant, Jr. *Knowing God's Will and Doing It!* Grand Rapids, MI: Zondervan, 1976.

Huffman, Douglas S., ed. *How Then Should We Choose? Three Views on God's Will and Decision Making*. Grand Rapids, MI: Kregel, 2009.

Naselli, Andrew David, and J. D. Crowley. *Conscience: What It Is, How to Train It, and Loving Those Who Differ*. Wheaton, IL: Crossway, 2016.

O'Donovan, O. M. T. "Christian Moral Reasoning." In *New Dictionary of Christian Ethics and Pastoral Theology*, edited by David J. Atkinson and David H. Field, 122–27. Leicester, UK: Inter-Varsity, and Downers Grove, IL: Inter-Varsity Press, 1995.

Willard, Dallas. *In Search of Guidance: Developing a Conversational Relationship with God*. Ventura, CA: Regal, 1983.

SCRIPTURE MEMORY PASSAGE

James 1:5–6: If any of you lacks wisdom, let him ask God, who gives generously to all without reproach, and it will be given him. But let him ask in faith, with no doubting, for the one who doubts is like a wave of the sea that is driven and tossed by the wind.

HYMN

"Open My Eyes, That I May See"

Open my eyes, that I may see
Glimpses of truth Thou hast for me;
Place in my hands the wonderful key
That shall unclasp and set me free.

Refrain:
Silently now I wait for Thee,
Ready, my God, Thy will to see;
Open my eyes—illumine me,
Spirit divine!

Open my ears, that I may hear
Voices of truth Thou sendest clear;
And while the wave-notes fall on my ear,
Ev'rything false will disappear.

Open my mouth, and let me bear
Gladly the warm truth ev'rywhere;
Open my heart and let me prepare
Love with Thy children thus to share.

Author: Clara H. Scott, 1841–1897

General Index

Scripture Index

Also Available from Wayne Grudem

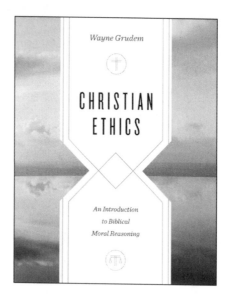

Best-selling author Wayne Grudem explains in detail what the whole Bible says about living as a Christian in this highly practical, biblically based volume on Christian ethics.

"Insightful, encyclopedic, biblical, and distinctively evangelical, this new book from Wayne Grudem is a massive contribution to Christian ethics."
R. ALBERT MOHLER JR.

For more information, visit **crossway.org**.

Also Available in This Series

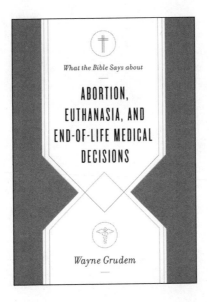

What the Bible Says about

ABORTION, EUTHANASIA, AND END-OF-LIFE MEDICAL DECISIONS

Wayne Grudem

Forthcoming Volumes:

What the Bible Says about Divorce and Remarriage
What the Bible Says about Birth Control, Infertility,
Reproductive Technology, and Adoption

For more information, visit **crossway.org**.